REDEFINING HIGHER EDUCATION

REDEFINING HIGHER EDUCATION

HOW SELF-DIRECTION CAN SAVE COLLEGES

MELVYN L. FEIN

Transaction Publishers
New Brunswick (U.S.A.) and London (U.K.)

This book is printed on acid-free paper that meets the American National Standard for Permanence of Paper for Printed Library Materials.

Library of Congress Catalog Number: 2013031178
ISBN: 978-1-4128-5357-6
Printed in the United States of America

Library of Congress Cataloging-in-Publication Data

Fein, Melvyn L.
Redefining higher education : how self-direction can save colleges / Melvyn L. Fein.
pages cm
Includes bibliographical references and index.
ISBN 978-1-4128-5357-6
1. University autonomy--United States. 2. Education, Higher--Aims and objectives--United States. 3. Educational change--United States. I. Title.
LB2331.4.F44 2014
378.101--dc23

2013031178

Contents

Preface

So many books about reforming higher education have appeared in recent years that it has become customary for authors to explain why they have written yet another one. I am no exception. Just as my predecessors felt a need to justify contributing to such an extensive literature, so do I. After all, a great many sensible things have been said about the current crisis confronting our colleges and universities. What have I to add that deserves the attention of interested readers? What makes me different?

As might be expected, I believe I differ on important fronts. First and most important, I do not teach at a prestigious research university. Many influential commentators have been based at elite institutions, whereas Kennesaw State University is a regional school. Indeed, it was founded less than fifty years ago as a community college in a semi-rural part of Georgia. Still, located about thirty miles north of downtown Atlanta, it has grown as Atlanta has. Starting with about a thousand students, it transformed into a four-year college with student body of several thousand, and then morphed into a graduate-degree–granting university once it passed the ten thousand mark. Today KSU has over twenty-four thousand students and is the third largest university in the state. No longer a strictly commuter or teaching institution, it has thousands of on-campus residents, tens of thousands of continuing-education learners, and millions of dollars of applied research.

At this point, I have taught as KSU for over two decades—and I have therefore been privy to the school's growing pains. Today widely regarded as a first-rate, albeit non-elite institution, it is clearly not in the same league as Harvard or Yale. As a result, it does not address the identical problems. Although its students once referred to it as the "Harvard in the Pines," no one would mistake KSU for Ivy League. It is, however, representative of the state-supported colleges the bulk of

American students attend. As one of my manuscript's early reviewers observed, KSU has "as many students as the combined number [of undergraduates] for Princeton, Harvard, Swarthmore, MIT, William and Mary, and Williams, the six best colleges and universities in America, according to one of the latest rankings." As a result, I have been afforded insights into what non-elite learners need, but are, in fact, receiving.

Nowadays, when people worry about a college bubble, it is not Harvard or Yale about which they fret. These schools, with their huge cash reserves and select student bodies, are liable to weather even the most severe storm. Rather, it is schools like KSU they expect to founder. I, however, am in a position to determine whether and/or why this is likely. Moreover, my front-row seat enables me to assess the degree to which mid-range schools can successfully emulate the elite ones. Are their attempts to do so strengthening them or making them more vulnerable? I suggest that it is the latter. My thesis is that unless these schools understand their appropriate mission, they cannot fulfill it effectively. The same, of course, applies to the elite ones.

My professional background is also unique in that for the first half of my career, I was not an academic. Indeed, I started out as a clinical sociologist. My job, when employed by a welfare department, a group home, a psychiatric hospital, a methadone clinic, a community mental health center, and a state vocational agency, was to assist ordinary people in addressing real-world problems. This was far from the abstract universe occupied by many college professors in that it demanded theory work hand-in-hand with practice. As a result, my orientation has been toward the concrete and feasible—not pie-in-the-sky speculations.

Add to this mix the fact that I am a sociologist and I see things differently than most observers. Instead of a technical or psychological perspective, I view problems in social context. An awareness of cultural constraints and the power of enduring interpersonal relationships have sensitized me to the effects of social pressures and social evolution. These—not just personal decisions—are often decisive in determining what is done. Moreover, I have written extensively about the professionalization of society (e.g., *The Great Middle Class Revolution: Our Long March toward a Professionalized Society* and *A Professionalized Society: Our Real Future*), the relevance of which will shortly be apparent. While I know this is not the whole story, it is one that is often neglected.

I must also admit to being an unusual sociologist. Unlike most of my colleagues, I am not a liberal, but neither am I a traditional conservative.

I have no desire to return to an idealized past. Instead, my goal is to understand how change occurs. As I make clear in the text, I believe that individuals are rarely the conscious drivers of significant social transformations. To use a metaphor, we are all in the same leaky skiff, with many of us frantically rowing in different directions. As a result, we are bound to get somewhere—but exactly where, we cannot tell.

Nevertheless, I am about to make a number of educated guesses. By looking at social trends as well as the nature of change processes, I have attempted to project ahead. As important, I ask a question the answer to which many commentators take for granted. To wit: what is the "current" mission of higher education? My assumption is that if we do not know where we are going, it is difficult to plot the best way to get there. I further assume that history is a useful guide in determining the proper mission. Still, I do not assume that the elite universities and those like my own are engaged in exactly the same enterprise. While there are important parallels, there are also differences. Moreover, change has been occurring for millennia. The issue is, therefore, in which ways is it headed? More particularly, how is higher education evolving? Will the emerging modifications be the same for all? If we can figure this out, we may be able to fix what is broken.

My first concern is thus: is there a genuine college bubble? Many people respond that there is, but are they right? Have costs gone up and quality come down to such an extent that our colleges and universities are in trouble? Likewise, will enrollments continue to rise or have they reached an upper limit? The answers are mixed and depend upon whom you ask. Much hinges on the values of the commentator. Much also depends upon which schools one examines. In any event, my initial chapter is dedicated to reviewing the possibilities.

Presuming there is a problem, chapter two reviews a broad range of potential solutions. These, however, vary with the expertise of the person making the proposal. Too often, people conclude that their own specialty provides the best answer. Thus, business people propose business answers, computer whizzes advocate computer solutions, and moralists favor moral reforms. Which of these make the most sense depends upon what we are attempting to achieve.

Consequently, chapter three delves into the question of goals. It begins by observing that the mission statements of universities are vague political documents that are too idealistic to serve as suitable guides. History, however, is a better source of counsel. Virtually all civilizations, from ancient China through classic Greece and Rome, the European Middle Ages, and colonial America have employed higher education to prepare their young for leadership positions. What differed were the skills needed and the individuals educated.

Ours has, in fact, become a mass techno-commercial civilization. As a result, we need leaders who can contribute to our joint well-being within this unprecedented context. Given that we depend on millions of strangers for personal survival, these others must possess the skills and motivation to assure our security. The question is, what sorts of individuals best accomplish this? Historically, societies have varied in the mechanisms utilized to maintain cohesion. By and large, what is appropriate is contingent on their size and technological sophistication. Thus, hunter-gatherer societies depended on family connections, while industrial ones have relied on bureaucracies. Our society, however, in becoming post-industrial, has witnessed a more professionalized mode of organization come to the fore. Its emergence therefore dictates that those who direct and coordinate contemporary activities be *self-motivated experts*. Unfortunately, this often pits professionals against bureaucrats—as is frequently the case in the modern university.

Because I come down hard on the side of the professionals (e.g., college professors), the rest of the book is dedicated to exploring how higher education can instill the traits necessary for them to operate effectively. One of the most, if not *the* most, essential is *self-direction*—therefore the title of this work. Individuals who are delegated crucial decisions must be competent at making independent choices. This implies a need to socialize middle-class individuals capable of self-supervision. Parents achieve much of this, but their efforts can—and should—be supplemented by formal education. Fortunately, colleges and universities inculcate not just technical information but also knowledge of the self, others, and social conditions. They can likewise implant the motivation to apply this learning.

By the time we arrive at chapter six, the details of how best to achieve this are explored. The starting point is the core curriculum. Because the young are generally too naïve to know what they must know, they have to be pointed in the right direction. This is especially true at lower-level institutions. The humanities, the social sciences, and the hard sciences all have a role to play in this process. Eventually, students must be encouraged to choose majors and electives from within a suitable range. Extracurricular activities likewise provide vital life preparation. Online learning, however, although it has a place, has been grossly over-sold. Meanwhile, the explosion in for-profit schools is scandalous. The bottom line is that the fundamentals must not be jettisoned. What is more, it is at schools like KSU where they are most in need of protection.

The professionalization process has, however, been undercut by the prevalence of an entitlement culture. Similarly, if every potential student is deemed worthy of a college credential, irrespective of preparation or talents, these degrees become worthless. Standards can remain high only if they are enforced. Yet something more is necessary. Good students (i.e., intellectually able and personally motivated ones) must be allowed to explore what works best for them. Being young, their knowledge of themselves and the world is limited. Accordingly, schools must provide the time and room to discover the optimum fit. Students can achieve this by testing their strengths within a supportive peer culture. They must correspondingly be provided with opportunities to practice self-direction.

Faculties likewise have a role to play in facilitating the development of self-direction. Professors have historically functioned as role models and mentors and should continue doing so. Once more, it is at mid- and lower-level schools where this service is most vital. Ironically, one of the greatest obstacles to the inculcation of professionalism is the ambition of college administrators. Their desire to maintain control has impelled many to curtail professorial discretion. Rather than encourage faculty self-direction, they promote unnecessary forms of standardization and misguided efforts at "accountability." More expedient is a professionalized faculty that applies its expertise assiduously and fairly. Therefore, while a significant proportion of professors should be encouraged to pursue research, not all ought be compelled to do so. Universal standards of "publish or perish" are a prescription for mediocrity. On the other hand, all academics should be obliged to teach. The central mission of education cannot be attained if instruction is relegated to the back burner. Nor need professors be forced into Procrustean beds. If they are not allowed to teach in their own ways, they cannot bring their expertise to bear. As a result, tenure must remain protected. This is essential for preserving both academic freedom and faculty self-direction.

Chapter nine contends that a professionalization and self-direction are in the process of evolving. Utilizing an evolutionary paradigm derived from Daniel Chirot, it explains how long-established practices are upset by social stressors and are then addressed by adaptive radiation and social selection. More particularly, it analyzes the problems that colleges and universities face, the suggested solutions, and why some are working better than others within this evolutionary context.

Not surprisingly, I come to the conclusion that the self-direction model works best. But I also conclude that higher education must create and protect both a community of learners and a marketplace of ideas. These are not new notions, but they have fallen into eclipse with the political "moralization" of higher education. As a result, many values crucial to inculcating self-direction, such as merit, responsibility, and universalism, have been neglected. This has had dire consequences that must be recognized and addressed.

1

The Bubble

A Bubble?

The bookstores are filled with tomes describing the problem (Selingo, 2013). Both the *Chronicle of Higher Education* and *Inside Higher Education* routinely publish articles that warn of the impending debacle. The National Association of Scholars and many other professional organizations make dire predictions about what will occur if there is no reform (Marks, 2012). John Leo's blog, "Minding the Campus," as well as dozens of other Internet postings, keep tabs on the foibles and failures of the contemporary university. Even the lay media have taken to printing stories that suggest American colleges are in deep trouble.

So widespread have forecasts of academic doom become that the predicament has received a name. It is called the "bubble" in emulation of the dot.com and housing bubbles (Barone, 2011, 2013; Agresto, 2011; Shaw, 2011; Reynolds, 2012). Just as Internet stocks rose to perilously high heights and then fell with a thundering crash, and just as housing prices increased to dizzying levels only to recede more quickly, so higher education is expected experience a sharp decline following years of giddy growth. Pundits on both sides of the political aisle worry that the amazing expansion in college enrollments cannot be sustained and that if it isn't, the nation will suffer. Should this occur, they fear that the expertise needed to support our economy will deteriorate and that an entire generation of Americans may be robbed of an opportunity to engage in upward mobility. If so, our nation will be poorer and less democratic than the American dream has traditionally promised.

The housing bubble left millions of people shaken. These individuals expected investments in their residences to pay off handsomely. No matter how much they expended on the initial purchase, the risk would eventually provide a profit over and above their outlay.

Nor would the buyers have to worry about meeting mortgage obligations. With the economy roaring ahead, rising incomes would continually outstrip interest rates. Yet we know what happened. Too many people took on commitments they could not meet and when they defaulted, the financial system collapsed. Many thousands of houses went into foreclosure, and the declining market value of millions of others wiped out the savings of innocent bystanders. So bad were the losses that the economy went into a tailspin. Unemployment climbed to heights not seen since the Great Depression, and it became clear that years would need to go by before the lost ground was recovered.

No wonder that people grow nervous when contemplating another bubble (Shaw, 2011). It is therefore no surprise that they seek solutions to the dangers they suspect are lurking around the corner (Taylor, 2010). But is it true? Is higher education riding for a fall? Have enrollments risen faster than the current institutions—or the nation—can bear (National Center for Educational Statistics, 2001)? Moreover, if our colleges and universities do crumble, will dire effects ripple through the community?

Maybe, however, people are merely recoiling from the uncertainties inherent in change. Perhaps they have allowed their anxieties to get the best of them because they cannot predict the future. Certainly colleges are not what they once were. The number of institutions of higher learning has escalated far beyond its historic peaks. At the moment, there are well over four thousand. Furthermore, far more students are attending college than previously. Nor are they studying what their parents and grandparents did. So what does this mean? Do these developments indicate that higher education will not be able to cope with the challenges? Are they evidence that our universities are failing?

Predictions of doom are nothing new. Ever since their inception, people have fretted about the impending collapse of American colleges. Today we take pride in how soon after the arrival of European settlers higher education took root on our shores. But it was a fragile beginning. Harvard University may have grown into a powerhouse, yet it started by teaching a few dozen scholars. The Puritans, who launched the college in an effort to provide themselves with well-educated ministers, could only manage a pale imitation of the established universities they left behind in England. John Harvard, himself no scholar, had the misfortune of dying young. He lent his name to the new academy, not because of his pedagogic achioevements but by virtue of willing it his modest library. Yet despite this generosity, neither he nor the school's faculty could do much more than keep its doors open during the formative years.

Small numbers of enrollees trooped to Harvard, as they did to Yale, William and Mary, and what later became Princeton, not because these outposts were bastions of scholarship but because there was no viable alternative. In many ways, we moderns would not recognize these institutions. Most of us, for instance, would be surprised to discover that their unexceptional student bodies were even more unruly than those of contemporary universities. Still, these citadels of learning hung on despite the downbeat predictions. Indeed, during the early part of the nineteenth century, a host of tinier colleges sprang up like mushrooms. Most of these were also sponsored by religious denominations in hopes of providing their members with sound leadership and economic opportunity. Even so, many were so brittle that large numbers closed their doors.

Nonetheless, by the middle of the nineteenth century the idea that higher education was noble had been firmly established in America. So romantically were colleges regarded that eventually there was sufficient congressional support to pass the Morrill Act. Such well-known institutions as Cornell, MIT, and Ohio State got their start this way (Christy and Williamson, 1990). Yet in the beginning, these land-grant colleges were also fragile affairs. Their goal of fostering agriculture and mechanics was honorable, but in practice they were distrusted. As a result, students were disinclined to enroll. The upshot was that many folded into more traditional universities.

Meanwhile, places like Harvard and Yale gained reputations as playgrounds for the spoiled scions of the rich. Parents, such as those of William Randolph Hearst (Nasaw, 2000), sent their sons in the hopes of instilling social polish. What they got instead was networking opportunities. Most enrollees preferred to party rather than study. As far as they were concerned, a "gentleman's C" was good enough. Actually, studying was reserved for the few nobodies who depended on what they learned to later earn a living.

It was only toward the end of the nineteenth century that Johns Hopkins led the way toward the modern research university by emulating developments then taking place in Germany. Thankfully, Harvard also began to institute the reforms, such as allowing students to take electives, that saved it from irrelevancy (Thelin, 2011). We today know that these correctives worked, but observers at the time bemoaned the problems with higher education as loudly as does the current generation. Furthermore, such schools as existed were barely able to survive on student tuition; hence, many depended on the contributions of local communities and well-heeled benefactors.

Eventually, as the economy grew, colleges adjusted to fit a new set of realities. Instead of teaching Latin and Greek, they began to provide instruction in the sciences and modern languages. It was at this point that the humanities and social sciences, which many moderns regard as the hallmark of higher education, began to acquire their present shape. This, however, did not certify the progressive reputation of these institutions so much as a concurrent innovation. Football had entered the nation's collective psyche as emblematic of a collegiate education—with Harvard and Yale more broadly regarded as sport powerhouses than academic strongholds.

By the 1920s, the image of the collegian was that of a raccoon-coat–wearing, jalopy-driving, hip-pocket flask-drinking rowdy who was more concerned with celebrating when his team won a championship than reading books. Nor was he ashamed to carouse with the growing numbers of co-eds then making their appearance on campus. College had become cool—yet not a place that encouraged serious learning. Naturally, this too worried those concerned about the fate of higher education. Was this sort of frolicking really meaningful?

Soon, other shocks, albeit of a different order, traumatized the universities. First World War II required them to adjust their curricula so as to prepare soldiers for the technical demands of modern warfare. Happily, this was managed with aplomb. Then there was the influx of millions of a different sort of student following the end of hostilities. With the implementation of the GI Bill, hordes of middle- and working-class men and women decided to pursue a college degree. Not familiar with the pleasure-seeking ways of the upper classes, and serious about improving their economic prospects, they speedily settled into studying with a vengeance.

Once more, commentators fussed about whether universities had the resources to cope. Yet these fears too proved overdrawn. Not long thereafter, the children of newly professionalized parents descended onto campuses. Having been told from the cradle that they would be going to a university, the experience seemed natural to these middle-class students. Accordingly, it was at this point that the modern university came into being. It was now that the numbers of students, including women, began to approach their current proportions. Where higher education had once been reserved for a select elite, it came to be regarded as the birthright of any person who sought social mobility. This soon included the children of the poor.

Mind you, apprehensions about the viability of universities lingered (Bosquet and Nelson, 2008; Delbanco, 2012). Having proved that they could cope with higher enrollments, the new question was whether they could teach the appropriate lessons. After the Soviets launched the first Sputnik, the fear arose that American colleges did not have the wherewithal to train the scientists to keep up with a technologically sophisticated adversary. The response was to direct greater funds to larger numbers of colleges and graduate schools. The federal government literally dumped billions of dollars into campus-based research projects, while additional billions in student loans enabled the financially disadvantaged to earn a degree.

So here we stand with our colleges and universities having expanded to a degree their founders could not have envisaged. One might imagine that this would be cause for celebration, yet we humans, being what we are, have fresh doubts. Today we are again concerned that we have reached an impasse. Have we risen to such heights that we cannot sustain the achievements bequeathed us by earlier generations? Can we build upon the foundation currently in place?

Exactly what has, or is, liable to go wrong is in dispute. After all, few observers evaluate the contemporary scene with the identical yardsticks (Fukuyama, 1995, 1999). Nor do they harbor the same hopes. Nonetheless, many share common anxieties. Having witnessed too many bubbles, they are terrified of a new one. Accordingly, they worry about a shapeless catastrophe. The question is, are they right? Should we be alarmed because a series of shocks are about to swamp our leaky skiff? One thing is certain: the changes will continue. The real issue is, what these will be.

Towards a "Self-Directed" University

Whether or not we are facing imminent disaster, there can be little question that the times are in flux. There can also be little doubt that the answers to our current challenges will differ from those inaugurated by our ancestors. Just as they made alterations as their world became more industrialized, so we have to adjust to a post-industrial world. The question is, what will this world look like and what sorts of demands will it make of higher education? Fortunately, while the future cannot be known in its entirity, it is possible to make educated guesses about its general outlines.

To begin with, ours is a mass techno-commercial society. We are surrounded by hundreds of millions of strangers upon whom we depend for survival. These others, most of whom we never meet, provide the food, clothing, shelter, and protection that enable us to live comfortably. Indeed, without their assistance we would literally starve. But how can we be sure that these others will continue to deliver what is needed? Can we, in fact, trust them to supply the essential goods and services? Are we right to be certain that they are the sorts of persons who have the skills and the motivation to keep doing this over the long haul?

Much of our confidence rests upon how well these others are prepared to fulfill the responsibilities assigned them. If they learn what they need to know and internalize a desire to perform the required tasks competently, our fears may be allayed. As important, if those who supervise the activities of these people are similarly knowledgeable and motivated, there is a better chance that the complex occupations upon which we rely will be successfully executed. In short, we require many individuals—many more than in the past—who are prepared to exercise expert leadership in a host of challenging endeavors. As a consequence, we likewise need an effective means of grooming these leaders for the duties they will assume.

As it happens, our colleges and universities are on the front line of readying young adults to undertake leadership roles. It is these institutions upon which we rely to instill the kinds of knowledge and determination these positions demand. The shorthand way to describe what is needed is "professionalization." Professionals are *self-motivated experts* in the complex specialities upon which techno-commercial societies depend. They are the sorts of persons who are capable of making the difficult decisions needed to direct and coordinate the enormously complicated pursuits that keep our market-based economies and democratically organized governments functioning.

But in order to become professionalized, individuals must undergo a rigorous socialization. There is a great deal of information to be absorbed and many arduous skills to be mastered. Yet there is something more. Professionalized leaders need to be proficient decision makers. They must frequently make independent choices within environments of uncertainty. As a consequence, they must be capable of skillful discretion. If others are to be governed by what they decide, these persons must have the courage to make ambiguous choices, the wisdom to make these prudently, and the integrity to correct the inevitable errors. These abilities may be summed up by describing such persons as "self-directed." They are self-starters who possess the personal qualities needed to exercise intelligent initiative without having to resort to detailed directions from adminstrative superiors.

Grooming such individuals is itself a challenging mission; nevertheless, it is the central task of contemporary higher education. Because the need for professionalization has expanded exponentially, not just elite institutions (such as those of the Ivy League) but many less select schools are now charged with promoting self-direction. For the latter in particular, this may include fostering social mobility. Individuals whose families of origin did not prepare them to exercise discretion must be assisted in growing into the sorts of individuals capable of it. This is no easy feat; still and all, it can be accomplished by schools that are aware of this mission and adjust their programs accordingly.

Fortunately, what is needed to make our colleges and universities more effective in achieving this goal does not imply a drastic overhaul. In many ways, today's academies have already been evolving in this direction. Confronted with students, parents, and politicians demanding the fruits of professionalization (even if these pressure groups are only dimly aware of its specifics), schools have developed much of the machinery to promote it. Peter Wood and Michael Toscano (2013) of the National Association of Scholars have succinctly put what until recently has been the direction higher education defined itself as pursuing. They describe this aim as "a complex forstering of knowledge, motivations, character, skills, attitudes, and commitments." Still, there have been missteps. A lack of clarity about the nature of self-direction has impeded efforts to instill its constituents. Accordingly, higher education needs to refocus its exertions. Those seeking reform must therefore alter their perspective so as to facilitate its most vital objectives. As such, they must worry less about promoting novel pedigogical techniques and more about understanding the social context in which they operate.

A useful analogy has been provided by the All-Star baseball player Ken Harrelson. In his current role as an announcer for the Chicago White Sox, he often explains that what converted him from a journeyman hitter into an outstanding one was a change in attitude rather than in mechanics. As long as he went to the plate worrying about where his hands were positioned, his batting average was pathetic. But when he switched to thinking in terms of what he intended to do, what the pitcher intended to do, and what the context of the moment demanded, he quickly led the league in runs-batted-in. Educational planners, if they are to be credible, would benefit from a similar mental adjustment. In their case, it is the larger social context, the one requiring self-direction, that must be appreciated. Specific pedagogical methodologies, while they are not irrelevant, are secondary. It is in being professionalized and being comfortable with encouraging professionalization that academics—and those counseling them—will have their most constructive impact.

But first it is necessary to investigate the nature of the problems confronting contemporary higher education. There is, it turns out, not one problem but a tangle of related problems. Nor are all of these consistent. Moreover, because different commentators have different objectives, how they evaluate these snags varies. By the same token, their recommendations for reform are typically contingent on a variety of values and competences. Pundits frequently support improvements in accord with their personal beliefs and abilities. It is therefore necessary to review the range of proposals before sorting through them to determine the most advantageous. This sorting process itself is contingent upon clarifying the mission of higher education, which in turn is best achieved by reviewing the history of such endeavors. It develops that advanced forms of education have long concentrated on preparing social elites for leadership positions. What has been taught, however, has differed with the nature of the society and its needs.

Only at this point will we be able to turn our analysis to examining the sorts of knowledge and skills our society requires. The closer inspection of these made when we arrive at chapter four will quickly reveal that small preindustrial societies, industrial ones, and our post-industrial one make different demands. With respect to colleges and universities, the most crucial of these confronting us follows from the changeover from a bureaucratic form of organization to a professionalized one. It develops that to a large extent, the challenges bedeviling contemporary academies derive from a failure to make this transition. Still mired in bureaucratic forms of governance, schools, often unintentionally, hobble efforts to expand self-motivated expertise. This then is the larger picture that must be kept in mind when addressing the college bubble.

All of this is preamble to scrutinizing the nature of self-direction so as to identify how best to implement it in our colleges and universities. What sorts of specialized knowledge do their curricula need to emphasize? And how do these schools go about instilling the appropriate forms of motivation? Much of what is in place need not be disturbed; nevertheless, a renewed concentration on the human dimensions of leadership and decision making ought be put into effect. It also must be understood that different schools, because of their differing student bodies and academic concentrations, may need to pursue these objectives in their own way.

In any event, what is taught, how students are encouraged to learn, and the role that professors and adminstrators play in these endeavors will be considered in the final chapters of this work. In doing so, it will become evident that while generalizations are valuable, so are specifics. How, we must ask, is a professionalized attitude operationalized at ground level? Furthermore, while some approaches may be better than others, does this indicate that a one-size-fits-all approach is appropriate? Almost surely not! Because many desirable changes entail cultural modifications, off-the-rack structural innovations handed down from on high generally interfere with the give-and-take in which new ideas are developed, tested, and adopted.

To put the matter baldly, improved ways of doing academic business are apt to *evolve* rather than derive from social engineering. Hence, we must eventually examine the evolutionary process itself. When we get to our final chapter we must therefore look back to see how our colleges and univseritities have coped with the stressors created by becoming more professionalized. We must also review the solutions suggested and evaluate how well these have fared in the testing process. A self-directed perspective may be vital, but its particulars will emerge slowly and from multiple sources. As a result, we must scritinize these and judge their efficacy.

This said, let us get on with a step-by-step examination of what, if anything, is wrong with contemporary colleges and universities. In what follows I will be casting a broad net in an effort to reconcile the many conflicting recommendations. Although a few of my own ideas may stike some readers as extreme, bear in mind that they too are part of a much larger process that of necessity entails assessing and modifying a variety of incompatible proposals. Observers coming from different directions may therefore be uncomfortable with discordant viewpoints. This too, however, is in the nature of the evolutionary progression in which we are enmeshed.

Straws in the Wind

Some educational problems are agreed upon. Commentators of different ideological stripes may differ regarding their severity or how they should be handled, yet a majority regard a core set of issues to be problematic. It, therefore, behooves us to inspect these to determine whether they are indeed acute. In the next chapter, we will ask about the appropriate sorts of response, but first, what has gone wrong?

Everyone agrees that costs of a college education have been rising astronomically (Hacker and Dreifus, 2010; Barone, 2012; Bennett and Wilezel, 2013). People may not concur as to why this is so or on how to control the increase, but there is no disputing that the number of dollars the government, private foundations, parents, and students have poured into university coffers has grown faster than the economy. As a result, people wonder whether this surge can be maintained. Will one or another of the current financial spigots go bankrupt and be forced to shut off the flow? Or will the funding continue but in the process, deny other projects the resources they require? Perhaps the nation will not have enough money to repair its highways, or provide welfare, or keep the military in modern weaponry. Worse still, maybe we are wasting money on underwriting unproductive educational efforts. Indeed, might we get more bang for the buck if we channeled expenditures elsewhere?

Clearly, tuition costs have been growing at an alarming rate (Nelson, 2013). Many of our elite universities charge over fifty thousand dollars per annum, and that does not include living expenses. Even some state schools now charge over ten thousand a year. For most families, this is beyond their means. In fact, only the very wealthy can afford to pay the freight for the best schools out of their own pockets (Armstrong and Hamilton, 2013). For most others, some sort of financial assistance is required. The question, therefore, becomes, are university endowments large enough to absorb these costs? With the present decline in the economy, they certainly have fewer dollars available than previously. Yet what about the future? If short-term funds can be found, will these be available for the long term?

Even the government, however, has limits on what it can provide. In point of fact, as the recent recession ate into state and federal budgets, the assets directed toward colleges markedly decreased. State legislatures were undertandably reluctant to provide the same largesse as formerly. Consequently, most trimmed what they allocated to working budgets and a majority eliminated capital projects. In addition, in order to make up the shortfall, they approved tuition increases—often large ones. They also had to cut back on scholarship programs; frequently by making their requirements more stringent. There was little choice. With many states facing huge deficits, the only way to balance their budgets was through reduced spending. As it happened, higher education seemed more expendable than prisons or grammar schools.

Some believe that the answer to this problem lies in increased taxes. Nonetheless, the resistance to this is substantial, because many voters are concerned about the ultimate impact of large-scale deficits. As for student loans, those that are outstanding are approaching the trillion-dollar mark. The question, therefore, is, can these be repaid or will defaults produce another economic bubble? Since many loan recipients have uncertain vocational prospects, they may never earn enough to pay back what they receive. What is more, with ever-growing numbers of for-profit schools encouraging growing numbers of poorly prepared enrollees, the ability of their graduates to earn sufficiently high incomes may be compromised. How, for instance, will the student who was promised a remunerative career in law enforcement but finds himself a security guard manage to keep up his payments?

Then there is the issue of whether such monies as are available are wisely spent. Many fear they are not. They fret about the so-called "frills" to which colleges seem addicted. Nowadays, sundry institutions of higher education expend scarce resources on spas and fancy athletic equipment in order to attract students. This penchant even applies to state schools. They too invest in Olympic-size swimming pools, expensive workout equipment, and rock-climbing walls. Then there are the exotic menus of college dining halls and the less-than-Spartan appointments of university dormitories. Where once undergraduates were crammed into sardine-sized rooms and gobbled down tuna fish sandwiches to make ends meet, today they demand the space to stretch out and play with their electronic devices before they head off to lunch on sushi or Moroccan lamb stew.

As if this were not enough, rather than invest in old-fashioned academics, many colleges prefer to erect monumental edifices. They engage in multimillion-dollar fund drives so they can put up an administrative building that boasts a breathtaking atrium filled with delicate tropical plants. Add to this the hundreds of millions expended on new football stadiums and the resultant bills include more extras than are peddled by automobile dealerships. In truth, many schools squander far more on sports than on the humanities. Only a few football teams make money, whereas many colleges spend hundreds of thousands on coaches they hope will elevate their program into the big leagues. The goal is to attract so much publicity that enrollments rise and costs are off-set. Yet for most institutions this remains an elusive ambition, especially if their teams do not win—which most don't.

Even when it comes to academics, administrative hubris knows few bounds. In the hopes that one day they may rival Harvard and MIT, presidents and provosts authorize state-of-the-art laboratory facilities intended to vault their schools to the apex of the intellectual map. They also lust after a faculty replete with nationally and internationally recognized experts. The latest computers, telescopes, and DNA-testing devices likewise find their way into already bloated budgets.

Since what goes up almost never comes down, the balance sheets of many universities resemble that of the federal government. They too have inbuilt deficits their administrators are forever scrambling to erase. The question is, how long can this orgy be sustained? Spending cannot rise indefinitely, so what happens when the projected outlays are not met? Will college campuses become an academic version of Greece? Will they too fall into a genteel decline or explode in a bacchanal of self-flagellation?

Enrollments

Just as with the housing bubble, many universities imagined that their enrollments would continuously rise (Vedder and Gillen, 2011). They always had, and so the green-eyeshade accountants in the backroom did what they usually do. They predicted a future grounded in the past. On this basis, even if growth did not accelerate, it would be sufficient to cover anticipated expenses. Since more folks craved a college education, the pool of potential customers was not close to being exhausted.

Except this mind-set seems to have been as injudicious as that of homeowners who took a flyer on edifices out of their price range. Here the question is, has the normal optimism that afflicts human beings when things go well set the stage for difficulties when conditions change? So far, the elite universities have managed without inordinate trouble. Their waiting lists are long enough to keep their numbers up. Some lower-level institutions, however, have seen enrollments decline. As of now, the reverses are modest, nonetheless this was not expected. It had been assumed that in hard economic times, more students would arrive on campus. Having been laid off from their jobs, they would seek improved skills so as to become more employable.

This latter did not occur to the extent imagined, because potential enrollees made an unwelcome discovery. They came to realize that advanced degrees were not automatically remunerative. With so many others boasting advanced credentials, these no longer stood out from the crowd. In much the same way that a good rain helps after a long dry spell but makes things worse in the wake of torrential downpours, so a glut of degrees makes each of them less valuable. Ivy League graduates are still in good shape, but even they find the pickings less robust.

Some reformers, such as Bill Gates, predicted that eventually nearly every American would earn a college degree and that a majority might obtain a master's or doctorate (Fain, 2013). But the slowdown in enrollments made many onlookers realize the limits might be reached sooner than expected. Still, optimists forecast a resumption of the upward trend. Indeed, some, such as Gates, aggresively promote college training for everyone. Nevertheless, doubts crept in. Could small changes in a negative direction be a harbinger of disasters to come?

Time

Another unexpected development was the amount of time students were taking to get their degrees. Back in the days when going to college was a minority pursuit, traditional students finished their studies in four years. They traveled to a campus some distance from their homes, took a full load of courses each year, did sufficiently well to pass them, and then were awarded their sheepskins on the anticipated date. So routine was this that an incoming class was identified by the year it was expected to graduate.

Some students, of course, did not follow this schedule. Many went to night school where the time required was extended due to the need to earn a living. A significant number of these scholars were older and came from disadvantaged backgrounds. If they took longer than traditional students, this was because they encountered greater obstacles. Still, a by-product of this delay was a relatively inferior education. Few considered the alumni of a night law school the equal of traditional law schools. With less time to study under the tutelage of less well-respected professors and probably struggling under the burden of insufficient talent, they learned less. Had they been more gifted, they would surely have obtained the financial support to go to a better place.

It therefore came as a surprise when the normal time needed to obtain a bachelor's degree rose to five and then six or more years. Most of those who attend the elite schools continue to follow the customary timetable, but even students who enroll in flagship state universities began to take longer. When it comes to colleges lower down the pecking order, the slowdown is more apparent. Many of their students take time off during their college careers, attempt fewer credits each the term, especially with regard to difficult courses, and drift from one major to another. It is not unusual for some intentionally to stretch out their college careers. Not yet ready to assume adult responsibilities, they hope to make their childhoods last as long as possible.

Yet this too increased the burdens on universities. With more superannuated students on campus, the resources needed to meet their demands rose. The ranks of undergraduates now also include professional students who jump from one campus to another. They likewise embrace older students attempting to rectify mistakes made earlier in life. Thus, many women who left school to raise a family return to campus to get a degree once their children achieve independence.

All across the nation, college administrators ponder what they consider dismal graduation rates. Time and again, often at the behest of state legislators or regents, they institute policies designed to speed students through the system. Yet time and again, the improvements are modest. Is this because there are now too many students who do not have the intellectual horsepower to complete the required course load in the requisite timeframe? Or is it because average students will not be rushed? As full-fledged adults, many decide to take courses suited to their schedules, not to a school's. Or maybe people just need more time to decide what they want to be when they grow up in a world replete with thousands of imperfectly understood opportunities.

Whatever the problem, the new attitudes toward college challenge the traditional model. Is this too a harbinger of revolutionary change? Does it mean that universities need to be reorganized to deal with these developments?

The Humanities

Irrespective of the costs of a college education, or the trends in enrollment, or the time it takes to finish, the sorts of programs students choose has also undergone dramatic revision. Where once the core of a higher education was located in the humanities, these are in serious decline (Ellis, 1997; Agresto, 2011). By 2008, the percentage of English majors had fallen to 3.5 percent of all graduates. This compared to 8 percent in the 1970s. As for history majors, they now comprise 2.13 percent of graduates. Most college students are no longer interested in mastering English literature or fathoming the causes of the French Revolution (Schama, 2000). They are more interested in something practical. Parents across the land warn that if Junior majors in philosophy, starvation awaits upon graduation. College is not supposed to be about taking a subject you enjoy but finding one that leads to a realistic vocation. This is especially so at lower-level institutions.

Indeed, the single most popular major is now business. By 2008, this had grown to 22 percent of all majors. Clearly, there is an enduring need for accountants and marketing managers, but for many students, the golden ring is ascent into the executive suite. Even before they reach their senior year, they imagine themselves becoming the CEO or CFO of a vast corporation. Some day, they too will sit in a Lear jet, winging their way to a business summit in the Caribbean. It is merely a matter of time and lucking their way into the right connections. This is why courses on business policy are so popular. Students taught how to create a winning business plan dream of being hired to guide an organization into prosperity. Then they too will make decisions that have broad impact.

Other practical, or apparently practical, majors also beckon. Among these are nursing and education. A career in teaching has long been considered a sensible choice for a woman who expects to have a family. Meanwhile, careers in nursing have soared in earning potential and social esteem. Where once nurses—most of whom are female—were perceived as helpmeets to male physicians, the occupation acquired greater respect and autonomy as its practitioners became professionalized. No longer limited to emptying bedpans or changing bandages, an accretion of technical skills amplified the demand for well-trained caregivers. The problem for many potential nursing majors, however, is that, unlike teachers, the required intellectual aptitude is substantial. As a result, many who seek jobs in the medical field must settle for a paraprofessional niche.

Those students with a more theatrical flare often migrate into becoming communications majors. Many eventually hope to find a slot as a newsreader on television. Despite the fact that there are very few such positions, not to mention the declining number of posts available as newspaper reporters, journalism and quasi-journalism retain a romantic aura. So does criminal justice.

Here too both men and women flock to crowded classrooms in hopes of becoming a profiler or crime-scene investigator. Having grown to maturity entranced by the exciting police narratives on the home screen, they crave a piece of the action. Many of the male students indeed find work in policing, but many women discover that a life on the streets dealing with criminals does not suit their self-image. The closer they come to translating what they learn in the classroom into an actual job, the more they realize that the romanticism they expected is an illusion. Thus, despite the fact that there are more openings for female law enforcement agents, they shy away at the moment of truth.

It might be supposed that given the prestige, demand, and compensation associated with engineering occupations, these majors would be teeming with male aspirants. This, however, is far from the case. While there are large numbers of such students, a significant proportion come from abroad. As a consequence, many leave the United States when they complete their studies. Engineering, it seems, is too difficult to attract young adults seeking a rocket ride to the top of the social heap. Medicine, of course, also qualifies as prestigious vocation, but it is even more difficult to get into med school. And besides, the effort required to become a physician is daunting.

This leaves law as an attractive alternative. It is also one of the traditional professions and as such retains social panache. Moreover, in an era where television dramas depict attorneys as champions of truth and justice, it too boasts a romantic aura. In addition, becoming a lawyer takes less time than becoming a doctor and demands lesser academic talents. The trouble is that law schools are churning out more attorneys than the available legal work requires. As a result, the nation has twice as many lawyers as physicians, with many of the former unable to obtain work in their field of choice. Large numbers instead become executives, journalists, and even college professors (e.g., in criminal justice).

As for the humanities, they have been left in the dust. What is the point of studying literature if the few available jobs are with a handful of publishers, and these pay minuscule salaries, thanks to an oversupply of applicants? The only viable alternative is teaching, but the college ranks are also overcrowded, while teaching high school holds few allures for academic stars who imagined themselves the next great American novelist. The same problem afflicts potential historians. Few carve out a niche comparable to Newt Gingrich. The rest frequently settle for an academic career that is not nearly as fulfilling as the glories on display in the historical sources. Nor are graduates of non-elite schools liable to find even these jobs. Given the oversupply of candidates, those from the best schools get first crack at them.

Potential artists, of course, know even when they are young that they and their ilk are liable to starve in a Greenwich Village garret. Nevertheless, many still feel called upon to sacrifice for the sake of their art. Gifted with a talent few others possess, whether as painters, sculptors, actors, or musicians, they accept the fact that they must suffer on the way to discovering whether they will be among the lucky few stars.

With regard to the social sciences, sociologists can become social workers, psychologists can become clinicians, anthropologists can obtain a positions studying South Seas tribes, and political scientists can become elected officials. Still, most do not end up where they imagined. Either their actual jobs are not what they foresaw or there are fewer openings in the ones they desire than the supply of aspirants can absorb. In any event, like humanities majors, most wind up in slots they never heard of. Colleges may offer useful information, but little of this turns out to be directly germane to the vocations they enter.

All in all, the lack of relevancy of the humanities, arts, and social sciences calls into question the validity of a traditional college education. Why spend the time and money acquiring knowledge that will soon be forgotten? Why not instead seek an entirely different route to adult success? For many, this is not an academic question but one that will affect their lifelong trajectories. As for the universities, it matters to them in that this attitude could cause their enrollments to come crashing down.

Quality

Another indicator that a college bubble is imminent is the declining quality of much of what passes for higher education (Bloom, 1987; Johnson, 2002; Buarlein, 2009; Kolwich, 2011; Mansfield, 2013; Voegeli, 2013). The elite universities boast faculties with international reputations; nevertheless, these are not the pedagogues with whom most undergraduates rub elbows. The academic stars may deign to teach one auditorium full of lower-division students per year, but many prefer not to converse with unwashed quasi-adolescents at all. This task is delegated to graduate assistants. Themselves merely beginning to learn their disciplines, these novice scholars are assigned to guide the breakout sessions where questions can be asked and answers provided. As almost everyone involved with prestigious colleges understands, their students learn mostly from one another. Luckily, because these neophytes are generally the best and brightest of their academic cohort, their peers are also academically talented. As a consequence, their collaborative explorations are, in fact, capable of expanding intellectual horizons.

Moving down toward the less prestigious institutions, the academic resources are less consistent. Many possess brilliant teachers and researchers, but they also employ a host of mediocrities. While their students can get a good education, much depends upon their personal motivation—a condition not always met. By and large, these schools don't provide an intellectually charged atmosphere. Often infused with a party ethos, few of their professors expect more than a tiny minority of their pupils to become academic giants. Nor do many students aspire to this outcome. Their goal is to receive a useful credential as painlessly as possible. In the meantime, they seek to get by without having to read too many boring books.

Indeed, one of the lessons most professors at mid-level schools learn is that a majority of their students hate to read. Classes can be assigned several books, but once students are examined it becomes evident they have not opened a single page. The faculty can, of course, compel students to do research papers. Yet when these are read, they either exhibit a woeful ignorance of standard grammar or reveal the unmistakable mark of having been cribbed from the Internet. A love of learning per se is ordinarily regarded as geeky. Much like the elite students of yore who were satisfied with passable grades, these more democratic student bodies are not inclined to devote themselves to assiduous study.

Then, there is the pervasive issue of adjuncts. As costs have risen, the problem of getting qualified instructors into the classroom has been solved by hiring untenured personnel. These lecturers are frequently graduate students or individuals with master's-level credentials. Most are relatively inexperienced, although some have years engaged as practitioners. In any event, it is not unsusual for adjuncts to be tepid teachers. Having no investment in the schools where they are temporarily employed, and generally less knowledgable than tenured professors, the information they impart is usually of a lesser caliber. Nor should it be overlooked that they are typically paid non-living wages. Were they not supported by student loans and/or other jobs, they could not afford to put food on the table. Unfortunately, this too lowers the incentive to give one's all in the classroom.

For years, colleges have argued that their central mission is to foster "critical thinking." They proudly claim to open minds to the glories of a intellectual endeavor. Instead of just passively listening to professors, their learners are presumably encouraged to consider meanings and implications. As a result, these proto-scholars learn to think things through and not take anyone's word on faith. Putting two and two together, they notice when these do not add up and quickly reject bogus arguments. While they might not remember every jot and title of what they read in English or history classes, practice in analyzing challenging materials is generalized to other aspects of life where they delve deeper and more searchingly.

Once, about a century ago, scholars argued that it was essential to teach college students Greek and Latin. Latin was deemed to be especially valuable in disciplining the mind. Because its construction was considered uniquely logical, it was assumed that this would be transferred to other intellectual tasks. Unfortunately, the newly emerging academic psychologists decided to test this proposition. They found that the supposed benefits were a myth. There was no crossover effect to mental discipline as a whole. This was one of the reasons the classical languages went into eclipse.

Recently, a similar shock traumatized the modern university. Researchers decided to test whether college studies actually improved critical thinking. As documented in the widely read *Academically Adrift* (Arum and Rosca, 2011), the answer turns out to be no. While there is a small effect for some students, it is nothing to write home about. What is more, such improvements as occured seemed to have more to do with who the students were than what they were taught.

As will shortly be argued, much of what is labeled critical thinking is a species of ideological indoctrination. Students are often judged to be thinking analytically when they are critical of the belief systems their professors reject. Paradoxically, students are not allowed to come to independent judgments but are asked to parrot what they have been taught. Their mentors then evaluate these efforts as intellectually astute because they reflect their own thought processes.

Yet another blow to quality education has been grade inflation. With so many students embarking on higher education with an entitlement chip on their shoulders, they fully expect grades consistent with their bloated self-opinions. If they do not get them, they blame their instructors. Often coming with cap in hand, they plead for a higher grade—lest they lose a scholarship or fail to achieve a grade-point average sufficient to get into graduate school. With tears in their eyes, they explain that if the professor does not provide relief, their lives will be ruined. Many faculty members then capitulate. Unwilling to be bad-mouthed to the adminstration and oftentimes sympathetic to a student's plight, they do what many of their colleagues are doing. They take the easy way out and submit a revised grade. So frequently does this occur, that the grade curve has been skewed upward. As a result, many students believe they are learning more than they are because their grade-point average suggests accomplishments in excess of those actually achieved.

This overestimation is further facilitated by the attitudes of parents and administrators. With no one desirous of looking bad in comparision with the competition, an unspoken alliance conspires to maintain feelings of entitlement. Thus, students told for years they are brilliant come to believe this. Meanwhile, their parents, intent on maintaining family reputations, are displeased when professors do not cooperate. As a consequence, they make their irritation known to adminstrators who, as political animals, do not want funding streams disturbed. The next step is for these presidents, provosts, and deans to appease the critics. They do so by cautioning faculties to refrain from being provocative. And the best way to prevent inflamatory reactions is to provide the inflated grades that make students look good.

The sad part is that overblown self-images do not equate to authentic accomplishments. Students and parents, convinced that they should not have to endure damaged egos, are rarely motivated to put in the work necessary for genuine learning. Is it any wonder that achievement tests routinely reveal that American students are not as good in math, science, or history as the foreign competition? The universities they attend may be churning out more graduates, but this does not mean their output matches what was once considered a college level education.

One additional nail in the coffin of quality learning is provided by student evaluations. Once upon a time, the teaching ability of faculty members was assessed by their colleagues. Today, in the name of responsiveness, virtually all institutions of higher learning stipulate that teachers be evaluated by their students. These professors are then subject to what amounts to student-based report cards. The goal is to provide feedback for all concerned in the hope that problems can be identified and corrected.

This sounds like a good idea, except for several concurrent factors. The first is that, as research demonstrates, students tend to award the best evaluations to teachers they like. Popularity, not academic rigor, is the touchstone of their appraisals. This means that many faculty members pander to students. This is frequently achieved by lowering classroom reqirements, while simultaneously hiking grades. Keep things fun is the watchword for these educators. Some even resort to giving almost every student an A. Naturally, this sort of leiniency does not encourage academic excellence. Nonetheless, this fails to scandalize most administrators. Charged with judging the effectiveness of their underlings, they feel comfortable relying on apparently objective measures. Student evaluations offer this. In the end, faculty reviews are often skewed by the numbers provided by such evaluations. The upshot is that nondemanding pedagogues often look better on paper than their more demanding peers. This is especially problematic for controversial professors. They may force their students to think, but if a significant percentage are offended, they can obtain their revenge at the end of the term. All in all, this process is not calculated to enhance academic objectives. Although it is lauded as promoting "accountability," an absence of quality argues otherwise.

The Gender Gap

Another problem that is not always perceived as a problem entails the gender skew of contemporary universities. Where once males dominated colleges, the situation has been reversed (DiPrete and Buchmann, 2013). Only decades ago, women were not regarded as suitable candidates for a higher education. They weren't deemed as intelligent as men, nor was what they learned thought applicable to their subsequent careers. After all, they were going to marry and become mothers. While their potential husbands benefited from additional schooling, they would do so only indirectly.

Times have changed. Few currently suggest that women should not go to college. Even fewer contend that women cannot hack it in the classroom. Nor are there many who claim that females cannot benefit professionally from a university degree. Indeed, the triumph of feminism has exposed those who make such assertions to withering rebuke. With women continuously told to be "all they can be," the suggestion that they limit their aspirations is interpreted as sexist. Surely women too should aim for a slot in the executive suite. Why must an accident of birth preclude them from becoming CEOs?

Next, there is the small fact that women are doing better academically than men. On average, their grades are significantly higher. They are also more likely to read assigned books, write assigned papers, and show up to hear lectures. They are similarly less trouble in the classroom. More polite and less acerbic, they offer less of a challenge. Then, once they graduate, many get jobs comensurate with their education. There may have been a time when most women became stay-at-home housewives, but this is no longer so. Even if they get married and have children, most enter the vocational arena. Indeed, the number of women employed outside the home is nearly identical to that of men.

So what is the problem? For starters, it must be admitted that few observers interpret this evolving gender imbalance as problematic. Indeed, many hail it as a healthy development. So again, what is the difficulty? Well, it is that, far from being excluded from higher education, women now account for nearly two-thirds of enrollments. While there are differences in the disciplines that attract men and women, many classrooms have become female ghettoes. This is especially so in the humanities and social sciences, as well as traditional female specialties such as nursing, social work, and elementary education.

Once more, what is wrong with this? The answer lies in the potential consequences of higher education. For years, it has been argued that a college degree is a ticket to vocational success. Those who graduate are described as earning more money and exercising greater power. Let us, for the moment, assume that this is correct. If it is, what does this imply for the future. Will women shortly be earning higher incomes than men? Likewise, will more rise to the helm of great corporations than their male counterparts? If a college education is the gatekeeper to occupational success, does this project a gender realignment in the workplace? Few make this forecast, but if this shift does not occur, what are the implications for universities? Will they no longer claim to be the royal road to professional advancement? If so, will they lose their social cache and with it their lofty enrollments?

Then too there is the current impact on male students. Recently attendees at the annual conference of NASPA: Student Affairs Administrators in Higher Education were surprised by the results of a dissertation that inadvertantly measured the attitudes of male adminstrators (Greenspan, 2013). Sandra Miles, herself a college adminstrator, reported that many of the men she questioned felt discriminated against. The fact is that straight white males are frequently depicted as oppressors within college precincts. Why then should they, or male students, feel comfortable in such places? And if they are not, will they find the education that these provide to be relevant to their futures? Furthermore, if it is not, will they continue to enroll in comparable numbers?

The Culture Wars

So far most of the problems discussed have elicited broad agreement. With the exception of the gender skew, a majority have been widely remarked upon. Thus, commentators tend to agree that costs, time, enrollments, humanities programs, and declining quality present major challenges. Exactly what they identify as most troublesome differs, as do the preferred solutions; nevertheless, most are in accord about most issues. There are, however, areas of serious contention. Ideological differences often impel observers to stress divergent sources of trouble. Thus, the values people hold and the strategies they promote combine to produce diametrically opposed recommendations.

We in the United States are in the midst of a culture war (Hunter, 1991). Partisans from the left and right are regularly at each other's throats. Is it any surprise therefore that higher education should be a bone of contention? And indeed, liberals and conservatives interpret the challenges facing our colleges differently. Both sides warn of storm clouds, but they identify problem areas as worlds apart. Each faction tells us that reform is essential, yet they advocate incompatible modifications.

Liberals tend to favor what they describe as "progress." They also insist on the importance of social justice. As a result, they conceive of higher education as a mechanism for disseminating their views (Deveaux, 2000). They assume that once young people understand the world as they (i.e., the liberals) understand it, they will inevitably flock to the side of fairness. For liberals, college is a place to both educate and mobilize forces that advance their moral agenda (Wood and Toscano, 2013). Hence to the extent that universities do not foster this, they are perceived as in need of restructuring.

Obviously, conservatives dissent. Their central concerns, which they too conceive of as moral, are advancing individual merit and traditional values. For them, colleges fail if they do not facilitate academic achievement and/or if they trample on standards inherited from previous generations. As a consequence, conservatives do not so much perceive themselves as reformers as the champions of established ideals. From their perspective, the bubble will burst if time-honored objectives are not protected. Colleges would then have nothing worth teaching and hence would slide into irrelevance.

Liberals

Liberals believe in social justice (Sowell, 2009). They are convinced that they have a duty to rectify the moral ills that plague humankind. They further believe that universities provide one of the best tools for achieving this. In addition, they are certain that were they to sit on the sidelines, they would be complicit in perpetuating unspeakable evils. As a result, they press for a variety of correctives. Their objective is to midwife a society that is more honorable than its predecessors. To do less violates their conviction that they are good people.

For this reason, when liberals survey the state of higher education, they bemoan the fact that it has not lived up to its potential. According to them, colleges are in trouble because they have not expedited the transition to a more just society. They regard merely theoretical knowledge as impotent and useless. As they see it, that which scholars learn about the world must be applied to making positive changes or it will be as inconsequential as determining the number of angels that can dance on the head of a pin. Moreover, were this the case, this updated version of scholaticism would be as impotent as its medieval forebear and thus destined for oblivion. The only way out is to restructure universities so that they impliment their proper mission.

Among the areas in which justice is to be pursued are social class, race, gender, and sexual orientation. Let us begin with social class. Colleges have long been percieved as gateway to social mobility. While it is true that they often provided the polish and networking needed to solidify upper-class status, they also enabled the children of the poor and working classes to acquire the knowledge and cultural attributes necessary to succeed in business and politics. Individuals who were not born into privledge could, if they were talented, parlay four years at a selective institution into a lucrative career. The problem was that this avenue was unduly restrictive. Only a few of the most gifted could avail themselves of it. This, however, left millions of deserving youngsters struggling to catch up. Through no fault of their own, they did not obtain the credentials to compete on an even playing field.

Such discrimination clearly demands correction. If universities merely promote a token opposition to an entrenched aristocracy, they are scarcely worth support. Higher education therefore needs to be democratized if it is to promote the American dream. Not only must the numbers enrolled continue to expand, but the lessons taught have to produce social mobility. Indeed, in the long run almost everyone should obtain a college education (Fain, 2013). To foster an artificial exclusivity literally denies countless Americans their birthright.

For the same reason, liberals argue that college curricula have to be drastically overhauled to make them more useful. Highbrow courses no longer make sense. The materials imparted must either be practical or grounded in the experience of ordinary people. These are the lessons that can be applied in the real world. Instead of flights of ethereal poetry or tributes to the fictional achievements of the great and powerful, information derived from actual events must occupy central stage. This celebrates truths that matter, instead of fabricated narratives that discourage accomplishments by those striving to improve their lot.

The need to assist those attempting to overcome adversity applies even more so to minority groups. Historically consigned to the lowest rungs of the social-class ladder, it is not enough to open the same opportunities to them as to whites. They also have to be provided with "affirmative action." African Americans, in particular, as the victims of soul-killing discrimination, deserve special attention (Bowen and Bok,1998). They, along with other ethnic and religious minorities (e.g., Hispanics, Pacific-Islanders, Amerindians, and Muslims) require institutional adjustments designed to improve their chances. Anything less is both callous and unjust.

Among the interventions liberals deem necessary are admission policies that compensate for previous injustices. These are typically depicted as targets to be aimed at, whereas they generally take the form of unacknowledged quotas (Sander and Taylor, 2012). Minority members are thus allowed entrance even if their test scores and high school grades fall below those of majority students. Much of this is done in the name of "diversity" (Wood, 2003). Elite students are said to benefit from ineracting with peers who come from different backgrounds. This presumably broadens their outlook and makes them more sensitive to the needs of those who have been socially harmed.

Other techniques are also to be employed to accomodate the requirments of minority students. Thus, because some blacks claim to be uncomforable lodging with whites, they are allowed segregated dorms. Additional funds are likewise allocated to support race-based activities. These include clubs, conventions, and sensitivity programs. Also added to university menus are black studies programs and concentrations in Hispanic studies. These are intended not only to increase the knowledge of minority issues but to demonstrate respect for disparaged groups.

Women, of course, are not a minority, but they too are said to have endured millenia of oppression (Lorber, 1994). As a result, they are also alleged to deserve a hand up. Despite the fact that they outnumber their male colleagues and do better academically, they are to command special attention. Not only is consciousness raising to be sponsored on college campuses, but so are sensitivity programs designed to teach men to eschew their hegemonistic tendencies. Women may not require skewed admission policies, but they allegedly benefit from programs in women's studies. These, in conjunction with campus-wide events celebrating the achievements of women, are expected to educate recalcitrant males about the moral rights of women. Among the measures undertaken are to be take-back-the-night demostrations intended to affirm female solidarity in the face of male intimidation (Whittier,1995). The goal is to teach women that they must no longer allow themselves to be passive victims.

Nowadays sexual minorities have been added to the greivance queue. They too are supported in demands for university assistance in promoting their moral agenda. Once more disciplinary majors are to be established so as to investigate the injustices done to gays and lesbians. Many colleges have, in fact, joined the bandwangon to create departments of gay, queer, and/or LGBT studies. As with women, college-wide programs designed to disseminate the message that sexual oppression must be resisted have become a fixture on campuses. Indeed, support for gay marriage and equal rights for gay couples is nearly universal among faculty members and course offerings.

Other liberal causes are also to be the recipients of university backing. Preeminent among these are peace and environmental studies. College professors are almost uniformly opposed to war (Chatfield, 1992). To this end, they once participated in ejecting ROTC programs from their schools. In many cases, they also insisted that military recruiters not be allowed on campus. Meanwhile, they continue to clamor for majors in peace studies. As might be expected, they likewise sponsor events intended to spread the message that war is evil. And given the idealism of college-age students, these find a ready audience.

With respect to environmental concerns, these too are to be enshrined in courses, majors, and programs. And given the political climate, these have been well received. Not only have professors promoted environmental theses, but schools have been reconstructed along pro-environmental lines. This has entailed minor alterations, such as seperating out recyclible trash, but also major initiatives, such as sustainability. Thus, new college buildings frequently incorporate environmentally friendly elements (Bonevac, 2011). They are, for instance, stingy in their energy requirements and organic in the materials with which they are constructed. Some even include showers stalls so faculty members who bicycle to campus can clean up before going to class.

Overall, progressive reforms are intended to discourage an emphasis on the accomplishments of "dead white men" and re-engineer university programs to venerate the contributions of those previously excluded. As the standard-bearers of community values, colleges are asked to redefine these in accord with the demands of social justice. In this, they should not only educate students to be better citizens but nudge society in directions from which all will benefit. This is to be achieved not only by refurbishing what is taught but by altering how it is taught. Faculty members are thus encouraged to create and then take advantage of "teachable moments." As liberals see it, this opens the minds of students and introduces information that serves them—and society—better than the traditional fare.

Conservatives

Quite naturally, conservatives are appalled by many of these proposals (Sowell, 2007). Their reform agenda starts from the proposition that liberal innovations would destroy what generations of educators labored to construct. From their perspective, the university bubble will burst from an excess of novelties. According to them, with colleges pumping up their curricula with trendy nonsense, the time must come when this foolishness is found out. Eventually, these ideological excesses will become so egregious that their emptiness can no longer be disguised. At that point, their lack of quality will be unmasked, and public support for colleges will collapse.

The way conservatives see it, liberals engage in indoctrination. According to them, the goal of self-described "progressives" is not transmitting knowledge but converting the next generation the liberal party line. This business about seeking social justice is actually "justice" the way liberals define it (Wood and Toscano, 2013). Portrayed as collectivist, this objective is spurned as a version of socialism. Since most conservatives are market-oriented, they bridle at a point of view that disparages economic freedoms. Where, they ask, are competing interpretations? Why aren't capitalist views afforded a greater presence on campus?

More concerned with promoting liberty than an equality of results, conservatives also argue for a marketplace of ideas. Their ideal is for thinkers of various stripes to defend their positions on an even playing field. The objective is to have contrasting ideas battle it out so that the best rise to the top. Of course, liberals too support a marketplace of ideas; nonetheless, conservatives protest that this is mere lip service. They claim that liberals believe in freedom of speech—for liberals. Conservatives also insist that political correctness supresses opinions liberals find objectionable, whether these come from students or faculty members (Lukianoff, 2012). Thus, professors whose viewpoints are out of the liberal mainstream allegedly find their job security tenuous, while students who advocate unacceptable perspectives are silenced, graded down, or expelled.

Conservatives contend that this is possible because of a blatant faculty skew (Graybar, 2013). The overwhelming majority of professors are, in fact, leftists. Not just liberal but often Marxist in their allegiances, they are accused of being intolerant of those with whom they disagree. Especially in the humanities and social sciences but also in specialty areas such as social work and education, upwards of 90 percent of faculty members profess progressive ideas. As a consequence, many disdain and punish the opposition. Thus, research shows that whether in hiring new faculty, making tenure and promotion decisions, or selecting articles for publication, the assumption is that conservatives are dimwitted. As a result, right-wingers tend to be excluded, which further serves to homogenize political opinions.

Conservatives further allege that professors who agree with them have to be careful about making their views known, lest they find themselves unemployed. Since liberals understandably believe they come closer to the truth, they interpret dissent as dumbing down the university. Conservatives, however, want to get back to a more time-honored curriculum. Thus, many promote a reliance on what are characterized as "the great books" (Adler, 1952). These are the works of the classical thinkers (e.g., Plato, Aristotle, Shakespeare, and Darwin), who have long been regarded as intellectual innovators. In other words, they want to rescue these dead white males from the oblivion to which liberals intend to consign them. Conservatives speak of a "canon." These are works that have purportedly survived the test of time. They are described as having been vetted by thousands of academics and found to contain profound ideas worthy of preservation. It is likewise contended that only this sort of orientation can save the humanities from the slow death to which political correctness is leading them.

Conservatives also fear that an emphasis on social justice dilutes demands for merit. Much more likely to be absolutist than relativist (Norris, 1997), they scorn fashionable course materials as devoid of genuine value. When liberals return fire, arguing that calling for merit is merely a disguised technique for keeping elites in power, conservatives dismiss this as a rationalization for preserving liberal biases. They insist that some ideas are superior to others and that competent professors can make valid distinctions between what has importance and what does not. In their view, were this responsibility tossed aside, a reduction in quality would ultimately proved fatal to higher education. If, in the final analysis, the information disseminated in college is not superior to that available on the street, why, they ask, should anyone bother with the expense and effort of attending a university?

Thus, while the liberals are busy installing new courses in peace studies, women's studies, and environmentalism, conservatives describe these as harbingers of mediocrity. Yes, some of these offerings may be popular, but this is no reason for incorporating them into a rigorous curriculum. According to conservatives, the real goal should be to give students what they need, not what they want. College, they insist, should prepare the young to be successful in the world they are about to enter—and this is not the world of which liberals dream.

Nor are conservatives shy about advocating something like the *in loco parentis* attutudes of the past. Where once colleges enforced moral standards as if they were taking the place of students' parents, a desire to respect the diversity and adulthood of attendees devolved into vulgar sexual and interpersonal norms. Who, the liberals have trumpeted, are college authorities to set the standards for others? This argument, conservatives quickly responded, bespeaks a lack of confidence in historic values that is both dangerous and repellant (Wood, 2011). Obviously, although traditionalists claim to admire intellectual tolerance, this does not always translate into unqualified moral tolerance.

All in all, conservatives seek to preserve what they percieve as the best aspects of the historical university. Most are not reflexively against change, but they want proposed improvements to be well considered. To do less is considered a waste of valuable resources, as well as an invitation to unsuspected troubles. Colleges, no doubt, can benefit from some reforms, but this does not mean that every innovation is an enhancement. Critical thinking, for instance, is probably useful. Nonetheless, what sorts of practices actually foster it? Care, and mature judgment are clearly needed, lest reformers be hoisted by their own petards.

Summing Up

Well then, is there a college bubble? And can a self-directed perspective prevent it from bursting? There is certainly reason to believe some things have gone awry. But what they are and how serious they are is open to intepretation. This clearly varies with the commitments of the observers. As a consequence, judgments of what is required to save higher education vary. Much depends on the purported mission of the university. Obviously, what works best at achieving what we desire depends on what we desire. It is therefore necessary to elucidate the central purpose of higher education. This will be considered in chapter 3. Chapter 2, however, is concerned with evaluating suggested improvements.

In the meantime, a cautionary tale is worth telling. Once upon a time there was school widely respected for its progressive attitudes (Will, 2007; Schwartz, 2009). Dedicated to innovation, Antioch College was more broadly admired than its small size would seem to have merited. Founded in the nineteenth century, by the mid-twentieth century it had become a magnet for middle-class students whose parents wanted them to receive an education in line with their permissive attitudes. This devotion to "modernism" extended to the faculty members and trustees. Almost all were deeply committed to creating the fairest and most stimulating educational environment available.

To this end, the school instituted a multitude of pioneering practices. One was co-ed dormitories. So co-ed were these that they featured co-ed bathrooms. At the same time, the school wanted to make sure there was no sexual oppression. Men would not be allowed to force their attentions on unresponsive women. In order to promote this, a dating policy was instituted, such that before a male touched a female, he had to ask for explicit permission. Thus, he had to say—out loud—may I touch your arm, your breast, etc. She, in turn, had to provide explicit permission before he could proceed. Ergo, she had to say, yes, you may touch my arm, my breast, etc. In practice, however, males and females who shared the same bathrooms occasionally had sex out in the open in communal shower stalls. No doubt, some students found this disconcerting—not to say confusing.

Even more alarming, however, were the implications of the school's racial policies. As an almost lily-white school that ardently believed in racial intergration, it was decided to engage in aggressive affirmative action. Not only would black students be allowed entrance, but they would be actively recruited. Inner-city youngsters, who were ill prepared for a rigorous academic program, would be sought, provided with financial assitance, and offered remedial services. But then once these fish-out-of-water complained of being disrepected, the progressive ambiance of the college demanded that their complaints be heard and addressed. Quite soon, whatever these students wanted translated into efforts at appeasement.

This, however, did not reduce campus tensions. Not only were there angry confrontations, but physical violence and criminal activities proliferated. In short order, the white students began to fear for their safety. Then when they did, their parents, who were paying a hefty freight for the privledge of saving the downtrodden, made sure that their offspring withdrew so that they could attend more welcoming institutions. So frequently did this occur that Antioch's enrollment declined precipitously. And with the loss of paying students went the college's financial viability. Despite numerous stopgap efforts to staunch the hemoraging, these were too late. Antioch, despite its vaunted reputation, had to close its doors. Other schools were increasing in size, but it, in its historic form, disappeared from the landscape as a result overly ambitious idealism.

The moral of this story is that good intentions do not always produce good results. Innovation per se is not improvement. It is therefore necessary, when addressing the difficulties of our universities, to be careful. What at first sounds like a good idea may not, in the end, have the desired outcome.

2

All the World's a Nail

Hammers and Nails

Higher education may be in trouble, but it does not suffer from a dearth of potential saviors. Many of those who participate in it and many of those who believe themselves affected by it have rushed forward to offer advice on the best ways to effect reform (Arum, 2012). How then are we to decide between these often-contradictory recommendations? Just as commentators tend to identify what has gone wrong based on their moral commitments, so they frequently base suggested solutions on their personal experiences. Although scores of these ideas are helpful, what is remarkable is how regularly they correspond with the specialties of the persons promoting them. There is an old saying that if you are a hammer, all the world looks like a nail. Likewise, if you have a particular skill, it appears to unravel nearly every problem.

This, in fact, is the situation in which we find ourselves. While there is broad agreement that our universities require restructuring, the manner in which this should be realized is widely disputed (Dewey, 1943). Moreover, given that many of those most concerned are academics, they assume that their personal proficiencies hold the key to fixing what is broken. As a result, rather than spend time analyzing what has gone wrong, they rush forward poised to pound colleges into the proper shape. Of course, laypersons and politicians likewise assume that their perspectives are the most appropriate. Somehow everyone feels they know best (which, in all candor, includes this writer).

Not surprisingly, as with assessments of the academic bubble, much of this certitude derives from the values of the potential rescuers. Too often, what seem to be objective difficulties are a reflection of the moral allegiances of the supposed redeemers. A great deal of this confidence also stems from their individual histories in problem solving. What people perceive themselves to be good at doing provides the evidence regarding what they think will succeed. To begin with, that something is problematic is a value judgment. Thus, we humans first decide that a circumstance is "bad" and then we demand it be corrected. From our perspective, a particular status quo violates intensely held standards; hence, it must be altered. This is why liberals and conservatives disagree so vehemently. Those who insist that social justice is the central concern obviously differ from those determined to reward merit. Moreover, because these outcomes are incompatible, the preferred remedies diverge.

The expertise of would-be reformers also matters in that perceived solutions generally derive from a repertoire of familiar answers. Most problem solving does not start from scratch. Having had previous involvement in the world, mature adults do not confront a novel puzzle, as might a young child. They favor some approaches rather than others because these have paid off in the past. This is especially true if a person is an expert. To be an expert is to be skilled at achieving particular goals. It, therefore, follows that parallel triumphs should occur if formerly successful strategies are implemented in a new situation. Indeed, this way of thinking does often produce the best results.

With respect to the impending college bubble, there is a broad range of favored remedies. These may be classified as belonging to several categories. One of them is *efficiency*. An array of proposed antidotes is based on improving the effectiveness of academic services. It is assumed that upgraded productivity can both lower costs and enhance quality. Just how this is to be achieved, however, varies with the competence of the author.

Another remedial approach seeks to provide greater *relevance*. Here it is assumed that what has gone wrong is that higher education is not delivering the product that our society needs. Were it to do so, the demand would surely increase and the impending collapse in enrollment disappear. Obviously, what is believed relevant is usually in accord with the values and competences of the individual reformer. Somehow, these persons contend the colleges should offer more of what they deem important.

A third approach is explicitly moral. Here the central concern is with increasing *fairness*. The focal objective in this case is to facilitate a better society by promoting outcomes that are more ethical. What is thought to achieve this, however, likewise varies with the master values of the activist. As we have seen, liberals and conservatives champion different versions of morality. It must also be noted that there are other versions of what is best, most notably those associated with religious convictions.

Last, many reconstructive strategies are *structural* in nature. These would reorder universities in terms of their organizational components. Many such proposals concentrate on reforming the roles of college faculties and administrators. Here it is assumed that the problem with higher education derives from defective job descriptions and/or supervisory arrangements. Were the composition of these altered, the end product would allegedly be improved. Yet in this case, too, there is disagreement regarding what constitutes improvement.

With so much to choose from, it is difficult to know which strategy to adopt. In the next chapter, we will analyze the fundamental mission of our colleges and universities so as to use this as a filter in sorting through the alternatives, but in the meantime, we must examine these to ascertain what they propose.

Efficiency

In contemporary Western societies, efficiency has become iconic. Few challenge its value on the assumption that improved effectiveness inevitably produces more of what is desired at lesser cost. Initially promoted in order to increase economic profitability, demands for efficiency skyrocketed with the successes of capitalism and industrialization. Indeed, the modern world could not be as wealthy as it is in their absence. It is incontestably true that we would not otherwise have been able to build commodious homes, construct comfortable automobiles, or produce foodstuffs in their current quantities.

Max Weber (Gerth and Mills, 1946), one of the most influential defenders of efficiency, also championed bureaucracy. He believed that rationally constructed organizations more effectively achieve the goals for which they were created. He further believed that they facilitate the sensible coordination of complex activities by permitting those at their apex to control the contributions of thousands of subordinates. This is to be accomplished in compliance with the motto *sine ira et studio* (without fear or favor). Of course, there are downsides to bureaucracy, including a loss of worker freedom. But the upside includes a reduction in the violence and favoritism that characterized earlier forms of organization. Bureaucracies are, therefore, able to accomplish their purposes with less wear and tear. This is critical for understanding what takes place within universities in that they too share this mode of association. In other words, if higher education is to become more efficient, it presumably needs to incorporate the techniques that enable bureaucracies to elevate their game.

If this is so, then many reformers believe we need to revise our attitude toward higher education. Instead of regarding it as a social service, they argue that it makes more sense to adopt a businesslike stance. Whereas government agencies and charitable institutions can take a warm-and-fuzzy approach to what they do, businesses need to be hard-boiled. In having to endure the ravages of two-fisted competition, they eventually learn that only the lean and mean survive. The same, these activists assume, applies to colleges. They too must offer products that others desire in a manner that reduces the costs to create them. As might be expected, this approach appeals to business-minded commentators. This applies to the capitalists who make generous donations to universities, the executives who sit on the boards of regents that control university systems, and the faculty members of business colleges.

This orientation begins by regarding students as customers. From this perspective, learners are to be considered consumers to be satisfied, as opposed to neophytes to be educated. Customers have demands. Those who choose to attend a university have desires that have to be satisfied if they are to generate repeat business. Persons engaged in commerce understand that they cannot dictate what their patrons will purchase. Yes, they can influence people via advertising and promotional endeavors, but they cannot force buyers to purchase what they do not want. In the long run, the marketplace determines which products develop a following and therefore which companies are profitable. The same should apply to higher education. If colleges do not provide instruction in the subjects students favor and in a manner they approve, these schools deserve to go out of business. There is no inherent right for them to teach whatever they decide. They too must therefore be sensitive to public preferences.

This outlook finds the *in loco parentis* orientation of the past objectionable. College students are not to be regarded as children, nor are college authorities to be perceived as quasi-parents. To the contrary, persons old enough to attend a university should be accorded the respect due adults. They presumably know what they want; hence, their judgments about whether they are receiving it ought to be honored. If they are, colleges will be richly rewarded with additional patronage.

A businesslike attitude also proves receptive to improved technologies (Wildavsky et al., 2011). Commercial enterprises have learned that new inventions and updated procedures usually produce quantum leaps in efficiency. Simply doing things the same old way, because this is the way they have always been done, is a prescription for stagnation. From this standpoint, those in charge of universities are rightly disparaged as hide-bound obstructionists. Accustomed to looking backward toward the intellectual achievements of their predecessors, they fail to perceive the benefits of palpable innovations.

Thus, professors tethered to the lecturing techniques of yore frequently stand in the way of progress. As they ramble on, reading from yellowed class notes assembled decades ago, all they succeed in doing is boring new generations of students. Often achieving no more than imitating the academics that irked them in their own youth, they reproduce cultural artifacts that have outworn their usefulness. Updated pedagogical practices are therefore desperately needed.

As it happens, the business-oriented reformers insist a superior model is at hand (Christensen and Eyring, 2011). Just as bureaucracies require their employees to utilize the most effective procedures in doing their jobs, colleges are now asked to follow suit. In the same manner that time and motion experts dedicate themselves to establishing the most effective ways of manufacturing products, so professional educators must also study the most effective ways of transmitting information. They too have to accumulate an array of "best practices." Then, instead of allowing professors to marinate in their idiosyncratic juices, schools need to enforce these standardized teaching policies.

To begin with, colleges should not allow professors to create their own curricula. This invites mediocrity. Only the best-vetted syllabi ought to be adopted. Moreover, these must clearly state learning objectives. Because it is nearly impossible to determine how much students have learned if the standards are ambiguous, these must be operationalized. Well-tested syllabi must also incorporate standardized rubrics (Bradley, et al., 1012). Not just what is taught but the sequences in which it is taught need to be clarified. Quality is impossible if lessons are not scrutinized to make sure that they include only what is necessary and that this is conveyed via a well-defined format.

Next, professors have to be tutored in the best in-class techniques. Not all forms of presentation are equally effective; hence, efforts should be made to instill those that achieve the best results. As of now, pedagogues are permitted to follow their own lights. But because not all are gifted teachers, how they teach has to be standardized. Thus, all faculty members must come to appreciate the value of visually arresting

PowerPoints. Unless their students' attention is captured by graphic means, they may miss the gravamen of what is taught. Learning must also be enhanced by providing study guides, sample test questions, and pictorial aids. Utilizing classroom exercises, engaging in lively debates, and fostering in-class discussions must similarly seduce students into keeping up with their lessons. Talking heads alone cannot do the job. Traditional lectures are worse than old fashioned—they are mind numbing.

Of course, the classroom itself is a holdover from a bygone era. The modern university, it is alleged, cannot be businesslike if it eschews the benefits of electronic technology. Advances in computers and distance learning have been so profound that if fully exploited, they are capable of vaulting higher education onto a previously impossible plane. Not only are these able to make learning more effective, but they can make it available to a broader constituency. In the process, this would multiply the socially available skill set, which would make for a more democratic society.

First of all, more courses can be taught online. Instead of requiring students to attend brick-and-mortar facilities, they can learn at home. The very best professors, utilizing the best teaching techniques, can share their expertise with more individuals—at a fraction of cost. In addition, this sort of education is convenient. It can be integrated with the learner's schedule, without him or her having to endure the expense and troublesomeness of automobiles or mass transit. Students will also have a broader selection of subjects from which to choose if fewer of them are required to make courses profitable.

Other potential benefits also accrue from electronic technologies. One is the electronic text. Traditional schoolbooks have become so expensive that once all learners possess laptops and notepads, they can bypass this expenditure by downloading what is required for a fraction of the cost. With words, graphics, and hyperlinks available at the strike of a key, students can similarly benefit from a wider range of materials. This goes for the chapters and articles they are required to read, as well as the library research for assigned papers. Gone will be the necessity of trekking to the stacks in quest of a volume that may not even be in a school's collection. Expanding the available resources will thereby enhance educational quality.

But wait; there are further benefits. In-class laptops make note taking easier. No longer must students depend upon illegible scrawls. Professors will also be able to distribute specific materials merely by forwarding them to pupils—in real time. This capacity may, in fact, render the old-fashioned blackboard obsolete. Then too, electronic networking makes it easier for students to participate in joint projects. They can thus work together to learn together. In addition, requiring classes to collaborate on multi-person writing assignments fosters cooperation. Learners thereby discover that pooling their talents produces better results. They can even do so internationally, with the added advantage of fostering world peace.

These capacities are said to advance efficiency on a number of fronts. First, they lower costs. It is obviously possible to learn more if each increment is cheaper. Consequently, although electronic devices may not be free, they are a wise investment. More versatile than books or chalkboards, they can be used for diverse tasks. As a result, the overall expense is reduced. Additionally, laptops and inkjet printers can follow students and therefore be utilized for other projects after graduation. In this case, the efficiencies migrate from the classroom into the public domain.

Second, flexibility is enhanced. A textbook deals with only one subject, whereas an e-reader can deal with thousands. All one must do is download new materials. This way it is possible to stay current no matter how rapidly knowledge advances. Nor does one need to be shackled to a single mode of transmission. As electronics become more sophisticated, it becomes possible to switch—at will—from sound, to graphics, to text, to pictorial narratives. Ergo, if one avenue does not get a point across, another can be substituted. This even goes for who is doing the teaching. Given the national and international networks that are up and running, schools may be able to mix and match their faculties to keep pace with student needs.

Third, advanced technology enables colleges to serve more students. There will no longer be worries about how many seats a classroom holds. As long as each learner can plug into the same system, the sky is the limit. There will thus be no difficulty in sustaining greater enrollments. Indeed, the goal of allowing every American to obtain a college education will become achievable. As a consequence, instead of elites monopolizing knowledge, good ideas will become a universal patrimony.

Fourth, electronic innovations make it possible to exploit the available talent more effectively. By common consent, technical expertise is not evenly distributed. Some professors know more than others, and some are more stimulating. Just as electronic music enabled us to hear world-class symphony orchestras at the touch of a button, so online college courses place world-class professors within reach. No longer will universities be at the mercy of faculty members gone to seed; no longer will they have to reduce costs by hiring ineffectual adjuncts. Only the best and brightest need be tapped to share their wisdom. Moreover, even they will benefit if their lessons are electronically recorded. This way they can be freed to pursue cutting-edge research without mindlessly repeating old-hat lectures.

Fifth, convenience will be improved. Distance learning technologies allow lessons to be absorbed when students are prepared to absorb them. As a result, family and vocational responsibilities need not dictate educational programs. Nor will some students be denied a higher education because they must earn a living or raise a family. The notion that college courses need to have definite start and end points will be a thing of the past. So will the number of hours dedicated to receiving a fixed number of credits. It may even be possible to interrupt a particular program without penalty, should life events divert a student's attention.

Sixth, efficiency oriented innovations promise to be more stimulating. Many jokes have been told about how soporific college lectures can be. Even after decades, graduates reminisce about how old Professor Smith rambled on so endlessly that they thought his course would never end. The razzle-dazzle of the new media should put an end to this torture. It will keep students awake and allow them to participate in class discussions as never before. With learners tuning in when they are ready, they should be more alert. Likewise, with conversations mediated electronically, even the shy or inarticulate can make contributions without fear of ridicule. This way they will be engaged to a degree never possible in traditional university settings. Accordingly, they will learn more than otherwise.

Seventh, with students learning at their own pace, many will graduate more quickly. If they do not have to wait for slower classmates to catch up, they can vault ahead. Indeed, if they are up to the task, they can simultaneously enroll in more subjects than classroom attendance would permit. By the same token, slower students can take the time they require without interfering with the schedules of others. Absent the need of students to drop out of one course and then into another, but only when the latter is available, universities will incur fewer administrative expenses. The pressures to improve graduation rates will thus evaporate, as will feelings of guilt for going too fast or slow.

Eighth, the need for support services will diminish. With fewer students on campus, there will be less need to feed or entertain them. Nor will they require the same athletic facilities. If colleges have gone overboard on frills, stripping them down to the bare essentials should reduce the temptations to overdo. Assuming that higher education is thereby made more convenient, this should also keep enrollments healthy. Even remedial programs can be reduced if students are given the requisite practice online. In other words, by being responsive to student needs, colleges can provide more bang for the buck.

Ninth, technological advances have opened the marketplace to for-profit institutions (Rosen, 2011). Part of the difficulty with contemporary higher education is that government-run colleges dominate. But because these obtain taxpayer-funded subsidies, they do not have to worry about keeping up with the competition. If they are inefficient, they merely go cap-in-hand to their state legislatures. Private concerns, however, must be responsive. If they do not adjust to evolving conditions, they go out of business. As a consequence, an expansion in private schools may provide the public ones with the challenge they require.

All in all, educational reforms that aim at improving efficiencies are expected to improve quality. According to the productivity mavens, merely because higher education has a long history of embracing obsolete practices does not mean it should resist modifications. Professors and administrators who have grown accustomed to the status quo ought not be allowed to sidetrack progress. Too much is at stake for their intransigence to dictate events. Whether the optimistic projections of the technology enthusiasts will prove accurate, however, is open to debate. As we will later see, there are reasons to believe that electronic innovations are far from a cure-all and that they may introduce a host of problems all their own.

Greater Relevance

Still, other observers have different priorities. They wonder what good it is to be efficient, if that which you achieve is not desirable. Naturally, these folks do not always agree among themselves as to what is most advantageous. As is often the case, people tend to believe that what they treasure is vital for others. Perceived relevance is therefore a matter of personal values; this is so despite the fact that these differences are frequently described as involving objective truths. As might be supposed, reformers deeply immersed in divergent aims usually identify their own preferences as universal facts.

Moreover, what is sought varies on many dimensions. Thus, activists who crave efficiency are liable to regard economic goals as most relevant. Social justice partisans, in contrast, reserve the place of honor for a multicultural curriculum. Their conservative adversaries, however, are more concerned with strengthening our democratic traditions (i.e., in the manner they understand them). Then, too, moral entrepreneurs emphasize the need to institute economic, environmental and/or international justice. Which of these goals gets the most play normally varies with the social salience of the moment. Still other reformers are, in contrast, spiritual in their aspirations. As a consequence, they often promote religious indoctrination in line with their beliefs.

Some secular commentators, to be sure, perceive relevance as a matter of student choice. They assume that the more comprehensive a learner's alternatives, the more likely he or she is to gain knowledge germane to his or her circumstances. These advocates tend to favor a wide range of courses and majors. They also champion electives. On the other hand, some reformers prefer the opposite. They want to limit student choices in the belief that the young must be exposed to essentials they may not yet recognize as beneficial. These folks frequently campaign for adjustments in the core curricula. Finally, other activists endorse interdisciplinary studies. They fear that too narrow a focus on particular subjects handicaps learners. Instead of exposing them to the full scope of knowledge, they become over-specialized. In this case, higher education is thought less than relevant when it does not impart information that might alter a student's life experience.

Economic Relevance

When the land-grant colleges were established in the nineteenth century, the legislators were clear about their aim (Christy and Williamson, 1991). The reason government was getting involved in higher education was to stimulate an already robust economy. The Industrial Revolution was well under way in the United States, while westward expansion had simultaneously expanded the acreage under cultivation. These new schools were intended to accelerate these processes. By concentrating on agriculture and engineering, they would make the nation more competitive. In the end, it would become an economic powerhouse.

Similar arguments are made today. The recommended adjustments differ, but the focus is comparable. What has changed is the nature of our economy and those who participate in it. Once the need was to reorient farm boys so that they could either increase the productivity of their fields or seek employment in the burgeoning factories. The current requirement is to maintain manufacturing productivity in a competitive international marketplace, as well as to facilitate the social mobility of those in poverty. To this end, the curricula of universities are to be modified so that their offerings are congruent with business demands. Still, where during the post-Sputnik years the emphasis was on science and mathematics, it has shifted toward engineering. This is an area in which American students are considered deficient compared with the rest of the world.

Nowadays, writings skills have also acquired greater prominence. With more people occupied in managerial and commercial endeavors, the need for clarity in written communications has increased. Participants in complex economic activities cannot effectively coordinate their contributions unless they accurately convey what is intended. By the same token, an ability to engage in cooperative activities has grown in significance. Schools are therefore urged to provide practice in interpersonal collaboration.

The greatest changes advocated for the sake of economic relevance are, however, modifications in the types of schools supported. While the professoriate is fixated on expanding research universities, a growing chorus of reformers contends that this is unwise. They assert that we already have enough graduate schools. With many PhDs nowadays reduced to working temporary jobs, they suggest that programs they regard as designed to inflate faculty egos be eliminated. On this view, there are enough specialists in Shakespearean sonnets. What is needed instead are programs that inculcate business skills.

Parents have long encouraged their offspring to major in disciplines that can be converted into employment, but now the call is also for colleges to concentrate on what is in economic demand. For many, this translates into multiplying community colleges. These two-year institutions have long served as a gateway to traditional four-year colleges, but they also teach competences that lead directly to gainful occupations. Thus, with computers becoming more prominent, an ability to service these is required. Hence, why not invest in schools that provide courses in this, rather than English literature? If we, as a society, respect only irrelevant cultural competences, aren't we greasing the skids to the poorhouse? A technologically dependent society, it is argued, that does not foster hands-on proficiencies must soon find the wheels of commerce grinding to a halt.

There is also another supposed benefit to expanding community colleges. Historically, higher education has been reserved for the socially advantaged. They have been regarded as the ones who benefit from acquiring a cultural competence. But we live in a democracy. Ours is a society that theoretically provides an opportunity for everyone. Yet if it is to do so, it must furnish openings for the poor as well as the affluent. Nonetheless, not everyone can be the chief executive of a major corporation. Some will find their circumstances improved by a job involving automobile repair. It is these prospects in which community colleges specialize. As a result, they distribute social resources more broadly and more democratically. This is regarded as in our national interest because the larger the number of people who have a stake in our institutions, the more secure we will all be.

As it happens, community colleges are not the only innovation in higher education that supposedly furthers these objectives. In recent years, we have witnessed an upsurge in for-profit schools. Business colleges have long been part of the educational landscape, but they have of late enlarged their portfolio so as to compete with the traditional universities. Although some warn that this is a harbinger of ill, others applaud the development. They claim that because these schools must be efficient in order to remain in business, their achievements often surpass those of their rivals. As a result, they accomplish that to which others schools merely aspire. Furthermore, unlike ordinary colleges, for-profits have no entrance requirements. They take all comers; hence are more democratic. In this, their economic relevance derives from serving an underserved market, thereby making additional talents available to the business community. They also decrease social jealousies by facilitating more wide-ranging vocational success.

Multicultural Relevance

Another chorus of reformers is more concerned with the social dimensions of higher education. Indeed, they often dismiss economic considerations as crass. For them, the issue often boils down to Rodney King's question: why can't we all just get along? They wish to promote the brotherhood and sisterhood of humankind—or at least of all Americans. They further assume that exposing everyone to a broad array of cultural differences can advance this goal. One of their watchwords is *diversity* (Wood, 2003; Dobbin, 2009). In their view, we, each of us, benefit from interacting with others whose ways of life may diverge from our own.

Once America was described as a melting pot (Wattenberg, 1990). Immigrants arrived from around the world and after a period of acculturation blended in with earlier arrivals. Ultimately, all described themselves as "Americans" because all partook of a homogeneous lifestyle (Alba, 1990; Sowell, 1991). By the mid-twentieth century, however, this notion seemed quaint. The United States was relatively tolerant of diversity, but that did not mean various ethnicities relinquished their heritages. Nor was there any reason they should. Instead, they could live peacefully side by side, while continuing to celebrate their unique customs. They constituted, as it were, a tossed salad. The ingredients might differ, but their distinctiveness made the whole more savory.

This insistence on the value of diversity reached a fever pitch when university entrance quotas were challenged in court (Sander and Taylor, 2012). If racial minorities were to receive preferential treatment, a rationale other than equalizing their representation was required. This was found in the thesis that exposing white students to black culture made them well rounded. Not only would they learn that African Americans are fully human, but they would discover that there are many virtues embedded in their lifestyle. This way our society would be better integrated, while preserving the integrity of its constituents.

Multiculturalists are often committed ethical relativists (Knight, 1998). They insist that no way of life is superior to any other. As a consequence, they believe that the United States, as a nation, benefits from adding arrows to its quiver. Not just blacks, but Hispanics and, to a lesser degree, Asians, theoretically bring perspectives that enhance our overall outlook. Much as Mexican and Caribbean foods enliven our diets, so the historical experiences of minority groups democratize our political system. Thus, freed from ancient prejudices, the intrinsic talents of millions of individuals will be unleashed to augment our common future.

Furthermore, our universities are regarded as the perfect place to bring divergent traditions together. With most college students teetering on the brink of adulthood, they are open to learning about the virtues of strangers. Having come together precisely to expand their horizons, universities have an obligation to exploit this opportunity. They can do so by offering courses in minority studies. They can also do so less officially. Thus, students with different backgrounds can be encouraged to interact in class, as well as in extracurricular activities. When they, on their own, discuss their differences or participate in shared social events, they learn more than from dry academic exercises.

In this way, diversity becomes a way of life that informs their endeavors once they graduate. This, then, is said to be democracy at ground level.

Democratic Relevance

Nowadays, of course, college campuses are overrun with multiculturalists. Less prominent are the voices of traditional democrats. Often silenced within academic precincts, albeit more vocal off campus, are individuals who identify themselves as political conservatives. They too take pride in our nation's egalitarian achievements; nonetheless, their focus is elsewhere. For them, the central issue is preserving the machinery of democracy (Putnam, 1993; Elshtain, 1995). These reformers hope to reinforce the democratic processes they believe essential to defending a government of, by, and for the people.

There was a time when most Americans believed civics lessons played a crucial role in primary, secondary, and higher education. Convinced that a well-informed electorate was indispensable if democratic institutions were to endure, they promoted courses that celebrated the nation's achievements. Far from seeking to unmask the country's feet of clay, they proclaimed its exceptionalism (Lipset, 1996). America was a shining city on a hill. It was different—genuinely freer than other nations. Yes, there were defects. And yes, there were hypocrisies. But people dedicated to perfecting the legacy bequeathed from the Founders could correct these (Bailyn, 2003). First and foremost, this entailed instilling a delight in what had been achieved. Instead of teaching endlessly about the injustices of our ancestors (Loewen, 1995), their aspirations deserved greater attention. The story of America was about its sometimes-messy evolution toward greater justice. This might, at times, have been exaggerated, but the core of the narrative remained valid.

As to a university education, it ought to include a more detailed exposition of this history than was possible with less mature students. The Constitution, in particular, ought to be emphasized (Morris, 1985). This should incorporate an analysis of its limitations, not just its virtues. What must not take center stage, however, but often did, was a muckraking attack on the nation's missteps. Courses in history and political science, but also in English literature and sociology, ought to be balanced. Conservative commentators were appalled by the degree to which neo-Marxist ideologies permeated the college classroom. To their minds, this was an assault on democracy. Little was more germane to the protection of our liberties than educating the young about the vulnerabilities of democratic institutions.

Social Justice Relevance

Liberals, in contrast, throw up their hands in disgust at having their patriotism challenged. They insist that they too are democrats. The difference, as they see it, is that they believe laying bare the historical duplicity of the American experiment. The rights of blacks, women, gays, and the poor are all said to have been trodden upon by the rapacity of capitalist elites (Humphrey, 1964; Zarefsky, 1986; Jencks, 1992). Either under-represented or unrepresented, their voices were rarely heard. Liberty might be important (Mill, 1857); nonetheless, liberty without justice was a sham. America's ideals are largely valid, but their implementation often left much to be desired. The future must consequently be different. It must take Thomas Jefferson's promise of equality seriously.

For liberals, morality without fairness is not morality. It is instead a rationalization for vested privilege. Consequently, multiculturalism is a good place to start teaching the next generation about rights of those previously excluded. But this is not enough. The inequities built into a perverted economic structure require excision. Unregulated capitalism is incompatible with authentic democracy (Schumpeter, 1942). Government of, by, and for the people requires that the poor and disrespected be rescued from their misery. They too must be empowered and provided with the resources to live in dignity. An education that leaves this truism out of the mix is not worthy of being called an education. It is propaganda disguised as wisdom.

But not just the poor need to be given their due. Women have also been egregiously misused by the male hegemony. They too have been denied an opportunity to develop their talents or control their destinies. What, then, could be more relevant than providing them with justice (Brownmiller, 1975)? When more than half of all Americans are treated as second-class citizens merely by virtue of their gender, something has to be done. The victims have to be armed with the skills to take their rightful place on the worlds of business, politics, religion, and the family.

The powerless, regardless of the origins of their plight, have to be instructed about the inequity of their situation. If they are to participate in correcting what is wrong, they first have to be made conscious that it is wrong. By the same token, those who have perpetrated these offenses have to be made aware of their predatory behavior. This is more important than any technical skills a college education might hone. After all, what good is it to be rich or well fed if one is in chains?

Those intelligent enough to be admitted to college are surely bright enough to grasp this elementary truth.

And so higher education must be reformed so as to highlight the ravages of inequality. Students must be made aware of how badly the poor, the minorities, the sexually different, the handicapped, and women have been abused. They must also be instructed as to the appropriate remedies. Mere knowledge that cannot be translated into action is a waste of time. Implementing transfer payments from the rich to the poor, clipping the wings of bloated corporate tycoons, electing women to the highest political offices, and allowing gays to participate in matrimony—these are what count. These are what universities should promote.

Yet that is not all. Justice is more than an individual concern. That which impinges on our collective welfare is also crucial. Matters having to do with peace and the environment must therefore be addressed by an advanced education. As to peace, what good is wealth or democracy if millions of lives are shattered in conflicts that serve only the egos of those who initiate them (Chatfield, 1992)? Military glory is an illusion. Not even remotely related to the requirements of justice, it destroys the happiness and well-being of populations that have no idea of what is being contested. No sane person can defend such indiscriminate killing. To even consider it is absurd. What, then, can be of more importance than studying ways to prevent this madness?

Similar considerations apply to the environment. Raping it is also hazardous to our shared happiness. There can be no doubt that preserving our planet from an ecological catastrophe is one of the most important tasks educated people can undertake. Indeed, we owe it to generations yet unborn to make this a top priority. To this end, liberal activists assert that universities must promote sustainability (Bonevac, 2012). They must make the future stewards of our ecosystem aware of the fact that the earth's resources are limited and that squandering them would condemn our great-grandchildren to privation. It would also poison the atmosphere and oceans, not to mention set off a runaway greenhouse effect.

To prevent this, universities must teach students about the impending disaster. This means that courses other than those dedicated to studying the environment must incorporate an ecological component. However, colleges must do more. They have to set a good example. They must live by sustainability, not just preach it. When they build, for instance, they must do so in accord with green standards. They must not waste energy or unnecessarily pollute their habitats. Only in this way can they be good citizens of the earth.

Spiritual Relevance

There was a time when most American colleges had a religious affiliation. They were founded by particular denominations and insisted on mandatory church attendance. This focus was frequently symbolized by the presence of a handsome chapel at the center of the campus. Nor should it be forgotten that the European universities upon which the American schools were modeled had their beginnings under the sponsorship of the Catholic Church (Haskins, 1957). This legacy, however, has fallen into disrepair. Most contemporary institutions of higher learning are secular. Strange to say, this often includes schools ostensibly affiliated with a specific faith (Hendershott, 2011).

This drift has inspired some reformers to recommend adding a spiritual component to college programs (Palmer and Zajoc, 2010). These commentators consider it at least as vital to protect the souls of students as to advance economic or environmental concerns. According to them, the good life, both here and in the hereafter, depends upon the cultivation of non-physical dimensions. While the number of persons who stress this aspect of higher education has declined, those so committed insist that our moral welfare is contingent upon a return to ancient verities. Doing otherwise might increase our wealth, but it would deplete the internal resources upon which our happiness and welfare depend (Hunter, 2000).

Curricular Relevance

With a vast universe of subjects from which to select, our universities must concentrate on just some. With only so many hours and faculty members at their disposal, they need to engage in what amounts to triage. Consequently, some topics are deemed so essential they are integrated into a core curriculum every student must take in order to obtain a degree. Meanwhile, other specialties are grouped together so as to create concentrations in which particular students major. This enables learners to develop an expertise in a circumscribed area. Were this strategy eschewed, it would be impossible to develop multifaceted proficiencies. Despite the years dedicated to advanced studies, ours would thus be a society composed of dilettantes. The fact is that there is too much to know for people to become truly knowledgeable without attending to some subjects more diligently than others.

This obliges universities to sponsor some majors, while excluding others. The question therefore becomes which concentrations are most relevant? Which simultaneously achieve the central objectives of individual students and those of the larger society? This is a knotty problem. So difficult is it that well-informed observers come to diametrically opposed conclusions. Whereas some favor adding as many majors as possible, others warn against a proliferation of subjects. Those who wish to expand the range of concentrations insist that all are worthy of inclusion. As a rule, they do not lobby for multiplicity per se but for additional majors in seriatim. The width of their vision is revealed only in practice. Meanwhile, their opponents argue that too many majors dilute the quality of each. They contend that students are best served by having fewer concentrations, while simultaneously refining these offerings. According to them, different universities should focus on different majors, thereby making a broad range of specialties available to the public at large.

Similar arguments are put forward with regard to particular courses. Some reformers reason that the more courses from which students have to choose, the more likely they are to discover subjects that serve their needs. Because no one can anticipate all that might be useful, they think that it makes sense to be inclusive. The opponents of this strategy respond that this is a recipe for mediocrity. Just as with majors, they contend that too broad a range of possibilities makes it difficult to determine what is appropriate, while simultaneously ensuring that individual courses will not be taught often enough to be taught well.

Almost exactly the same considerations are brought to bear when deciding how many electives students should take. Those falling on the extended side of the divide submit that students are best situated to determine which are relevant for them. Consequently, to force a large array of required courses upon learners is tantamount to denying them what they need. The other side, however, maintains that this does not factor in the immaturity of most students. These individuals may not, in fact, be the ones who can make the best decisions regarding what they require. If anything, when given wide latitude, they are apt to choose what is easy and/or trendy rather than valuable. Greater relevance is therefore achieved by limiting discretion.

Interdisciplinary Relevance

This chapter began by declaring that those with hammers in hand see nails everywhere. Some point out that if this is true of reformers, it is even more true for disciplinary specialists (Mead 2011). Professors who have dedicated their careers to accumulating an expertise in a circumscribed subject area are liable to regard it as applicable to more problems than those who are less committed. The cliché of the moment has it that they are trapped in "silos" that prevent them from seeing the bigger picture. Instead, they concentrate on ever more arcane issues such that what they study loses contact with real-world concerns (Hamilton, 1996). In the end, only they care about their chosen topics.

The solution to this difficulty is thought to be in encouraging interdisciplinary programs. Instead of trapping faculty members in departments where they only communicate with like-minded scholars, universities ought to be reorganized so that professors with different interests engage in cross-fertilization. If, let us say, a biologist and a sociologist share the same department, the sociologist will learn more about the genetic factors influencing human behavior, while the biologist will get better acquainted with the interpersonal aspects of biological communities. This way each will be better prepared to expand his or her intellectual horizons.

More to the point, faculty members who are less parochial have more to share with their students. Having removed their disciplinary blinders, they are inevitably better communicators. The increased sensitivity acquired by having been removed from their ivory towers thus redounds to the benefit of all concerned. In this way, the university can be brought back to a more productive relationship with the community. Even the research efforts of an open-mined professoriate will become more relevant.

Fairness

Before proceeding, it must be admitted that fairness and relevance are not entirely discrete categories. Both are clearly driven by overlapping value considerations. Social justice, for instance, may be promoted because it is relevant to shared social needs and/or because it promotes greater fairness. Moral commitments so pervade our decision-making processes that it is impossible to create reform classifications that are completely unconnected. That said, the proposals assigned to the fairness heading are sufficiently distinctive, sufficiently action oriented, to merit separate attention. As will shortly be seen, most concentrate on programs that directly assist the weak—which no doubt are also perceived as relevant.

College for All

If individuals who attend college are liable to earn a million dollars more over the course of a lifetime than those who do not, how fair is it that only some people are allowed to attend? Doesn't a true democracy demand equal opportunity for all? Doesn't it also posit equal results (Coleman, et al., 1966)? A positive answer to these questions implies that the current practice of admitting only the best students is unjust. Egalitarian moralists consequently insist that a college education should be open to everyone (Williams, 2012). No persons should be denied the chance to succeed, merely because they are less intellectually able.

Besides, say advocates of universal higher education such as Bill Gates (Fain, 2013a) or Barack Obama (2006), we humans are more mentally alike than different. If some do better in school than others, it is because they have endured fewer environmental handicaps. Thus, remove the barriers bedeviling them, and they too will thrive. According to this theory, genuine fairness obtains only when everyone learns the same amount. Anything less is evidence that the appropriate steps needed to ensure a competent education for all have not been taken. Persistent inequalities indicate, for instance, that institutional discrimination is still operative. This bias may be unconscious, but it is nonetheless egregious.

The answer to this problem is said to be the elimination of admission requirements (Lavin and Hyllegard, 1996). There must instead be open enrollment. If this means that we, as a nation, have to invest in more college classrooms and/or in more professors, so be it. Excuse making only puts off the day of reckoning. In the long run, no democracy can endure if it saddles too many citizens with a legitimate grievance. Ultimately, those excluded demand their fair share, and the piper will have to be paid.

Few, however, believe that all must attend the same schools. One hears few recommendations that the elite universities be dismantled. It is thus the mid- and lower-level colleges that are asked to open their doors. They are told that they should eliminate virtually all admission requirements so that every potential student gets a chance. They are also to install programs that allow unprepared students to acquire the foundation they need to succeed in college.

Affordable Schooling

Unfortunately, even if admission standards are eased, a significant proportion of the population will be unable to afford college. Truly universal schooling, therefore, entails providing students the wherewithal to pursue advanced degrees. This can be accomplished in at least two ways. The first is to make a higher education free. Just as the government underwrites the costs of K–12, so, it is argued, government-sponsored colleges should charge no tuition. Indeed, once, not long ago, many state-supported colleges were free.

The government might also commit to picking up the tab for books, supplies, and room and board. These too can be provided directly or indirectly. In the latter case, all students—not just the needy—can be provided with scholarships and/or assistantships. They might, for instance, be sent checks, sometimes for work performed, so they can purchase what is necessary for their studies. A failure to do so, it is alleged, is tantamount to denying the disadvantaged the ability to take what is offered with one hand but snatched away with the other.

Or if this policy is considered too expensive, students can be given access to low-cost loans. All students, not just those with high grade-point averages, can be offered this resource. In the same way that mortgages enable people to purchase houses despite a lack of ready cash, adult learners can likewise be permitted to acquire a better future. If anything, the interest charged should be minimal—considering that college students are only starting out on their careers. Of course, such loans are already widely available. Nevertheless, some politicians wish to curtail these. They say that their goal is to prevent another financial bubble, but this is a rationalization for limiting access. This ploy, say the open-admissions advocates, cannot be tolerated because it is self-defeating. In attempting to protect the national wallet, it impoverishes the country by denying it the talent required for long-term prosperity.

Helping the Weak

Yet if everyone is to attend college, it is essential that some be assisted in graduating. Every person may possess the potential for a higher education; nonetheless, not all start out with identical academic skills (Herrnstein and Murray, 1994). If this is to be rectified, the laggards must be provided with remediation. Merely throwing students into the deep end of the pool is a farce. It makes much more sense is to compensate for the deficiencies of stragglers.

Furthermore, this assistance must be comprehensive. Some of it will be purely intellectual. Thus, poor readers must be provided practice in reading, while the mathematically challenged have to be brought up to speed. Yet this too is not enough. Some students have learning and/or emotional difficulties that need to be accommodated. If, for instance, they require more time to take examinations, this must be furnished. Or if they need psychological counseling, this too must be made available. Additionally, for some the requisite support entails residential facilities, while for others transportation is the issue. In all of these cases, compensation for temporary infirmities should be provided.

Fewer Elitist Subjects

The poor rarely have the opportunity to visit museums or take summer vacations in France. As a result, some of their handicaps are cultural (Bourdieu, 1977). Through no fault of their own, they have not been exposed to the symbolic indicators of superior status. This, however, does not mean they are less intelligent. Nor does it imply that they are less ambitious. All it suggests is that they have not been able to internalize knowledge that has historically been employed for gatekeeper functions. Speak with the wrong accent or fail to distinguish between a Titian and a Canaletto, and in some circles you get the cold shoulder. Social mobility is thus denied on the mistaken assumption that a lack of familiarity with the social currency of the elites denotes a lack of ability.

This being the case, a genuine higher education cannot entail indoctrination in the cultural artifacts of those at the apex of society. A universal education that is truly universal respects diverse social standards. Caviar cannot be assumed to be superior to hamburger. This attitude should also apply to the subject matter taught in college classrooms. Shakespeare has his place, but so does Batman. Likewise, sixty-four–dollar words may make it possible to express subtle distinctions, but street-level expressions can usually do the same job. Advocates of fairness therefore insist that education not be confused with pretentiousness. To genuinely understand the truth is not the same as pretending to be smarter because one is versed in the argot of the powerful. If the weak are to be given an equal chance, college curricula must be overhauled to make them more democratic. Only this can remove artificial obstacles to an egalitarian society.

More Affirmative Action

The need for affirmative action has already been implied when discussing social justice and multiculturalism. Indeed, reformers who believe in *relevance* and those who desire *fairness* both insist on its importance. This is because justice is thought to be concerned with fairness, while multiculturalism implies a moral equality between cultures. Moreover, justice and multiculturalism are deemed relevant to democracy precisely because democracy is interpreted as promoting cultural fairness. It remains here to spell out mechanisms for achieving this. In fact, affirmative action is sought because it is widely regarded as the *sine qua non* of egalitarian activism (Bergmann, 1996).

Affirmative action signifies the active pursuit of a moral course (Bowen and Bok, 1998). Instead of passively awaiting social improvements, policies designed to achieve these are to be aggressively implemented. Thus, devotees of fairness maintain that it is not enough to refrain from evil. Simply refusing to participate in discrimination is not believed to hasten its demise. More muscular interventions are required. This is true both inside and outside academe. It is also true for modes of unfairness other than racial discrimination.

Nonetheless, the starting point for many activists is academic quota systems. Of course, given previous Supreme Court decisions, these are not so labeled. They are instead referred to as "targets" or "goals." Yet because these are rigorously enforced, they are indistinguishable from quotas (Lynch, 1997). This, however, does not trouble their partisans. They are so deeply committed to fairness that they consider reverse discrimination necessary. As previously noted, this is defended as providing diversity.

On the other hand, conservatives denounce systematic preferences (Bernstein, 1994; Clegg, 2011). They depict these as unfair to those who do not receive them. According to these commentators, students who belong to an unprotected category are denied admission so that less well-qualified minorities can be accommodated. What, then, of the victims' futures? Opponents of the practice also insist that affirmative action mismatches students with universities (Jackson, 2008). This means that individuals who are unprepared to meet the rigorous standards of elite institutions are liable to drop out when they cannot keep up. Should they do so, their admission was unfair even to them. In any event, special preferences supposedly lower the academic bar, which adversely affects academic quality. This too is said to be unfair in that it deprives students of intellectual excellence.

Intellectual Diversity

Conservatives are especially distressed at the ideological tilt of contemporary universities. They contend that favoring some students over others undercuts intellectual diversity. Instead of providing a marketplace of ideas, this imposes a one-size-fits-all mentality antithetical to scholastic ferment (Rausch, 1995). The critics of the political correctness maintain that knowledge is advanced when partisans of different perspectives are allowed to clash (Horowitz, 2007). It is in having to defend their positions that individuals are driven to develop them further. Likewise, it is in arguing with classmates that students determine what they believe. Intellectual uniformity is therefore the enemy of scholarly progress.

In order to rectify this, some conservative reformers propose what amounts to a quota system for professors. Since the current faculty is heavily stacked in one direction, they advocate efforts to recruit underrepresented thinkers. Unless this is done, they fear that liberal gatekeepers will only allow their brethren to achieve tenure and/or promotion. While conservatives regret such draconian measures, they conclude that exhortation alone cannot achieve the required changes.

Faculty Reforms

As just noted, if the professoriate, as currently organized, does not promote the reforms many critics favor, they would overhaul their composition and perquisites. They would, for instance, change who teaches and the conditions under which they teach. Rather than allow those currently dominating the classroom to set the standards, these pedagogues would either be removed from their positions or compelled to alter their methods. Nowadays, in fact, professors are regularly taken to task for being conformists. Whatever their political allegiances, they are criticized for resisting innovation.

For some reformers, this obstinacy cannot be tolerated. Where once professors were placed on a pedestal, they are now derided for being too imperfect. According to their detractors, they make mistakes; they have biases; and they grow old and rigid. It is therefore imperative that the dead wood be culled and replaced by vibrant and pliant successors. Only in this way can new knowledge and responsive teaching be stimulated.

End Tenure

Tenure is widely deplored as an outmoded form of job security (Riley, 2011). The notion that professors should be granted employment for life is decried as preventing the turnover essential to reinvigorating stale teaching. Thus, professors who know they cannot be fired are said to lose the spark with which they began their careers. Instead of actively pursuing additional knowledge, they recycle the platitudes of their youth. Notorious for droning on, they neither recognize nor care about the damage they inflict.

This arrogance, it is asserted, must come to an end. Just as with other professions, college teachers who are no longer productive ought to be terminated. Perhaps they should be offered time-limited contracts; perhaps just shown the door. This would open the way for fresh blood. It would also inspire improvements by providing the competition that works so well in the economic marketplace. Moreover, arguments that tenure is needed to protect academic freedom are spurious. The conceit that professors only entertain controversial ideas if they are protected from arbitrary dismissal is outmoded. First of all, most professors are anything but controversial. Having been vetted for their political correctness, they go along with the crowd (Ravitch, 2003). Second, the mavericks are already protected. Free speech is defended by the American Constitution; hence, there is no need for special academic freedoms. These are bogus protections intended to provide job security rather than to advance knowledge.

With tenure gone professors will be on their toes. No longer will they sit in faculty lounges sipping latte, smirking about how well they are paid for doing so little. Colleges will then be able to compel them to teach more courses, which, in turn, will lower costs. Nor will professors be able to ignore public pressures for reform. Having been forced into the same boat as other Americans, they too will be compelled to improve their productivity.

Utilize Adjuncts

College courses are not as difficult to teach as professors let on—or so say detractors of the current system. Many classes entail no more than a rehashing of what is presented in textbooks. This is especially so for introductory courses. As a consequence, instructors with relatively little experience can teach them just as effectively. In fact, their ability to do so can be enhanced by providing them with well-tested syllabi and media-based supplements. In this case, graduate students and/or master's level alumnae will do as well as PhDs. What is more, they will do so for less money. Happy to gain classroom experience, they can enthusiastically supply a better product than the traditional cicerones.

So why aren't colleges manned primarily by adjuncts? Since many of these part-timers have full-time jobs elsewhere, the experience they bring to their tasks is a welcome bonus. Besides, as temporaries, they can be hired and fired as enrollments change or course offerings are modified. They can thus provide a flexibility that improves academic quality.

If these benefits sound too good to be true, many critics insist that they are. They tell us that our universities are already overrun with adjuncts. They also claim that these temporaries are an inferior substitute for veteran professors. For the most part, such neophytes know less and are pedagogical amateurs. Far from compensating for their inadequacies with enthusiasm, they provide a second-rate education. They therefore represent the triumph of cost cutting over academic excellence.

Add to this the fact that experienced professors are apt to be active scholars who have more to share with students. Perhaps accomplished researchers, perhaps published authors, they know more about their subjects than beginners possibly can. This is no small advantage. Given that higher education is concerned with complex materials, those whose insights have been honed in practice can provide more detailed information than those merely informed by books. What is needed, according to the anti-adjunct coterie, are thus more full professors. They insist that quality cannot be had on the cheap, and the assumption that it can is a dangerous illusion.

Promote More (or Less) Research

Commentators who favor beefing up the full-time faculty frequently advocate increased research. They tell us that professors should be both good teachers and good scholars. To this end, more emphasis needs to be devoted to expanding our database. Universities that simply reprocess ancient wisdom are not places of higher education. They are cobweb-encrusted tombs from which nothing vibrant emerges. Yes, we must learn from the past, but doing so to the exclusion of increasing what we understand is a formula for stagnation. Like ancient China, we would become so enamored of our cultural accomplishments that we would decline as a world power. Continued prosperity and security depend on moving forward, which is one of the primary reasons we are concerned with preserving high-quality colleges in the first place.

Stressing first-class research also guarantees first-class instruction. Professors who rest on their laurels have less to offer students. After all, active minds are curious minds. Intellects that reach beyond what they already know have more to share. They are also enthusiastic minds that bring excitement to the classroom. If universities are about disseminating wisdom, then those dedicated to rigorous learning are the ones who can best inspire it.

As might be expected, there is a counterargument. Other reformers insist the above thesis is wrong-headed. While they do not dismiss the necessity of vigorous research, they deny that this is necessary to enhance classroom teaching. To the contrary, they maintain that the best researchers are frequently the worst professors. Focused as they are on intellectual investigations, their attention is not on student needs. All too often inarticulate, many researchers are not sensitive to how well they communicate. For them, course requirements are a diversion. As a result, many seek releases so they can spend more time in the laboratory. While they know more than less-accomplished colleagues, much of this is highly specialized and beyond the comprehension of beginning students.

If this is true, then perhaps teaching per se should be emphasized. Instead of attempting to follow the example of Harvard and hire a stable of world-class investigators, more weight might be placed on discovering and rewarding classroom talent. Let a few elite institutions specialize in research and scholarship. No doubt we, as a nation, would profit from the ideas they develop. Nonetheless, emulating their example everywhere could be fatal to higher education as a whole. It might mean that most students learned very little. What is required instead may be a division of labor. Perhaps some colleges should allow most of their professors to specialize in research, while encouraging others to develop pedagogical skills. Perhaps less elite schools should place the stress in the reverse order. This way we could have the best of both worlds. Indeed, inferior researchers who are not forced to do inept research would have more time to improve their teaching techniques. Research is important, but it is not the sole good provided by colleges and universities. Recognizing this might save funds squandered on copycat scholarship.

Less Scholasticism

Whether or not universities promote research, some contend that they must reduce their output of scholasticism (Mead, 2011). Back in the Middle Ages, scholars were immersed in a sea of trivia. Concerned almost entirely with theological hair-splitting, clerical scholars dedicated lifetimes to arguments so subtle that no one but those with whom they debated could understand them. According to some observers, contemporary scholars have entered a similar blind alley. They too are engaged in purposeless pursuits. Trapped in disciplinary silos, they have become so over-specialized that no one but a handful of academics shares their interests. Hence, they write books and articles no one reads, attend conferences where they are bored by irrelevant papers, and wind up holding the burned-out cinders of once-promising careers in their hands. It is therefore time to end scholastic games and encourage professors to be more productive. Instead of demanding that they establish academic reputations based on innovative ideas, we should recognize that this may promote inconsequential meanderings. The result has been thousands of learned men and women seeking to be different for the sake of being different and merely packaging old wine in new bottles.

Less Ideology

Finally, as should be apparent, there is a profoundly moralistic bent to contemporary academe. With professors hard-pressed to distinguish themselves intellectually, they frequently dedicate themselves to social causes. In an effort to be good people, they concentrate on advancing moral agendas. Gussying up personal commitments as universal truths, they then teach these as if they were beyond criticism. Despite assurances that theirs is a quest for empirical facts, they do not allow uncomfortable observations to get in the way of cherished convictions. Fortunately for most of these scholars, their principles are shared by a majority of their colleagues. With liberal worldviews having become the academic gold standard, they are rarely reproached. To the contrary, they are frequently applauded.

Nevertheless, ideologies are ideologies. However widely endorsed, they tend to be inimical to change. Ideologues, of course, are confident that they know the truth. They also believe that they know how to fix what they consider broken. This is because their belief systems provide both a theory about how the world works and an agenda for pursuing improvements (Sowell, 2009). And while there may be nothing wrong with subscribing to such theories and agendas, they can be too tightly held. We all need an intellectual map to understand the universe and a playbook to tell us how to act. Nevertheless, if the consensus upholding a particular viewpoint is too inflexible, it can prevent progress. This, unfortunately, has been the fate of the current liberal hegemony—at least according to their ideological opponents.

What is undoubtedly true is that liberal ideas pervade higher education and that their adherents are intolerant of dissent. Liberal domination is so complete that students or faculty members who question the prevailing wisdom face hefty sanctions. Thus, dissenting students get lower grades and unorthodox professors are shown the door. The result is intellectual skew. Ironically, professors who perceive themselves as progressive end up resisting change. Instead of questioning their convictions, the chief concern is defending them. Far from participating in a marketplace of ideas, they operate like priests who demand that the faith not be examined (Wood and Toscano, 2013).

Into the Weeds

The above is a long list of potential responses to the presumed academic bubble. They vary from technological innovations, to various forms of relevance, to concerns about fairness, to faculty restructuring. Plainly, many of these proposals are in conflict with one another. Just as plainly, when we trek into their weeds, we discover that moral agendas frequently color the judgments of their advocates. These diverse propositions address issues such as costs, enrollments, time, and quality, but their focus is largely determined by ethical considerations. As a consequence, onlookers may wind up favoring some proposals over others on the basis of their personal commitments. Instead of investigating the causes of the underlying problems and examining which suggestions best correct them, they tilt toward long-held allegiances.

How then are we to sift through these very many potential solutions? By what criteria should some be considered superior to others? The answer depends largely upon what we are attempting to accomplish. Whether a particular strategy is effective can only be decided by how well it achieves a desired end point. So what is the mission of higher education? If we can agree on this, the appropriate solutions may come into sharper focus. As should be noted, none of the answers so far put forward specifically claims to advance professionalization or self-direction. Whether technology, or affirmative action, or tenure will do so therefore remain open questions. It is even an open question as to whether professionalization and self-direction deserve to be the filter through which we decide what works. We must consequently explore the central mission of higher education before concluding which, if any, of the foregoing schemes is worth pursuing.

This, however, will take us into the tangled growth of university mission statements and the twists and turns of historical developments. Nonetheless, these can provide hints as to where we are headed and furnish a preface as to why a professionalized model of social organization is currently replacing a bureaucratized one and why it must eventually do so within higher education as well. We will also have to explore the nature of human hierarchies so as to gain a better grasp of what it means to be elite. Although it is anathema to many commentators, social leaders—of whatever sort—belong to an elite. One consequence of this—albeit a controversial one—may be that college is not for all. If not everyone possesses the talents and motivation to make important social decisions, perhaps, in the end, he or she is not college material.

3

The Mission of Higher Education

Mission Statement Mania

It is difficult to determine if you have arrived at your destination if you have no idea of where you are headed. If this sounds too trite to be stated out loud, it nevertheless suggests what is wrong with many current programs for college reform. These often tell us what we are supposed to do but not why we are supposed to do it (Kissel, 2011). Evidently, many passionately endorsed schemes assume that the appropriate objectives are so self-evident as not to require comment. This may be because their authors are so deeply steeped in specific moral agendas that they are convinced everyone else is too.

Nevertheless, as we have seen, many reforms start from different premises. Indeed, some are diametrically opposed in the end points they recommend. It is, therefore, imperative that we clarify what is sought before laying out yet another proposal. First off, our goals must be clear and justifiable. Likewise, their provenance and effectiveness must be substantiated. Without this information, there is little to choose between alternate plans. Furthermore, given how many interpretations of academic problems and their potential solutions are floating around, we need well-founded criteria for sorting through them. How are we to proceed when there are so many candidates, with so many persuasive advocates? The answer is not obvious.

As earlier suggested, the central thesis of this work is that as our society becomes more professionalized, we need more self-motivated experts to provide the services upon which we depend. But a mass techno-commercial civilization must also have ways to ensure that strangers deliver what is required. Higher education has been alleged to achieve this by developing a self-directed elite.

This leadership category may be more broadly based than historically privileged groups, as well as characterized by greater social mobility, yet all the same, its members will exercise levels of authority denied less proficient decision makers. This, however, makes sense only if these individuals are effectively socialized so as to be worthy of this responsibility.

The question is thus: are the above assertions true? Is the central mission of higher education to groom individuals who are capable of competent self-direction? Moreover, do our colleges achieve this? Indeed, are they geared to achieve this? Needless to say, it is not enough to allege that this is so. Evidence must be adduced to support this contention. Where, then, are we to find the appropriate confirmation? It might be supposed that a good starting place is the mission statements produced by colleges and universities. These are presumably transparent accounts regarding what schools are attempting to achieve. Unfortunately, this is not so. Because these declarations are political documents, they are generally too ambiguous to serve as useful guideposts.

Yet so universal is the need for an explicatory rationale understood to be that nowadays almost every college offers a detailed mission statement. Most of these texts, unfortunately, are remarkably nebulous. Because their primary goal is to legitimize what these schools do in the eyes of the public, they specialize in euphemisms. Their purpose is not so much to define what is done as to proclaim a list of aspirations in a way that diverse constituencies can read into them what they wish. This way, colleges hope to enlist support from multiple quarters.

How this is achieved can be garnered from the mission statement of my own college. Thus, Kennesaw State University says it "aspires to be a progressive and exemplary educational institution, respected for excellence and leadership in teaching, service, and research; [one] committed to continuous improvement in an increasingly diverse and constantly changing learning community." This document likewise touts the school's "diverse student body," claims that "effective teaching and learning are central institutional priorities," and maintains that its "research, scholarship and creative activit[ies] are broadly defined and predominantly applied."

These objectives are similarly said to make the school "distinctive." But how distinctive are priorities that promise to be all things to all people? KSU's mission statement is, in fact, a diplomatic instrument. As is the case with most public universities, it is designed to appeal to the voters and officials whose favor it must curry. School administrators know that if the budgetary spigots are to remain open, these constituencies must remain friendly. As result, it would be unwise to alienate them. All must therefore be left with the feeling that the university is attuned to their desires.

The upshot is a statement that is bloated and hyperbolic. Thus, it promises to foster "high-quality academic preparation, critical thinking, global and multi-cultural perspectives, effective communication and interpersonal skills, leadership development, social responsibility and lifelong learning." Also pledged is a research agenda that includes "improvement of teaching and learning; survey research for community and economic development; interdisciplinary studies in support of environmental, governmental, business or health interests; creative contributions to the arts and humanities; intellectual contributions; discovery research and publication; and the interpretation or application of academic research."

Obviously, the purpose of this exercise is to leave out as little as possible and to state this as brightly as possible. Max Weber (1947) thought bureaucratic goals were supposed to inform organizational members of their shared objectives. This, however, is only tangentially true for contemporary universities. For the most part, their mission statements are public-relations devices. The sunny embellishments in which they specialize are intended to tap into every market-tested cliché that might impress potential patrons.

This posture is understandable in that it promotes institutional survival. Nevertheless, it does not provide useful guidance regarding reform. A declaration of goals that covers every possible contingency does not distinguish between alternatives or provide reasons for emphasizing some directions rather than others. While it is true that universities can pursue multiple objectives, it is also true that this sort of ambiguity can be confusing. Still, universities are diverse institutions; hence, a misleading consistency could handicap their efforts and create internal discord.

Let us pause here to underline the fact that universities are political arenas. They are not isolated from the communities in which they are embedded, nor are they immune to internal stresses. As a consequence, what they do is often decided in extended negotiations during which competing factions espouse their own programs. These quasi-political coalitions bring pressures to bear in the hopes that these will carry the day. Yet complete victories for one side or another are rare. This means that what is pursued may be a hodgepodge of shifting objectives. Nevertheless, coherent reforms have to identify what is broken and how it can be fixed. While disjointed amendments can produce benefits, consistency reduces turmoil. To achieve this, however, it is necessary to prioritize. Which goals are most important? Which can be safely jettisoned? In other words, if there is a clash between competing directions, which take precedence?

This said, because no group's values are completely consistent, it is doubtful that any of them can reach comprehensive agreements as to their priorities. This stricture obviously applies to higher education. It, therefore, makes sense to place what is sought in historical context. History can tell us what people and institutions have done, not just what they claim to have done. Thus, if discernible patterns are evident, these may offer better evidence regarding organizational purposes than do verbal avowals. Let us therefore examine how colleges and universities have developed. What brought them into existence and what sustained them through the shifting currents of history?

History—The Beginnings

Higher education has a long pedigree. Most of this, however, does not include universities as currently constituted. It does, however, suggest the central purposes for which efforts at advanced learning were instituted. Yet before examining the roots of colleges in the West, let us to look East. China has long been noted for its commitment to scholarship. Even today, Confucian principles inform the cultural attitudes of contemporary Chinese. We also see this in the United States where a large proportion of our most accomplished students draw upon Asian traditions. Books have actually been written about "tiger mothers" who settle for nothing less than academic excellence (Chua, 2011). The effect has been to produce a generation of college students who are disproportionately Chinese, Japanese, Korean, and/or Vietnamese. They are admitted to elite schools in higher numbers than might be expected, and then they go on to obtain grades that reflect the seriousness of their resolve.

This attitude has an ancient lineage. It can be traced back thousands of years to the origins of Chinese civilization. Thanks to early inventions, such as the iron plow, the population of what is today China was much larger than that of any contemporary European or Mid-Eastern society. This crowding stimulated political innovation. Large nations require competent administration. Their rulers find that if they are to prosper, their underlings must be intelligent enough to deal with complex issues. Because family connections were not sufficient to ensure that the cream rose to the top, the Chinese instituted an examination system to identify those who, in recent years, have been described as "the best and the brightest." These tests were based on cultural proficiencies. Those who did best devoted years of study to the literary and scientific accomplishments of their forebears. Success therefore depended upon both intelligence and diligence. While what was studied might not be directly related to governance, mastery of it provided a useful means for distinguishing those fit to make difficult decisions. In any event, because political power was bestowed upon those with scholarly credentials, a good education was highly valued.

Events proceeded somewhat differently in Europe. Initially without comparably centralized administrations, what facilitated political advancement, of necessity, differed. Perhaps the best place to begin analyzing this disparity is Greece, and doubtless, the best example of advanced learning in Greece was provided by Athens (Fornara, 1991). As the commercial hub of a politically divided peninsula, it pioneered developments emulated elsewhere. One was in business; another in democratic governance. Not wholly disconnected, these innovations relied on well-educated citizens. Merchants, who bought and sold goods around the Mediterranean, needed to understand their customers, as well as to think swiftly on their feet. To do less was an invitation to be outsmarted by more able competitors. In some contemporary quarters, businesspersons are reputed to be dense, but the talents of those who rose to prominence in Athens belie this judgment.

Commerce is also replete with conflict. Buyers and sellers not only try to outsmart one another, but they sometimes resort to unethical shenanigans. Early on, a remedy was found in a court system. Cheaters could be sued to force them to make good on their promises. Nowadays complainants hire lawyers to protect their interests. Back then, the burden fell upon the merchants and artisans themselves. They had to go to court and make a persuasive case if they were to prevail. This is where education came in. Learning to speak well, which included a familiarity with cultural symbols, could be acquired from the appropriate teacher. As a bonus, these skills were useful in exercising political influence. With many governmental decisions made in the agora, an ability to make a persuasive speech could prove the difference between being a leader and an also-ran.

Democracy, in short, with its emphasis on verbal dexterity, was a seedbed for advanced scholarship.

Among the practitioners who catered to the demand for knowledge and verbal fluency were the Sophists. Although this designation is derived from the Greek word for wisdom, recent parlance has associated these peripatetic teachers with intellectual dishonesty. At the time, however, they could remain in business only if they provided a valued service. Customarily interested in instilling rhetorical polish, they were derided for what would today be described as a relativistic attitude. More concerned with what moved audiences than with deep philosophical insights, critics, such as Socrates, despised their alleged shallowness. Claiming, as they did, that "man is the measure of all things," they alienated absolutists such as Socrates and his disciple Plato.

Socrates was a relatively poor artisan who made a reputation by challenging the accepted wisdom of his peers and for collecting a devoted coterie of youthful disciples. He did not charge for his services nor have a fixed location in which he taught. Plato, however, changed the manner in which he disseminated his expertise (Plato, 1928: Edman, 1928). He created a school—the academy—where he propounded his theories. He also wrote a series of dialogues to provide a standardized account of his ideas. Himself an aristocrat, in these he promulgated a set of reforms that exposed an elitist edge. Thus, one of his most influential theses was that states should be governed by philosopher kings—much like himself.

One of Plato's most renowned pupils was Aristotle. Less aristocratic than his mentor and also more empirical, he opened new vistas of learning. Early on he applied these to tutoring the eldest son of King Philip of Macedonia. This young man grew up to be Alexander the Great. Once finished with this assignment, Aristotle returned to Athens to found the Lyceum. He also committed his encyclopedic knowledge to written form (Aristotle, 1941), where it eventually provided authoritative documents for medieval European universities and Islamic academics.

The Romans, who wrested political dominance from the Hellenes, were not as scholarly. More practical in orientation, they dedicated themselves to maintaining military discipline and to building the roads and aqueducts that enabled them to assemble a great empire. Nonetheless, their aristocrats—the so-called patricians—valued education. This was usually acquired by employing Greek tutors. Noted intellectuals also attracted ambitious Romans to their public lectures. These were appreciated because Rome, which started as a democracy, retained a tradition of learned court advocates. It similarly maintained a respect for gifted speakers who could sway their senatorial colleagues. Thus, Cicero, who stemmed from the equestrian order, parlayed an excellent education and rhetorical eloquence into an illustrious legal and political career (Everitt, 2001). Meanwhile, Cato the Younger used his position in the senate to elevate himself to the defender of Roman traditions thanks to his oratorical gifts. Even Julius Caesar (1980) depended upon his literary skills to produce commentaries that recruited other patricians to his cause.

Rome did not have universities of the sort that later arose in Europe, but its more celebrated educators systematized a curriculum that later became the basis of higher education for nearly a millennium. Thus, the trivium and quadrivium became the core of what every educated person should know. The trivium consisted of grammar, logic, and rhetoric. Here the central objective was to teach learners how to think and express their ideas with accuracy and clarity. The quadrivium, in contrast, concentrated on arithmetic, geometry, music, and astronomy. These subjects dealt with measurement and sought to instill numerical accuracy. Together they summed up a set of intellectual skills that could underwrite a successful political, military, commercial, or engineering career.

After the so-called Dark Ages that set in with the decline of Rome (Gibbon, 1993), organized learning virtually disappeared for over five hundred years (Pirenne, 1936). The rudiments of literacy were largely confined to the monasteries. With the Christian Church, the sole surviving continent-wide social organization, it sought to preserve the legacy of a more sophisticated age (Haskins, 1957). At the very least it attempted to ensure that the Bible and other sacred texts remained available to clerics. This, however, greatly restricted the sort of knowledge perpetuated, while simultaneously limiting its access to a very few.

Not until the reemergence of a vibrant economy was this to change. Fostered, in part, by the monasteries, commerce picked up and towns arose to dot the landscape. Soon the embryos of nation states consolidated their power and imposed a legal consistency on those governed. But first, the church itself sought to strengthen its administration. For this, it required educated clergymen. If the church's legal machinery was to provide consistent justice, some priests, bishops, and monks had to be more than literate. They needed to know the ecclesiastical law and to be skilled advocates. Also, with secular power centers rising to greater prominence (Elias, 1998), the church's spokespersons had to make persuasive arguments in its defense.

The cathedrals long had schools attached to them, but now some grew in enrollments and stature. In places like Paris, Montpelier, and Bologna, institutions developed that would later become universities. Initially the exclusive preserve of clerics, their most prestigious teachers and students specialized in theology. The Bible was regarded as the foundation of all learning, but it was supplemented by other sources. Where in earlier years faith was the sole arbiter of truth, learned men began to insist that reason could enhance it. These two highways to knowledge, they argued, had to be consistent; hence, what was discovered would never challenge church authority.

With the trivium and quadrivium having become canonical, logic was taught with Porphyrius's *Isagoge*, Boethius's *Topica*, and Aristotle's *Analytica Priora*. Similarly, grammar was conveyed by Prician's *Institutione Grammaticae* and Donatus's *Barbarismus*. Philosophy and natural philosophy were, however, dominated by Aristotle. His *Physica*, *Metaphysica*, and *De Animalibus* acquired the status of near biblical authority. Even his *Ethica Nichomachea* stood toe-to-toe with the ethical treatises of the church fathers. This is not to say that there was no original thinking emanating from university scholars. Indeed, Thomas Aquinas developed proofs of God's existence that continue to command theological respect. By the same token, William of Occam's razor still sets the standard of intellectual parsimony.

Alongside these developments, schools of law and medicine made their appearance. As the curtain of ignorance that separated medieval society from classical times began to lift, Roman achievements in the legal and medical domains once again commanded the attention of scholars. They began to realize, for example, that the technical proficiency of classical lawyers could profitably be applied to their own circumstances. As commercial endeavors multiplied, merchants benefited from regulations that resolved disputes. Hence, at first in Italy, where the economy revived earliest, academics sought to analyze and codify the Roman legacy. So valuable was this achievement that students from all over the continent flocked to Bologna to acquire the expertise needed to establish Roman-style legal systems in their homelands.

Something comparable occurred with respect to medicine. Health has always been a human concern; therefore, people have always valued techniques that preserve their physical well-being. As it happened, Roman physicians such as Galen and Greek physicians such as Hippocrates were far in advance of religious-based medicine. These classical doctors were primitive compared with their modern counterparts, but they were far better organized—and more scientific—than their competitors. In fact, they spurred empirical studies in anatomy previously forbidden by the church. Where cutting into human flesh had been disallowed as impious, now Renaissance autopsies revealed how human bodies were constructed. Soon, this would lead to a better understanding of human physiology.

It might be assumed that these university-based developments were isolated from secular occurrences, but this would be mistaken. While the church was the primary locus of educational innovations, their utility did not escape notice. As was the case in China, monarchs realized that educated retainers could improve their administrations. The intelligence and literacy of scholars enabled them to keep track of extensive domains and to improve communication with government subordinates. Rulers such as Philip the Fair of France deliberately recruited university-trained clerics to assist in consolidating control (Elias, 1983). They could and did develop policies that enabled Philip to suppress rival centers of power. Indeed, this was the origin of positions such as "secretary" of state and "secretary" of the treasury.

Nor were scions of the bourgeoisie excluded from these developments (Plumb, 1961). They too could see that educated administrators were good for the bottom line. Literacy skills were useful for communicating with customers and subordinates, and mathematical skills were advantageous when engaging in computations in the newfangled double-entry bookkeeping. While a proficiency in Latin and Greek was not as important as previously, these came to symbolize advanced learning. Eventually, when the vernacular replaced Latin in day-to-day transactions, this once lingua franca became semi-comatose. Nonetheless, it soldiered on as a cultural icon. As with other subjects studied in the universities, it served to identify those who were well educated. This, in turn, could be translated into social stature that greased the wheels of commerce. After all, a learned person must be a smart person, and a smart person made a better business partner—or at least a more dangerous adversary.

Interestingly, the cultural competence inculcated via a higher education became a symbol of aristocratic standing as well. Thus, Henry VIII of England took great pride in his theological knowledge and musical talents. So confident was he in his grasp of religion that he wrote a pamphlet in defense of the Catholic Church that prompted the pope to confer the title "Defender of the Faith" upon him. Henry was also proud on his ability to compose music on par with professional musicians. Later on, Edmund Spenser wrote a poem titled the *Faerie Queene* in praise of Henry's daughter Elizabeth that elevated both his and her status. At the time, well-educated folk of both genders routinely composed poetry to validate their intellectual credentials. So common was this, that several aristocrats have been identified as the true author of William Shakespeare's plays. Even Isaac Newton, a man of relatively humble birth, was rewarded with an aristocratic tithe to acknowledge his scientific achievements. He was appointed warden of the Royal Mint, despite being a lowly professor, because the entire nation was grateful for his insights regarding how the universe operated. It was as if his theory of gravity had provided a window into the mind of the Creator.

The American Experience

The American colonists were the heirs to this legacy (Rudolph, 1990; Taylor, 2010; Thelin, 2011). The New England Puritans, in particular, had a long-standing connection with Cambridge University. Primarily from East Anglia, many of their ministers received their training there. Consequently, when the colony's leading citizens decided to found an institution to train ministers, they used Cambridge as the model. The problem was that they did not possess the same resources. With less wealth to draw upon and fewer first-class intellects available to teach, they made do. Greek and Latin as well as theology were at the heart of their curricula, but the rigor of the Old World was largely absent. Still and all, many of their students benefited from this instruction.

One who did fairly well was John Adams of the Massachusetts Colony (McCullough, 2001). The son of a farmer, by dint of hard work and a clever brain he rose to become a successful lawyer, a moving spirit behind independence, an ambassador to France, the vice president, and ultimately the president of his new country. Adams's chief rival, Thomas Jefferson (Ellis, 1996; Mapp, 1987) was also college educated. The son of a wealthy Virginia planter, young Thomas was initially tutored at home but eventually enrolled at William and Mary, the premier Southern college. He too did fairly well politically, as did his admirer James Madison (Ketcham, 1990; Ellis, 1993). More bookish than either Adams or Jefferson, Madison went to the College of New Jersey, ultimately renamed Princeton

University. There he became so familiar with the contemporary European literature on history and politics that when the time came, he was up to the challenge of becoming the moving force behind the American Constitution (Morris, 1985).

Meanwhile, Madison's collaborator on the Federalist Papers, Alexander Hamilton (Brookhiser, 1999), followed a different trajectory. A poor orphan from the Caribbean, he was so bright that he was sponsored for a college education in New York City. Not only did he do quite well at King's College (the future Columbia University), but he caught the eye of General George Washington. After serving as Washington's chief of staff, he carved out a successful legal career in New York, participated in the Constitutional Convention, was instrumental in ensuring the document's ratification, and then became the nation's first secretary of the treasury. A brilliant writer and a compelling thinker, more than any other person he helped organize the administrative machinery of the fledgling government and set the agenda for the commercial triumphs in store for his adopted country. All in all, it can be said that America's crude young colleges did a credible job in turning out world-class social innovators.

Of course, not all of the new nation's leaders obtained a college education (Isaacson, 2003). Much to his embarrassment, Washington did not, although he sought to compensate by educating himself. Nor did Benjamin Franklin, Andrew Jackson, or Abraham Lincoln. The latter two, however, became lawyers as a result of being trained by other lawyers. Having started their careers on the frontier, they had little choice but to become autodidacts. Nonetheless, as the nation pushed westward, the motivation to establish new colleges was compelling. Those at the cutting edge of the westward advance had no intention of being left behind by their Eastern brethren.

A prime example of one who benefited from this impulse was James Garfield (Millard, 2011). After having been raised on an Ohio farm by his widowed mother, he complied with her wishes and attended Hiram and then Williams Colleges. Subsequently, himself an educator and a politician, he served many years in Congress, as well as a general during the Civil War. Although Congress has not been the ideal platform to rise to the presidency, his intellectual gifts and broad academic knowledge shown through in his sterling oratory. Drafted to run for the highest office in the land, he was tragically assassinated before he could accomplish very much. Today he is little remembered, but in his time, he was honored as a brilliant product of the nation's burgeoning educational system.

As earlier noted, the Morrill Act sought to bring a college education to the masses. Ordinary young men were to be afforded an opportunity to become skilled engineers and/or agronomists. Washington, among others, favored establishing a national university, but the land-grant colleges were to be as close as the federal government came to this. Nonetheless, they were a bona fide effort to democratize higher education. The military academies (i.e., West Point and Annapolis) also deserve mention for their democratic traditions. Often the only opportunity for a solid education that a poor boy, such as Ulysses Grant, could afford (McFeely, 1981), they were first-rate engineering institutions. The so-called Ivy League schools (Harvard, Yale, Princeton, etc.), in contrast, specialized in catering to the elite. Private and therefore relatively expensive, they may not have been admired for their scholarship, yet they set the standard for other schools, thanks to their prestige. Both old and comparatively rich, they provided a ritualistic transition to adulthood for the scions of the wealthy. Thus, the Vanderbilts (Auchincloss, 1989), the Roosevelts, and eventually the Bushes became synonymous with the gentleman's C's in which these schools specialized (Collier and Horowitz, 1976, 1984, 1987; Nasaw, 2000).

But the Ivies did not remain trapped in their snobbish slumbers. A series of reform-minded college presidents were determined to elevate their scholastic reputations. To this end, more prestigious faculties were recruited. In short order, Harvard (Douthat, 2005) was following the lead of Johns Hopkins. Hopkins, as a new college, sought to import the German-style university to the United States. Where universities such as Oxford were mired in sanctified medieval customs, the consolidating German nation was hell-bent on outstripping its rivals. It, therefore, pioneered universities dedicated to science and scholarship. What was to become the modern research university was intended to provide the knowledge for economic and political expansion (Schumpeter, 1942). This, however, required sophisticated forms of organization. Indeed, it was from this need that the division into different disciplines such as chemistry, biology, and psychology arose. Previous to this, they were lumped together as natural philosophy.

Johns Hopkins made such a splash with its research model that Harvard decided it could not be left behind. Harvard also introduced the elective system that has since become an international standard. Students would no longer be compelled to take a lock-step program decreed by the college but could choose many of the subjects they studied. This, together with updating instruction to include science and modern languages, made higher education more relevant to a burgeoning industrial economy. Later added were efforts to attract more intellectually gifted students. This, in turn, created a need to identify which students were, in fact, most promising. And so were born the college entrance examinations.

The next great modification in who went to college and what was learned occurred in the wake of World War II. After the soldiers returned home, they were encouraged to attend college on the GI Bill. Not only did this increase college enrollment, but it dramatically altered the composition of their student bodies. The children of the elite still attended the best schools, yet they were now outnumbered by classmates with less exalted pedigrees. These new students were not so much looking for polish or networking opportunities as skills they could convert into remunerative careers. They wanted quality and subject matter relevant to their circumstances. The colleges soon complied.

What eventually emerged was a more middle-class–oriented society. David Brooks (2000, 2004) coined a word to describe what the graduates of American universities had become. He called them "bobos." This stood for "bourgeois bohemians." Brooks began his book on this transition by telling how the society pages of the *New York Times* changed over time. Where once marriage announcements touted the family connections of impending spouses, these now flaunted their educational achievements. It was increasingly understood that how successful people became depended more on their university credentials than their family histories. Higher education had become the gatekeeper to social status and personal clout. In other words, colleges came to matter. More than ever, they made the difference between those who rose to the top and those who did not. Doctors and lawyers but also corporate executives, bankers, engineers, and advertising geniuses generally began their careers as top-flight students at first-rate colleges.

Richard Herrnstein and Charles Murray later documented one consequence of this in their book *The Bell Curve* (1994). They argued that as the entire American educational system became geared to selecting the ablest students for entrance into elite universities, intellectual abilities came to be concentrated at the apex of society. The best and brightest—or at least the brightest—could now get scholarships to good schools, even if they came from modest backgrounds. This was not welcome news for those fixated on achieving total social equality, but it underlined the importance that higher education had acquired in the modern economy.

Meanwhile, there developed an array of mid- and lower-level schools, many of which were state sponsored. A college education thus became available not just for the brightest students but for nearly everyone ambitious enough to seek a credential. The result was a multitier system with private research universities, such as Harvard or Stanford, and flagship state universities, such as the University of California at Berkeley, at its summit, and smaller private, state, regional, and community colleges lower down the scale. Often what differentiated these schools was their selectivity and academic rigor. Those at the top could limit their admission to the top 3 percent of high school graduates (and also some legacy and affirmative action choices), while those at the bottom took most comers. The elite schools also boasted more prestigious faculties and better research facilities.

Which leaves us where in determining the mission of higher education? History, if it shows us anything, suggests that colleges and universities have specialized in preparing elites to function within the societies that create them. Whether these were Chinese scholar administrators, Greek and Roman orators, medieval clerics, early modern merchants, colonial politicians, proto-industrialists, or contemporary professionals, those who received a higher education generally exercised greater social authority. They came to be respected for what they knew and were therefore delegated decisions upon which others were dependent. These learning facilities have never been for everyone, nor did they aspire to teach everything. History, of course, only tells us what these institutions have been. It cannot dictate what they will—or should—be. That is up to us to decide. Nonetheless, the past has been described as prologue to the future. As such, it provides clues as to what might lie ahead.

The Hierarchical Imperative

We humans are hierarchical animals (Fein, 2012). Always and everywhere, we rank ourselves in comparison with others of our species. We may abhor this fact, but as social scientists regularly remind us (Diamond, 2013), it is a universal aspect of human communities, especially when they are large. More than this, those who come out on top generally live more comfortable lives than those on the bottom. Few would contend that this is fair, but nowhere has anyone been able to eliminate these inequalities. As we have seen, however, many academic reformers are determined to alter this state of affairs. They insist that higher education can promote social justice. Whether or not this is true, history provides little comfort for social engineers. Clearly colleges have consistently maintained hierarchical distinctions. How they achieved this has differed, but that they did has not. At some point things may change, but it is up to egalitarians to prove that this is feasible. Given how great is the transformation they desire, they must demonstrate how conditions can be modified and why this would be beneficial.

Pierre Bourdieu (1997; Swartz, 1997) has been a prominent commentator on higher education. He observes that universities (especially the French ones with which he is most familiar) specialize in perpetuating cultural traditions. He also notes that the children of successful parents have a leg up in assimilating these materials. Already familiar with much of what is expected, they absorb it more readily than do less well-prepared classmates. This, says Bourdieu, is not fair. Why should schools be designed to favor students who beforehand possess social advantages? Curricula that accomplish this are therefore condemned as at best arbitrary and at worst prejudicial.

One of the concepts Bourdieu popularized is "cultural capital." The words people use, the examples they employ, and the recreations they prefer can all provide advantages in the struggle to get ahead. Like it or not, people are judged by the accents in which they speak. They likewise gain networking opportunities if they are proficient in golf. These may have little to do with their job performance, but everything to do with whether they are promoted. Sadly, while some students acquire this capital while attending university, others are shut out. Prejudged as not fitting in with the existing elites, they are never invited to the right parties. Nor do professors, who assume that crude communications are indicative of a defective mind, heed them. It is therefore the same old story: the rich get richer and the poor get poorer.

As with most critics of the present system, Bourdieu wants to alter it. But is this possible? Does he have a credible program to rectify its inequalities? There is reason to believe that he does not. If the goal is to eliminate all inequalities, this appears to be a hopeless quest. It goes against our nature as hierarchical creatures. Some people believe that if elites can be eliminated, their baleful influence can be excised (Rousseau, 1968). At the very least, we, as a society, can squelch the selfish impulses of these neo-aristocrats so as to allow the less well-off to flourish. Much as weeds must be pulled from a fruitful garden, snobs cannot be allowed to monopolize the nutrients others require.

This theory assumes that greedy elites cause inequality. Thus, if they can be stopped, the natural fairness of the majority will establish more equitable ground rules. Much as Jean-Jacques Rousseau theorized that a rapacious gentry caused the misery of the peasantry, so contemporary robber barons are accused of stealing the bread from the mouths of vulnerable minorities (Chernow, 1998). Rather than allow the latter to prosper, they invent ways to keep ordinary people from challenging them. Except that this is not entirely true. It is an attractive myth that assumes some people (i.e., the successful) are inherently less moral than those they allegedly suppress.

The reality is that we all seek precedence (Fein, 2012). We may not be equally ambitious, but virtually everyone wants to outstrip someone else. Certainly, no one hankers for a fall to the bottom of the social pyramid. No one wants to be a loser. This disposition is built into our genes. It is a legacy from our hominid ancestors that enabled us, as a species, to become what archeologist Ian Tattersall (2012) describes as "the masters of the planet." It is largely because we compete with one another that we developed the capacity to lord it over the rest of creation. This superiority was not bestowed on us from above but results from our skills at fighting for what we want.

Of course, it must be admitted that our conflicts are sometimes violent. Even so, most are restrained (Diamond, 2013). Yes, elites fight to maintain their higher status. Still, those lower down fight to move up. If they can, they hope to vault over their "betters." Moreover, while they resent their inferiority, they conspire to maintain it by respecting the superiority of those above them. Paradoxically, if people did not care who exercised precedence, rank would be impossible. If no one deferred to higher-ups, there would be no higher-ups. Just as Rousseau speculated that property rights came into existence when ordinary people made the mistake of respecting one man's claim to a patch of ground and would disappear once this was withdrawn, the same would apply to hierarchical differences were they disregarded.

But they are not disregarded. People care about who is more powerful and seek to improve their relative standing. What is more, this is functional for us as a species, even if it is not for every individual. We human beings, qua human beings, have survived as a species largely because we are hierarchical. The benefits of being so are manifold. Among the more important is motivation. Because we, as individuals, strive to get ahead, we accomplish things we would not, were we more placid. Just as Davis and Moore (1945) conjectured, people demand rewards for extra effort. What they failed to underline is that the most compelling reward for superior exertions is superiority itself. Our desire to be better than others impels us to outdo them, for in the process we gain respect—and deference. It is this, more than the associated wealth, we crave. To be "looked up to" is a daydream in which almost everyone indulges. Our biology is such that this feels good. So familiar is this fact that we discount it. We also discount how hard we work not to be losers.

Another benefit of our hierarchical nature is an ability to coordinate complex activities. We humans are social creatures. We frequently work together to accomplish objectives that are beyond our individual capacities. No doubt this can be traced to a long apprenticeship as social hunters. In order to bring down large game animals, our ancestors had to cooperate. If they did not synchronize their efforts, the enterprise would fail. The same is true today when we bridge great rivers or work on assembly lines that turn out thousands of automobiles. These undertakings are successful because we participate in divisions of labor organized from above.

Ralf Dahrendorf (1959, 1968) described what is required as "imperative coordination." Superiors give orders to subordinates, who then obey these. The latter comply because they respect and perhaps fear those who rank higher. In any event, the outcome is that many people are able to work together on the identical project. What they do fits in with what others do because they aim at the same objective. But this objective is common precisely because it is imposed from above. Similarly, their respective contributions mesh because they are directed to perform certain tasks, in a certain way, at a certain time, with certain others. Were each of the participants to go his or her own way, the resultant cacophony would be worse than the Tower of Babel. Unless each is compelled to do what he or she might not independently choose, there can be no such thing as a joint endeavor. In such an event, we humans would be like bears wandering through the forest, perhaps respecting each other's territories but doing little that required coordination. We would build no cities, highways, or rockets to the moon. In short, we would be at the mercy of natural forces we could not surmount.

Yet another function of hierarchy is to ensure our safety. This may seem to contradict the fact that we compete for status, but it does so only partially. Indeed it is because we are competitors that we require peacekeeping mechanisms. Thomas Hobbes (1956) sometimes makes it sound as if a single superior person—the so-called Leviathan—must be appointed to impose harmony. This, however, is misleading. No single person can achieve this goal. Even if he is selected by a conclave of others, he requires help.

Hobbes's hypothesized war of all against all overstates the case, but every society needs leaders to maintain communal peace. Much as parents prevent childish rivalries from getting out of hand, so leaders keep subordinates from tearing a group apart. But to do so, they must be strong enough and respected enough to intervene when conflicts arise. Since there are always conflicts, the capacity to contain them must also exist. The presence of stable hierarchies accomplishes this by establishing the bona fides of the powerful and by admonishing them to employ their strengths on behalf of the community. There are, of course, exceptions, but leaders derelict in this duty tend to be replaced (Ludwig, 2002).

Hierarchical leaders also organize resistance to external threats. Individuals compete to determine who is superior, while communities compete over scarce resources and relative priority. Battles over territorial supremacy have been with us for as long as we have records. We often bemoan the existence of wars, yet they are never in short supply. This makes it imperative that communities erect a stout defense. Just as complex activities and internal security require coordinated efforts presided over by respected figures, so does a military apparatus. We humans are not lotus-eaters. We are aggressive and selfish; hence, we need powerful protectors, lest more aggressive rivals brush us aside. This is not nice, but then we, as a species, are not especially nice. We are, after all, carnivores.

Last, hierarchies enable us to distribute scarce resources with less wear and tear. Neo-Marxists are fond of deriding the greed of elites, but if the truth be told, we are all somewhat greedy. And we need to be. The rabbi Hillel taught us that we must first be for ourselves—at least some of the time. If we are not, if we are totally passive with regard to asserting our needs, we will be paid no attention. Instead of getting what we require, we will be consigned the leftovers—if any. But if we fight too aggressively, the Hobbesian nightmare might be realized. The battles to control valued goods would be so fierce that few would survive. Hierarchies make this less likely by establishing some individuals as so much more powerful that they are not challenged. What happens is that those at the top are able to protect their wealth. They get more, and keep more, because they have the clout repel others. Meanwhile, the relatively powerless are left out in the cold. They do not appreciate this; nonetheless, they back down. This is not because they want to but because they recognize that if they pick a fight, they are apt to lose. The calculation is that if they accept a smaller share, it will avoid the injuries that might be suffered if they did not. In the end, the existence of hierarchies leaves them less well off at the same time that it preserves the community from internecine battles.

How then is hierarchical supremacy established? The answer will not please those who hope that the lambs will one day lie down with the lions. Pacifists and egalitarians must understand that the exercise of power entails contests over its use (Fein, 2012). We humans will never be as gentle as deer. We are not a prey species. As such, we are not on constant guard against predation. Rather, it is others, including our fellow humans, who must fear us. To reiterate, this is not nice; nevertheless, it is who we are. Those who deny this reality have a mountain of counterevidence with which to contend.

In any event, the central mechanism creating human hierarchies is the "*test of strength*." Individuals engage in contests to determine who is stronger than whom. Much as rams butt heads to establish which is more powerful, so do we. And as with rams, the losers recognize the winners and back down. Because of this, the skirmishes do not continue forever but subside once it is clear who is victorious. At this point, the winner acquires a reputation for being stronger, while the loser is stigmatized as weaker. Now the winner becomes dominant and the loser submissive. This is just another way of saying that the loser henceforth declines to issue another challenge. Unless circumstances change, the loser avoids subsequent battles, while the winner assumes he or she can overpower all comers. These attitudes are apparent even in the way the parties subsequently bear their bodies.

Hierarchies are then constructed from summing a great many tests of strength. Eventually, the participants, partly from engaging in these contents and partly from observing them, develop a sense of who ranks where in the larger scheme of things. On the assumption that power is transitive (which is only somewhat true), they fashion a stabilized status structure. Thereafter, while there remains some jockeying for position, the general outlines of where they stand are fairly constant. What, in a social class system, is referred to as social mobility is possible but difficult. Individuals can go up or down the scale, but a structural stickiness inhibits easy change.

One crucial difference between ram and human hierarchies is that we humans also engage in tests between groups. We do not rely exclusively on our personal powers, but recruit allies to overpower others. Our adversaries, of course, do the same, and the next thing we know is that we are enmeshed in political machinations. Politics is the art of assembling and deploying coalitions to defeat other coalitions. Therefore those who are skilled at doing so can enhance their own status. Their comparative strength is judged by that of the group to which they belong, as well as their ranking within this group.

This said, we have as yet to specify what constitutes a strength. What is it that is tested? Among rams, it is physical power as measured by an ability to butt with greater power and stamina. Yet what of humans? Physical power matters among us but not so much that bodybuilders dominate our societies. As it happens, we have many areas in which we compare potency. As a generalist species, we employ numerous skills in order to feed, clothe, and protect ourselves from harm. Any of these can be exploited to assert superiority. Furthermore, because we, unlike rams, can belong to different hierarchies, we are able to shop around to find one where our assets enable us to rise above others. Generally speaking, the particular strengths affirmed vary with what works to improve our survivability as individuals and groups.

Among the powers utilized to enhance status is, as implied above, physical power. A good boxer, wrestler, or weightlifter can assert superiority on the basis of defeating others in these endeavors. Meanwhile, other athletic skills can be honed to do likewise. The fastest runner, the highest jumper, the most prolific home-run hitter, and the most elusive running back can all claim to be the best in their respective enterprises. Nonetheless, these are not the strengths that earn the greatest respect in a society such as our own. Intelligence normally has a better payoff than muscle power. Being unusually smart provides the dexterity to excel in many different activities; hence, it is highly esteemed.

What concerns us here is that the strengths that produce high status fluctuate with changing social conditions. Abilities useful in one setting lose their luster in another. This has frequently been validated over the course of history. Thus, skill at wielding a spear or tracking a spoor were admired in hunter-gatherer communities but are less relevant in techno-commercial ones. By the same token, the mathematical competence needed to design a suspension bridge is esteemed among us but produces yawns among the Khoisan. This is because factors such as a society's size and technological sophistication alter what is needed for group survival.

Looking back upon the history of higher education, it is clear that what was taught related to what facilitated higher status within a specific community. If we look to Greece and Rome, we can discern the outlines of what later evolved into contemporary college programs. Ancient Athens, in particular, provided the rudimentary beginnings for academic learning. Central to this was information that enhanced rhetorical and commercial skills. Persons who bought and sold products among strangers had to be quick on their feet. They had to understand human differences and make adjustments accordingly. At the same time, if they were to influence their fellow citizens in the agora, they had to be fluent speechmakers. Democratic institutions, including the laws courts, placed a premium on intellectual dexterity. This is what the Sophists, the Platonists, and the Aristotelians provided. In this, they assisted individuals anxious to achieve elite status. The knowledge they imparted was thus specific to their conditions and admired because it was effective in producing the desired outcomes.

If we move to the Middle Ages, we find comparable hierarchical imperatives. Obviously, medieval Europe did not begin as a hive of commercial activity. As a result, its formative elites were not grounded in mercantile success. In fact, the hereditary aristocrats at its apex depended upon military skills and family-based property rights. These did not require literacy; hence, the most powerful personages rarely obtained academic training. Their strengths were honed in a martial apprenticeship and battle. Others might spend time learning to read, whereas they concentrated on what paid off in the interminable warfare of the period (Pirenne, 1936).

The few who acquired literacy were associated with the church. As the sole surviving continent-wide institution, it required a cadre of individuals that could maintain long-distance communication. It also needed leaders who could read the Bible and scribes who could see to it that the hallowed books remained available. As the stewards of sacred knowledge, this provided the underpinning of their social status. A presumed relationship with the deity also bestowed powers denied others. To be holy was to be powerful. The church fathers could even inspire crusades to rescue Jerusalem from the infidels.

Yet it was the economic growth fostered by greater social stability that instigated a resurgence of higher education. The gothic revival at first enabled churchmen to keep pace with laymen whose wealth inspired great pretentions. A firm grounding in religious knowledge enabled them to assert the priority of ecclesiastical law. This was achieved by converting cathedral-based schools into universities, a transformation facilitated by the revival of ancient knowledge. The rediscovery of Aristotle (1941) and the trivium and quadrivium provided legitimacy to fledgling scholars. They had their strengths boosted, as it were, by associating with the glory that was Rome.

But this academic resurgence did not stop at the church door. Better-educated clerics, in lending their skills to public administration, enhanced the powers of their sponsors. Their own comparative ranking was further improved when a quickening of commerce made literacy and a legal education more valuable. As in ancient Greece, extra business meant additional conflicts, but conflict was bad for business. It was at this point that the Roman law was rediscovered and its application appreciated. With this, the law schools rose to prominence and those who imbibed their teachings did as well. Legal knowledge became a strength that bestowed secular potency. Something similar occurred with the emerging medical schools. They too bestowed greater status on their graduates, given how highly health is esteemed.

But the greatest change in how stature was evaluated was reserved for the laity. This entailed another aspect of tests of strength that has not yet been fully explored. As societies grow larger, it becomes more difficult to compare relative powers. Hunter-gatherer societies are small enough for the participants to evaluate each other directly (Diamond, 2013). But once societies grow into the hundreds of thousands and eventually millions, this is impossible. No one can size himself up against all the others, nor can anyone be present to witness all potential contests. Something else is needed to ascertain comparative strength, and that turns out to be the "symbols" of power. These are not as accurate as actual tests, but they are frequently all that is available. They also have the disadvantage of being easy to manipulate. This makes possible—indeed, it invites—efforts at deception. Yet there is often no choice. Bourdieu disparages symbolic expressions of potency, but what other means is available for comparing the status of millions of strangers? The question is, therefore, not whether people will engage in this practice but how accurate it will be.

Nor are the symbols utilized utterly arbitrary. Those employed are usually associated with genuine strengths. In other words, they begin as a signs of power but are transmuted into symbols of it because they were good indicators of an ability to win interpersonal contests. In any event, this is what occurred with respect to medieval universities.

Their graduates were so skilled at administrative duties, whether for governmental or commercial purposes, that they acquired a reputation for power. As a result, a university education became prized, not just for clerics but for the scions of the aristocracy, mercantile princes, and those who hoped to compete with them.

Modern-day observers, when scrutinizing the curricula of the early universities, wonder at their emphasis on Greek and Latin. Why, they ask, would students be forced to master what were even then becoming dead languages? The answer is that these had acquired symbolic eminence. Having long epitomized what was taught in church-dominated schools, they became associated with an elite education. The new elites, whether they were a partially demilitarized aristocracy or an up-and-coming bourgeoisie, merely appropriated a long-standing indicator of dominance.

This key to elite status became so entrenched that the colleges founded by colonial Americans utilized them to provide the foundation of their efforts. Any boy aspiring to a college education first had to demonstrate a proficiency in Greek and Latin. Although times were changing and most graduates would not become ministers, the status conferred by a classical education retained its vigor. It indicated that someone was an educated man and therefore a person to be reckoned with. Clearly smart enough to master materials others might find daunting, he was probably clever enough to be a formidable adversary.

This attitude followed Americans as they migrated west. They might be more rustic that their Eastern contemporaries, but they were eager to prove themselves intellectually noteworthy. They realized that to be truly elite is to be "impressive" and therefore intimidating. Still, times were again changing. As the Industrial Revolution took hold and as American agricultural products acquired an international market, greater efficiency became a national mania. Superior know-how could be converted into superior wealth, which then transformed into higher social status. This was why engineering and agronomical skills rose in esteem. They bestowed commercial muscle and therefore status, as measured by financial success.

Soon the sciences acquired a similar prestige. Research universities took hold, as did curricula in the sciences. Once more college graduates who facilitated commercial success were in demand. But since intelligence was required to master the new subjects, those who could only manage a gentlemen's C found they had to make room for scholastic stars whose social origins were lower down. The strengths these upstarts brought to the table were such that they could intimidate their previous betters. As a consequence, they moved up in hierarchies where technological skills provided an advantage. Literally tested on their academic competences before and after they gained admittance to elite universities, their success eventually helped maintain the reputation of their alma maters.

Ultimately, the middle-class revolution—that is, the elevation of the middle classes to economic and political dominance (Fein, 2005)—raised their virtues to preeminence. To demonstrate these qualities thus became the ticket to social mobility. Now, a virtuoso acquaintance with Shakespeare brought fewer kudos than the business insights acquired in an MBA program. As previously, what enabled a person to succeed in the class system became symbolic of individual strength. Whether this strength was a valued skill or an emblem of it, it enabled those who went to college to beat the competition. This is not nice—but to repeat, it is a reality of the human condition.

Which brings us to the present and provides a hint as to the historical mission of higher education. Advanced learning has always been about servicing elites and/or enabling individuals to join their ranks. It has never been about knowledge for the sake of knowledge. What has been taught, and how it has been taught, have varied with the social needs. Since all societies are hierarchical, and since hierarchies fulfill vital functions, the question has always been how these functions can be facilitated under the prevailing social conditions. To wit: what skills best serve communal needs? Furthermore, what do individuals need to learn in order to rise to the top?

In addition, which individuals should be provided with these strengths? In our democratic society, this last question has achieved great prominence. Our techno-commercial requirements are such that heredity alone cannot be allowed to determine who has an opportunity to rise. With meaningful competences needed to perform complex activities, we have to determine who has the potential to perform these well. In this, merit (i.e., a combination of innate ability, superior motivation, and actual accomplishment) plays a larger role than previously. To put the matter plainly, contemporary universities are in the business of turning out an elite that can fulfill the hierarchical responsibilities assigned them. This is their mission! These are the strengths in which they must specialize.

What remains to be seen are the particulars of these strengths. Assuming we can agree on the central goal—admittedly a huge assumption—we may be able to agree on what should be taught, to whom, and how. Unfortunately, a consensus on these objectives does not ensure an agreement as to means. This too provides grounds for contention and therefore will also have to be addressed.

College for Everyone?

College is not for everyone! This must be insisted upon. Despite the growing clamor for everyone to be a university graduate (Rogers, 2013), this is neither possible nor desirable (Vedder, 2011). If colleges are to fulfill their mission, they must be selective. The notion that a democratic society can only be democratic if it enables everyone to rise to the top is both fatuous and self-contradictory. To contend that social justice exists only when everyone is completely equal flies in the face of our hierarchical nature. It asks us to become what we are not. The fully egalitarian society to which many aspire exists only in their imaginations. In the real world, we need elites; hence, the question is, what sort of elite?

First of all, not everyone is qualified for college. There is a reason universities are identified as "higher education," and it is not just that their students are older. A college education is more demanding than primary or secondary schooling. The subjects taught and the level of competence expected have historically set their graduates apart. Presumably smarter and more knowledgeable than others, they are delegated positions of power because they have demonstrated an ability to handle them. Sadly, not everyone is equally gifted.

Some radical egalitarians argue that IQ is equally distributed. They tell us that if some people do better on tests, it is because they are better prepared. If so, all we need to do to overcome disparities is provide everyone with equal educational opportunities. If measurable differences are subsequently detected, this presumably demonstrates we have not. Yet this is fantasy (Sowell, 2013). As with many genetically influenced factors, intelligence falls on a normal curve. Some people are smarter than others. They find it easier to master calculus than their less-able peers. This is unfair, but it is also unfair that some people are born taller than others. To ignore these differences—for instance, in height—and pretend that all can excel in basketball is to pave the way for mediocre basketball. The NBA does not and will not, because its existence depends on putting an excellent product on the court. Societies can do no less if they hope to survive. Since colleges focus on separating the best from the worst, they too must be selective.

There are also disparities in motivation (Jaschik, 2013a). Not everyone wants to go to college. Some know they are not intellectually qualified, whereas others do not enjoy academic pursuits. Still others labor under emotional or environmental handicaps. This too may be unfair, but it provides a good indicator of who will succeed on campus. We would not want to waste our time trying to teach someone to play golf if she hated the game. Why would we do something comparable with higher education? The fact is that potential students come from all sorts of backgrounds that cannot be equalized by assuming all are equally prepared to expend the necessary effort. If we do, we are not only wasting limited resources; we are also refusing to acknowledge the best performers. We are, in essence, declaring that merit does not matter and, in some cases, does not exist.

Nor do we have reliable techniques for overcoming motivational differences. Just as developmental programs have limits on how much they can compensate for a lack of intelligence, so they have difficulty surmounting emotional liabilities. Years ago, I participated in a national study of penal rehabilitation. We found that these programs made virtually no difference in reducing recidivism. Nevertheless, many reformers continue to disregard these findings. They are so eager to reduce crime that they are convinced they will find a way to do what others could not. Sundry educational reformers have the same bent. They too assume that someday, somehow, they will find a way to compensate for whatever disadvantages students have. And perhaps they may. But that day is not this. In the meantime, we must make plans based upon what we can do.

If disparities in intelligence and motivation are—for the moment—ineradicable, then demanding equal educational results can only be accomplished by diluting quality. The laggards can only catch up if what is asked of them is radically reduced. Because even below-average students would have to be accommodated, the standards would need to be set such that they too can pass muster. Although we have already moved a long way in this direction through grade inflation, we would have to go further if literally no one is to be left behind. Much like in some Little Leagues, we would have to jettison efforts to keep score.

Radical equality would also have the effect of diluting the value of a college degree. If everyone got one, their possession would indicate nothing about the knowledge or abilities of their possessors. Thus, employers would find them useless in identifying the best employees. If so, they would stop using them; hence, those who obtained them would gain no advantage. Were this to become the norm, people would stop going to college. The most talented would find they usually got better results from self-study. In this case, a university education would symbolize inferiority. In other words, making higher education universal would also make it worthless.

Some argue that college graduates secure a million-dollar bonus thanks to their degrees, but if everyone gets a sheepskin, there will be no bonus. Those who project ahead based on the current situation fail to recognize that in changing the nature of a college degree, they also change its economic implications. Indeed, we have already reached the point where many college graduates have difficulty obtaining employment. There are simply too many in the marketplace for all to find work commensurate with the skills a college degree should provide. This reality has not yet dawned on all potential college students, but one day it will.

This is not to say that people should summarily be denied a college education. In a society that values opportunity, everyone should have the possibility of obtaining a higher education. There need be no guarantee all will succeed, but all ought to be offered the chance to prove themselves. Some schools, albeit not the elite institutions, should provide appropriate openings. Nor need these entry-level schools specialize in the same skill sets as Harvard. College may be about developing leaders, but the areas in which people are prepared to lead need not be identical. In any event, if students do well in a lower-level school, they should be allowed to climb up. If they do not, however, they should be allowed to fall off. Standards must remain high if they are to mean anything.

Some people, of course, require second, third, or fourth chances. Inadequate preparation, poor motivation, or too few resources ought not, however, spell the end of the road. People who fall off the educational ladder should be able to get back on if their circumstances change. If they were rebellious when young but adjust to social realities when older, they need to be able to change course. Or if family responsibilities took precedence over academic pursuits, they should be able to take on new challenges when these concerns lessen. Or perhaps their interests change, and they find themselves motivated to seek a career that had not previously beckoned. These folks all ought to be offered an opportunity to rectify past mistakes. It is merely that whenever they are afforded the prospect of moving forward, the standards must remain lofty.

Nor should all persons be assumed to need a college education. Many have "technical" aspirations. The kind of learning that helps them obtain a suitable job may not be the sort in which universities specialize. In this case, technical schools should remain available. But whether these are called "institutes" or "community colleges," they must be distinguished from genuine colleges. Universities may be more prestigious, but they are because of what they teach. Merely misappropriating this honorific serves only to confuse issues. If you are not trained for a job that confers hierarchical status, you will not achieve that status, irrespective of what your school is titled. Too often, people believe they can confer equality through word magic. They cannot. Eventually, others see through the legerdemain, and connotations of inferiority reemerge.

The problem—and it is a serious one—is that in an effort to equalize schools, standards have been compromised. In order to facilitate the transfer of students from inferior institutions to better ones, courses get watered down. This, however, only succeeds in cheating everyone, including society as a whole. In the meantime, some students get to feel they have accomplished more than they have. Life will probably catch up with them, and when it does, they will have a right to feel resentful (Sander and Taylor, 2012).

A society that, in the name of fairness, does not allow winners to win is on the road to impotence. If it decides that hierarchical advantages must be eliminated, it simultaneously discards the advantages that hierarchies provide. No longer can it motivate significant effort, coordinate complex activities, protect itself from internal or external dangers, or distribute scarce resources. In an effort to help everyone, it arranges events so that it can help no one. Inequality is a fact of life. It is built into who we are. The question is whether merit will be rewarded. If the answer is no, then a society is sure to lose out in competition with other societies where the answer is yes.

The question therefore becomes, what sorts of strengths should higher education emphasize? This depends on the qualities in which we want our leaders to excel. So what are these qualities? The answer depends on the nature of a society. As we have seen, what counts as a strength differs with the challenges that communities face. Hence, we must also ask, what challenges are we, here today, endeavoring to overcome? It is these that higher education should address.

Ours has become a middle-class society. We are a mass techno-commercial civilization that requires a sophisticated leadership commensurate with this way of life. We therefore require a democratic and professionalized elite. In short, we need to develop competently self-directed leaders. Preparing these individuals for what lies before them is what our colleges and universities are about. Reforms that do not accomplish this goal are therefore not reforms at all.

Conclusions

We must not forget the central mission of higher education. The primary objective of a college and/or university education is to prepare graduates for contemporary leadership roles. Assuming that our techno-commercial society requires a greater supply of professionalized leaders, we must thus socialize larger numbers of self-motivated experts. This requires institutions of higher education to teach students how to be competently self-directed decision makers. They must therefore implant both the knowledge and the personal commitments to make good choices—choices upon which others are dependent.

The level of professionalism in which various schools specialize and the degree of self-directed expertise students require differ. The graduates of elite schools are thus likely to shoulder greater responsibilities than the graduates of lower-level institutions. Likewise, those who go on to become doctors, lawyers, and college professors require more intense preparation than individuals who become nurses or police officers. Nonetheless, the need for some form of professionalization is becoming more widespread. As a result, the graduates of even non-elite schools are more apt to exercise leadership than formerly.

Lower-level schools must also focus on social mobility. They may need to assist many of their students in becoming more professionalized than their antecedents. Students who come from elite backgrounds often, it is true, require less support in acquiring professionalized attitudes. Nevertheless, students with working- and lower-class roots frequently need to be explicitly introduced to these mind-sets. They may also require assistance in dealing with the stresses entailed in being self-motivated.

Goal displacement must likewise be avoided. With a cacophony of critical voices often demanding incompatible objectives, it is easy to be led astray. Goals are frequently displaced in directions deemed traditional and/or ideal. Moreover, bureaucratic imperatives can supplant educational ones. In these cases, means commonly override ends, with stereotyped practices taking precedence over genuine learning.

As we have seen, many reformers clamor for greater relevance. They demand social justice, environmental sensitivity, or interdisciplinary research. In so doing, they lose sight of what is most important. To repeat, the central mission of higher education is to foster self-directed competence. If this is neglected, then other improvements are of little value. This makes it imperative that we acknowledge that the primary purpose of a college education is to prepare the young to exercise social leadership. These individuals, to be sure, ought constitute a democratic elite, one that is routinely modified by social mobility. Still, unless they are groomed to be personally potent, they cannot serve the needs of the larger community.

Finally, many commentators insist that higher education be fair. They want everyone to be equally successful. Yet fairness without merit is not really fair. If students are not professionalized, then what they learn is of little value to them or to society. They may technically be equal, but they will be equally barren of the skills needed for all to prosper. Higher education creates inequalities, yet given our hierarchical nature and the challenges of a techno-commercial economy, the question is whether these inequalities will benefit the larger whole. Similar queries can be made of technological innovations. Do these foster the human qualities that enhance a self-motivated expertise? If not, they are ornaments as opposed to improvements.

Reformers tend to be moralists. They often judge problems and solutions based on their long-standing emotional commitments. But in so doing, they can allow their passions to obscure what is harmful, as well as what is helpful. Fixing the college bubble requires that we understand where we need to go and then testing the best modes of getting there. This is a complex enterprise; hence, it is these complexities we need to investigate in greater detail.

4

A Professionalized Society

A Techno-Commercial Society

Ours is a middle-class society, in large part because it is a techno-commercial society (Blumin, 1989; Fein, 2005). This, therefore, must be our starting point in evaluating appropriate educational reforms. Because many more of our contemporaries earn a living through jobs that incorporate a technical and/or commercial aspect, we have an interest in cultivating the skills and motives needed to perform these well. Having become dependent on a host of strangers to provide the essentials of life, it is crucial that they be dependable (Ladd, 1999; Moore and Simon, 2000). But to repeat, these others are strangers. In fact, we may never cross paths. How then do we exercise influence over their efforts? The simple fact is that because there are millions of them, we could not even begin to know them personally.

So what do we do? Our need to rely on an impersonal marketplace is so great that we cannot throw up hands up in despair. We must at least attempt to ensure the resources upon which we depend. As it happens, one of the mechanisms to which we turn is education. As an institution dedicated to grooming strangers to accomplish important tasks, it can serve as a useful surrogate, because it has the ability to inculcate the habits and proficiencies we hope to see instilled.

The next issue becomes ensuring that these schools perform as desired. Assuming that the central mission of higher education is to train members of a hierarchical elite so that they are capable of guiding and protecting us, what do these leaders have to learn (Fein, 2012)? As previously suggested, they must internalize the skills and motivation needed to coordinate and/or administer the creation of the goods and services required by a mass-market, democratically governed society. More particularly, our upper middle classes must become self-motivated experts in working with people and data (Demott, 1990). It is these difficult tasks in which they must become proficient.

Karl Marx (1967) taught us that economic activities are central to the organization of large societies. He had a point. Members of the upper middle class in a techno-commercial civilization derive much of their power from controlling economic uncertainties. They do not, however, need to own the means of production in order to achieve this. Nor need their higher status derive entirely from economic concerns. Max Weber (1947) was also correct when he insisted upon the importance of political and social power. These too serve as avenues toward advancement. Especially when we deal with densely populated societies where conflicts are endemic, elites must do more than coordinate business and/or distribute scarce resources. They must also protect people from internal and external threats and motivate greater effort.

This is why, in a world inhabited by millions of strangers, we need specialists in both political organization and marketplace regulation. Moreover, given that we live in a capitalistic democracy, our leaders must possess a democratic and professional orientation. What this entails is complicated; hence, a fuller explication will have to await our next chapter, which deals with self-direction. In the meantime, suffice it to say that members of our elite must be committed to middle-class values. Because they collectively set these standards, was this not the case, the moral compass we jointly require would be absent.

To this must be added the need to socialize the appropriate aptitudes in our young. No society can wait until adulthood to bend its eventual leaders in the necessary directions. This duty has to be entrusted to families. Even in our Gesellschaft society, the prime responsibility operates best at this level. Yet this, in turn, requires us to strengthen the personal allegiances between the consenting adults at the core of most effective families (Lareau, 2003). Good parents must first love and care for one another. Despite the dangers presented by intimacy, they must remain loyal and mutually helpful. This stability is vital to providing the environment in which the next generation can be prepared to take up the mantle of command. It is also vital in providing the emotional support adults require when dealing with the vicissitudes of a competitive society. Indeed, these objectives are generally decisive to maintaining social cohesion. So important are they that colleges and universities too must play a role in socializing leadership roles and strengthening personal attachments.

Many models of social organization have been employed to keep societies from fragmenting. Nonetheless, not all are appropriate under every condition. As societies have grown larger and more technical, paradigms that once served to bind people together no longer function very well. The organizational archetypes that arose and then sometimes stumbled can be classified a number of ways. Among the overarching categories are the pre-bureaucratic, bureaucratic, and professional models. The last of these is most appropriate under the current circumstances. Although many people continue to think in pre-bureaucratic and/or bureaucratic terms, they are asking these forms of regulation to accomplish tasks for which they are ill suited. If this is so, then the mission and methods of higher education must adhere to the professional model. If only this pattern can satisfy our needs, it must be understood and implemented with due diligence.

Pre-Bureaucratic Models

Hunter-gatherer societies were neither large nor complex (Lenski, 1966; Diamond, 2013). Their members invariably knew each other very well and hence could depend on their personal relationships to maintain social stability. Emile Durkheim (1933) called this mode of interaction mechanical solidarity. By this he meant that people who performed similar tasks understood each other and therefore could sympathize with one another. As a result, they were capable of cooperating harmoniously so as to further their mutual interests.

What he did not stress, however, was that these people were, for the most part, biologically related. Wandering their territories in bands of between one hundred and one hundred fifty, they were husbands and wives, mothers and fathers, aunts and uncles, cousins and grandparents. In other words, from birth they were governed by relationships that were traditionally defined and emotionally governed. These folks both knew and cared about one another. Oftentimes they loved one another, although, it must be admitted, hatred sometimes overwhelmed love. Rarely were they neutral. Their interactions were too close and their interdependence too crucial to be affectively dispassionate. After all, they had to rely on one another—and only one another—for survival.

Hunter-gatherers had no choice but to work together. The men set out in tightly coordinated hunting parties to furnish their families with meat, while the women stayed behind to gather berries and tubers and to watch over the children—also in groups. Then at night, when the sun went down, they, as a group, gathered around a common fire, frequently to hear stories told by the elder men and women. These tightly knit associates knew who could be trusted to do what and to whom they must show deference. Their familial and economic roles were clearly specified, as were their limited chains of command.

Theirs might be called the family model of social coordination. Since enduring biological relationships were at its core, these bonds were primary in enforcing interpersonal order. To some extent genetically determined, their attachments were reinforced by socialization, traditional norms, and long-standing personal contacts. On the other hand, their level of technology was modest, as was their store of knowledge; hence, these provided less adhesion. Likewise, they boasted relatively few types of roles and engaged in limited amounts of property exchange. They did, however, establish face-to-face hierarchies based on direct observations of which individuals possessed the greatest skills in tasks such as hunting or midwifery.

This family model had a long run. Our species is probably no older than about two hundred thousand years, but for almost this entire period our ancestors were hunter-gatherers (Tattersall, 2012). This provided ample time for the appropriate attitudes and customs to be built into their genes and social habits. As such, this mode of coordination provided a foundation for other forms of social organization. Even though later societies grew too large for everyone to know everyone else, strangers often operated as if they were related.

After agriculturally based empires appeared, the ground rules changed and the estate model of organization took precedence. Now, societies became stratified into rigid layers that often treated outsiders as if they belonged to different species. This was especially the case with caste systems. Nonetheless, identifiable tiers were also present in societies where aristocrats regarded themselves as genetically superior. Here, it was often the family relations of the upper crust, combined with coercion, that proved decisive in enforcing cohesion. Nobles, who thought of themselves as biological relatives, regularly showed no compunctions in terrorizing peasants into submission. Nor were they squeamish about exhibiting favoritism toward family members. Since the latter were the ones they most trusted, they typically functioned as allies during political maneuverings.

Given the mists of time, just how ruthless this mode of organization could be is often overlooked. The Assyrians, for instance, in assembling their empire, would capture a town and then build a pyramid of severed heads at its front gate. This served as a warning to other communities that might consider defying them. So stringent were the mechanisms used to intimidate potential rivals that the social distance between the rulers and the ruled was treated as unbridgeable. Indeed, peasants were regarded as sub-human—especially if they spoke a different language.

Also prominent in estate systems was religion. At first in nations but then in multiethnic empires, a belief in the gods was used to impose discipline even when rulers were not present. In nearly every instance, the gods were considered stronger than mere mortals. Furthermore, they were present everywhere. As important, they were viewed as the natural allies of the upper classes (Shermer, 2011). Thus, if members of the lower orders violated the strictures of their leaders, they might be punished by entities more powerful than their kings. Nor would these sanctions stop at death. They continued in the afterlife. This was truly frightening and therefore effective in maintaining social order.

The estate model worked well in large agricultural societies. In civilizations where most of the work necessary to maintain sustenance was relatively routine peasants did not need to exercise discretion. Terrifying them into compliance was sufficient to get the work done. The fact that this quashed initiative in no way undermined the effectiveness of subsistence farmers. This changed, however, with the invention of money. The commercial societies that replaced the agricultural empires required independent thought from a wider range of contributors. As a result, classical civilizations such as those of Greece and Rome pioneered a new mode of social organization (Crowell, 1961). This may be dubbed the patrimonial model.

Merchants and, to a lesser extent, independent artisans must make independent decisions. Especially with respect to long-distance commerce, this is necessary in order to make advantageous deals with strangers. Unless these are consummated sagaciously, profits evaporate. As a result, traders press for autonomy. This, however, cannot be complete. The likelihood of conflicts between venders and customers, as well as between rival commercial states, demands social controls. A number of such arrangements emerged, including the Athenian model of participatory democracy. Nevertheless, these were soon nullified by the success of Rome's patrimonial system.

The Roman paterfamilias was the designated head of more than his immediate biological family. He also participated in a chain of patrons and clients. These hierarchies of pseudo-familial relationships bound individuals together by loyalties ostensibly undistinguishable from those found in genuine families. Thus, the patron was to apply his superior strength to safeguarding the welfare of his clients, while these clients submissively did his bidding. When, for instance, a patron ran for office, his clients and their clients were to vote for him. They might even be called out on the streets to guard his physical well-being. This way, they constituted grand alliances that might grow in power when conjoined with similar patronage chains.

These pseudo-families were further supplemented by large numbers of slaves. In an era when industry was powered primarily by animal and human energies, slaves provided the muscle to create much of the wealth. Commercial societies, such as Rome, frequently satisfied the demands of their customers with goods that were reasonably priced precisely because low-cost workers were used to produce them. These laborers (i.e., slaves) were captured in war and regarded as property. They could be coercively controlled, in part, because they were deemed sub-human and, in part, because other workers could replenish them when hostilities brought in a fresh supply of bondsmen.

Rome also relied on the rudiments of a bureaucratic system of governance, as well as vestiges of an estate system. While its highest level patrons were patricians (i.e., the Roman equivalent of aristocrats) slave hierarchies in the employ of the state provided much of the empire's administration. Indeed, the fact that the emperor owned teams of minions ensured their loyalty. These administrative assistants exercised enormous power but only at the behest of their master (at least in theory). He gave the orders, and they obeyed on pain of harsh punishment.

In modern eyes, this jerrybuilt edifice seems rickety and cumbersome. Nevertheless, it managed to endure for centuries. Because it facilitated commercial flexibility in conjunction with military prowess, it was able to keep competitors at bay for over half a millennium. In the end, however, contradictions between its commercial and military requirements made it vulnerable (Gibbon, 1963). When the costs of fending off barbarians inspired the emperors to institute price and job controls, the economic wherewithal to finance an effective defense proved insufficient. This was when the Germanic hordes came pouring through the gates.

What followed was the feudal model of social organization (Gregorovius, 1971). This was essentially a variation on the estate model. It too depended upon theoretically impermeable social statuses to maintain stability. There were, however, a few new wrinkles. Once more agriculture became the primary source of wealth and therefore, those who controlled the land exercised the greatest power. In this case, the descendants of the victorious warlords took over, but because they descended from semi-nomadic farmer-pastoralists, they did not possess the skills to perpetuate the Roman system. They could not, for instance, maintain an administration dependent on literacy. Nor could they build new roads and aqueducts to provide an infrastructure for large-scale polities when they did not possess the requisite building skills. Even more important, they were commercially backward. Inexperienced in long-distance commerce, they could not sustain the Roman monetary system. Instead, they reverted to localized forms of control that depended upon family connections and personal loyalties.

At the heart of the feudal model was the concept of fealty. Individuals swore allegiance to particular leaders; hence, when their superiors died, the status connections that held them together also dissolved. This made for chaotic patterns of governance that promoted unending military conflicts. So customary did warfare become that close relatives were frequently at odds. Protected behind castle walls, they would periodically venture forth to storm the citadels of their enemies. So insecure did life become that Europe experienced a dark age, where learning and commerce nearly came to a halt.

Nonetheless, a Catholic Church that regarded itself as the arbiter of legitimate sovereignty supplemented the rule of these rowdy aristocrats. Widely respected religious beliefs, as interpreted by the church, held that pontiffs and kings occupied their positions by divine right. Having been anointed by God, they were not to be defied—that is, as long as they did God's bidding. There were, to be sure, ongoing disputes between lay and ecclesiastical authorities, but for the most part, social order was preserved.

There have, of course, been other models for maintaining social order. Among these was the Big Man societies that flourished in horticultural times, Likewise, sharecropping societies arose in the wake of slavery, and theocratic societies appeared where the religious authorities came to dominate secular affairs. Each of these, as well as other models, has provided the cohesiveness for at least short-term survival. Yet none proved sufficient to cope with the challenges of modernity. They could furnish neither the controls nor the expertise to deal with large-scale techno-commercial demands. The numbers of people requiring coordination and the tasks demanding synchronization introduced complications they could not master. Each therefore suffered fatal defects. Either they were too chaotic, too violent, or too unreliable to supply the necessary stability or direction. As a consequence, all lost out to bureaucratic arrangements.

The Bureaucratic Model

At first the needs of the church, then the military, then larger governments, and finally industry provided the impetus for the emergence of the bureaucratic model (Grusky and Miller, 1970; Hall, 1999). Max Weber (1947, 1958), this mode's most influential champion, attributed its ascendance to the triumph of rationality. As people began to calculate what was most effective in achieving their aims, they settled on a form of management grounded in logical calculations. Instead of flying by the seats of their pants, they learned to figure things out in advance. As a result, rather than rely on the emotional bonds of families, the coercive mandates of estate systems, the pseudo-familial relationships of patronage chains, or the ecstatic commitments of feudalistic religion, cooler heads prevailed. In Weber's terms, bureaucracy epitomized the triumph of *sine ira et studio* ethos. Usually translated as "*without fear or favor*," the point was that reliable hierarchical controls in large and complex groups could not depend on raw force or personal attachments. Something else—something that encouraged thoughtful planning—was necessary.

For Weber, bureaucracies furnished this control without resorting to brutality or unfairness. They provided a ranking mechanism for accomplishing complicated tasks that enabled large numbers of persons to cooperate in relative harmony. They did so by promoting an efficiency from which a society benefitted. Yes, there were downsides to the social restraints upon which this depended, but these were more than compensated for by the material advantages. Individuals might lose some freedom, and methods of operation might become unduly rigid, but the alternative was worse. Poverty, tyranny, and social disarray were not a happy substitute. As a consequence, bureaucratic arrangements became prevalent virtually everywhere in the modern world (Gouldner, 1954; Blau, 1963; Etzioni, 1961; Crozier, 1964; Perrow, 1970).

One of bureaucracy's primary loci has, of course, been education, including higher education. Most contemporary schools are bureaucratic and, generally speaking, the larger they are, the more bureaucratic. It therefore makes sense to illustrate the bureaucratic model by utilizing colleges and universities. The first feature of bureaucratic organization identified by Weber is "*organizational goals*." If organizations are to be efficient, they must be clear as to their aspirations. With multiple participants involved in advancing common objectives, the players must understand what is expected. Just as military units once maintained cohesion by following a pennant held high by a standard bearer, so organizations flaunt figurative pennants their members can focus upon so as to advance in unison. In other words, they have a mission.

Within particular universities, their specialties are fairly well known. Thus, "research" universities, such as Harvard, attempt to enroll elite student bodies, while simultaneously encouraging their faculties to engage in cutting edge investigations. Most such schools also aspire to first-rate graduate programs so as to socialize a new cadre of researchers into the disciplines in which they excel. Less often highlighted, but generally well known to the participants, are the subject areas they stress. One school, for instance, might be known for its prowess in mechanical engineering, whereas another emphasizes medicine—perhaps also accentuating oncology. Typically, schools have a limited array of disciplines in which they take pride.

In identifying the central mission of higher education per se, we are specifying the fundamental goals that colleges and universities, as a whole, ought to pursue. These are not the organizational objectives of particular schools but the institutional objectives to which individual schools, to a greater or lesser extent, ought to subscribe. Nonetheless, the purpose is similar to that espoused by Weber. The objective is to provide reformers with an understanding of where universities are headed, so that they can chart an effective line of advance.

A second hallmark of a Weberian bureaucracy is a "*functional division of labor*." Over two centuries ago, Adam Smith (1776) argued that complicated tasks are best accomplished by dividing them into distinct operations. In his famous pin factory example, he contended that assigning different people discrete duties enabled them to become skilled at particular operations, while at the same time avoiding distractions that might interfere with their concentration. Obviously, universities have taken this to heart. Since at least medieval times, they have divided teaching duties by subject matter. Back then, law professors and theologians were separate persons with separate areas of responsibility. As a result, each could become expert in his or her respective spheres. Eventually, as the subject matter became more complex, the territory was further subdivided. Disciplines multiplied and metastasized into sub-disciplines. No longer were faculties members merely philosophers or natural philosophers. Now, they became theoretical cosmologists or medical sociologists.

Any lesser division would have stretched professors so thin as to be hopelessly shallow.

The next aspect of the Weberian model concerns operationalizing the division of labor. Here the question is, who shall teach what? Once it is decided that distinctive subjects should be separated, it is necessary to delegate the best persons to fit these niches. Professors now come to occupy "defined offices." These slots entail elaborate descriptions of what is to be taught. Experts in particular disciplines are then hired to fill what are regarded as "jobs." Since no one can know everything, competent teaching requires recruiting individuals who demonstrate the appropriate knowledge for discrete pedagogical roles. They are the ones most likely to perform these duties effectively and therefore to achieve the objectives for which the university was designed. Moreover, these persons can be rewarded by promoting them from one level to another, thereby motivating them to do their best.

Still, it is presumed that an expert-driven division of labor cannot, by itself, ensure an effective coordination of diverse tasks. Also necessary in the Weberian model is a "*hierarchy of authority*." Some individuals are delegated control over others. These persons give orders that their designated subordinates are required to follow. Yet this is not all. What makes the bureaucratic model superior and less coercive is that this authority is limited. Supervisors are not permitted to give orders about whatever they desire but only issues within a restricted area. No more than a few tasks fall within their purview; hence, only in these areas do they receive organizational backing, should they be challenged.

Put another way, bureaucracies tame the coercive aspects of hierarchy by incorporating limited powers into clearly defined supervisory roles. The tests of strength that create and maintain dominance and submission are thereby kept within nondestructive channels. In this way, reliable specifications, wherein the participants know who is in charge of what, keep large numbers of persons, many of whom are strangers, from wreaking havoc on others to whom they have no personal attachments. They can thereby coordinate activities, motivate effort, distribute scarce resources, and provide internal and external protections without having to be brutal or irrational. This is no small achievement in the light of how much impulsive violence has often been employed to maintain order in the past.

Universities, as is true of all bureaucracies, exhibit hierarchical chains of command. Not only do they boast presidents, provosts, and deans, but they also have department chairs, full professors, associate professors, assistant professors, lecturers, and adjuncts. These individuals may occupy scholarly roles, but they also relate to one another in terms of their respective ranks (Ludwig, 2002). Herein, as we shall shortly see, are the seeds of conflict. As will also soon become apparent, university hierarchies are looser than other forms of imperative coordination. This is because the nature of the work demands more room for maneuver than in, let us say, an automobile factory.

In any event, Weber tells us that a rational bureaucracy requires rules and procedures that expedite the effective achievement of its goals. If the organization does not pursue its objectives by the best means available, it is liable to be replaced by more efficient associations. Consequently, administrators are charged with developing and implementing the best possible modes of operation. They must either create or emulate the most effective measures for achieving the job at hand. Then, they must make sure their underlings follow instructions. Only in this way can the available resources produce the best product with the least effort.

The apogee of this attitude was reached in Fredrick Taylor's (1911) scientific management. At the beginning of the twentieth century, when burgeoning factories competed to see which could produce the highest quality steel the most cheaply, its seemed self-evident that scientifically inspired technologies would produce the most material goods. It was only common sense that workers—who, in essence, were a unique sort of tool—should be subject to the same sort of upgrading. If efficiency experts (also called "time and motion" or "systems" analysts) could calculate the quickest and least costly methods for achieving defined goals, then managers could see to it that the workforce put these into effect. Those lower down in the hierarchy could now be ordered to carry out their responsibilities as specified. Because they (i.e., the bosses) cared most about accomplishing the organizational goals, it was up to them to engage in imperative coordination in a manner that best served the needs of all.

One last aspect of the Weberian model concerns files and records. Bureaucracies are notorious for the paperwork they generate. Entire buildings—or today, computers—are filled with evidence of their handiwork. Sometimes it seems that everything they do is committed to paper or a memory chip. With administrators engaged in churning out memos to which their subordinates are required to respond, "paper-pushing" has become an industry unto itself. Indeed, for many people it has become their raison d'être, although for others it is their bête noir.

Weber, however, conceived of files as a means of keeping track of what large organizations do. With so many people producing so much work, no individual could remember everything that had been done or needed to be done. An objective record that all of the participants could consult was thus mandatory. This would reduce conflicts over joint operations, as well as supplement fragile human memories. How otherwise could a huge manufacturer, such as Ford Motors, keep track of which automobiles had been produced, ordered, delivered, or paid for? The mind boggles at the chicanery possible without definitive documentation. A problem arises, however, in deciding what must be recorded and in what specificity. The devil, as they say, is in the details, and with respect to record-keeping, the details have been known to get out of hand and/or become impossibly rigid.

In any event, the bureaucratic model has proved singularly successful. Despite its drawbacks, it facilitated the emergence of massive corporations and even more massive governmental agencies. In the process, it demonstrated an unequaled capacity for coordinating complex activities and for producing uniformities bridging international distances. Often precise in its operations, lightning quick in effecting designated end points, remarkably effective in containing interpersonal conflicts, and unrivaled in reducing expenses, no wonder it dominates the organizational landscape. No wonder as well that few can imagine a viable alternative. Weber himself complained that bureaucracies incarcerated workers in an "iron cage." Nevertheless, he believed that modernity demanded this sacrifice. Only bureaucracies could provide the centralized control massive institutions required in order to function effectively. As such, they were vital for our individual and collective survival.

The Professional Model

But is this true? Are we condemned to a wholly bureaucratized future? More particularly, are universities inevitably bound by bureaucratic strictures? George Ritzer (2011), among others, implies that there is little choice. In *The McDonaldization of Society*, he suggests that bureaucracies are popping up everywhere. Much like crabgrass (or fast-food restaurants), they are persistent and almost impossible to eradicate. If he is right, then most people will ultimately occupy jobs little better than burger-flippers. They too will perform simple tasks according to strict instructions that are rigidly enforced. As cogs in a human machine, they will mindlessly reproduce the same outcomes, hour after hour and day after day. The logic of this is said to be inevitable as organizations seek to make their operations simpler, more routine and, in the process, more controllable. Thus, in quest of profits, they will continue to deprive people of their humanity in an effort to turn out cheaper burgers.

As Ritzer puts it, the simplified operating procedures of McDonald's promote efficiency, calculability, and predictability. They do this, in part, by substituting non-human technologies for human fallibility. Instead of having a cook decide when to turn a burger, a uniform patty placed on a standard grill is turned whenever a clock specifies that it should. A person might get it wrong, whereas the proper equipment operated according to tested procedures gets it right every time. The problem is what Ritzer calls "the irrationality of rationality." This sort of approach robs workers of their humanity at the same time that it reduces flexibility and lowers quality. Yes, the burgers are all the same, but that does not mean they meet the needs of individual customers who desire the tastiest product. That this bland uniformity comes at the price of turning workers into virtual robots is therefore unconscionable. It may be beef up a company's bottom line, but must we, as a society, do this to innocent human beings?

The answer, happily, is no! Ritzer's dire scenario is based on a faulty assessment of recent developments. It assumes that most large organizations are becoming replicas of McDonald's. They emphatically are not. Even McDonald's employees are not being turned into soulless clones. Why not? Because most do not remain burger-flippers. They either move up or out; that is, they are either promoted into management, or they go on to other jobs. The vast majority of the company's labor force is temporary. Young people work there while they are going to school in the expectation that they will move onto something better once they graduate. They understand that a college education is intended to provide the credentials to perform less stereotyped work.

No doubt, American employers are enraptured by modern technology. They see in it the sort of efficiency, calculability, and predictability of which Ritzer writes. But they see something else; they see the possibility of replacing finicky people with uncomplaining machines. It turns out that people hate routine work. They find it boring and unfulfilling. But it also turns out that these are the jobs most easily mimicked by machines. Yes, burger flipping is tedious, but one day a machine will do the flipping unaided by human supervision. Meanwhile, the people will go on to jobs that require greater discretion. They will be asked to perform tasks that are so complicated even smart machines are unable to do them. In this, their judgment, as human beings, will be employed to make decisions that cannot be easily routinized.

Herbert Simon (1947), in his Nobel Prize-winning critique of scientific management, argued that many tasks are too complex to be reduced to exact calculations. Decision makers often find that they do not know all of the alternatives from which they must choose or all of the consequences of these options. They cannot even be certain of the values people use in favoring one outcome over another. Humans, says Simon, have "bounded rationality." They cannot do what Taylor and Ritzer imply they must. Instead, they make do with "satisficing," as opposed to optimizing. Then, if things go wrong, they fix what is broken. Simon might also have stressed that many decisions are arrived at via social negotiations. No single individual, however smart, settles on them. Rather, it is groups of individuals, often with divergent interests, that push and pull until these largely unpredictable maneuvers bring about a consensus. This is not calculation of the sort Weber or Taylor envisaged.

As it happens, discretion is more necessary the more complicated decisions become. Indeed, a need for discretion is one of the chief characteristics of a techno-commercial society. With more people performing tasks that entail interacting with people and/or data, the mechanical work of dealing with things, as exemplified in old-fashioned factories, is going the way of the dodo. This, in fact, is why a college education has become so highly prized. Its specialty is socializing students so that they can exercise competent discretion. The goal is not to fill their heads with trivial information but to convert them into effective decision makers. Universities have acknowledged this objective by boasting that they teach "critical thinking." But as *Academically Adrift* (Arum and Roska, 2011) demonstrated, although this is not exactly true, the aspiration is appropriate. Even so, it is more accurate to say that universities specialize in—or should specialize in—preparing students to exercise "self-direction."

This brings us back to the professional model. Individuals, who are liable to be successful in a techno-commercial society benefit by virtue of becoming professionalized. The simple truth is that Gesellschaft institutions put a premium on the qualities characteristic of professionals. Consequently, our universities, if they are to cultivate a suitable hierarchical elite, must instill these characteristics. They themselves have to be professionalized. They must, as it were, be organized in a manner that facilitates teaching the skills and attitudes that produce professionalized graduates.

Professionalization—as with universities—has its roots in medieval Europe (Larson, 1977). The original professions were few in number but crucial to social subsistence. This is why their occupants were the chief beneficiaries of the first colleges. Doctors, lawyers, and priests had to be good at what they did. The health of their communities' bodies, economies, and souls depended upon it. As such, these persons needed to be competent in their specialties (i.e., they required focused knowledge). But they needed something more; they had to be dedicated to what they did. What they "professed" was regarded as a "calling." God had selected them to fulfill his purposes; thus, they must take their occupations seriously. These were not merely jobs; they were ways of lives to which their occupants must personally commit themselves.

Modern professionals are obviously not as comparably religious in their dedication (Hughes, 1958). Although their occupations are also regarded as elite, their commitment is secular. Doctors and lawyers are still numbered among them, but scientists, engineers, architects, and college professors have joined their ranks. Generally speaking, these positions remain high-powered vocations that demand intelligence and personal devotion. Where to draw the line between them and lesser endeavors is arbitrary, but the fact that some jobs are more demanding than others cannot be doubted. Physicians may therefore be used as their paradigm. Indeed, it is fair to say that other occupations are professionalized to the degree they approach the attributes to which doctors aspire.

We may begin with the specialized, often theoretical knowledge that physicians control (Greenwood, 1957). Almost everyone considers doctors as smart. Because they need to know more about the body, disease, and medical procedures than others, they command the respect of lesser mortals. More than this, they participate in developing this knowledge. Many physicians are not practitioners but researchers. They are in the laboratory or out in the field running trials, developing the improved forms of intervention to which their fellow physicians will hold an almost proprietary right.

Because of this unique knowledge and the fact that its efficacy has been corroborated in action, doctors are granted exceptional authority (Bruhn, 2001). The government, for instance, licenses them to prescribe medications that were they distributed by others would land them in jail. More than this, ordinary persons follow medical instructions with nary a word of dissent. Their attitude is that "the doctor knows best"—even if this diagnosis derives from a "second opinion" (which, of course, is also medical). Doctors are not merely listened to because what they say is interesting. Rather, their authority is commonly treated as if it were biblical. Indeed, for some people doctors are the closest thing to terrestrial deities. So superior is their medical knowledge deemed that neither it nor they are questioned.

The uncommon competence that provides doctors control over life and death also provides control over their working conditions. Because only physicians have the insights to judge the performance of other physicians, they get to determine whether malpractice has occurred. Even if this issue is decided in a courtroom, their expertise is typically decisive. When coupled with the fact that MDs are committed to a stringent ethical code, they are trusted to make decisions laypersons are not.

It is because of this that physicians get to coordinate activities, motivate effort, distribute scarce resources, and provide internal and external protections much in the way that bureaucratic authorities do. Whether they are dealing with patients or their own working conditions, the respect they command is thereby translated into operational leadership. Moreover, while their hierarchical precedence rests less with their organizational connections than does that of bureaucratic leaders and relies more on their demonstrated abilities, it is nonetheless effective.

How then do physicians acquire their knowledge and hierarchical authority? Clearly, they are not born with these but must attain their elite credentials. The key is a lengthy and demanding socialization, followed by induction into an exacting cultural community. Prospective doctors must go to college, where they are required to do unusually well in a difficult intellectual program. Only then can they compete for admission to highly selective medical schools. Here, they also must do well in another stressful program that includes an internship of diabolic proportions. Yet even after this, an apprentice physician's education remains incomplete. Now comes a residency during which he or she may function as a physician—albeit one essentially in training. If a board-certified specialty is also desired, there will be even more training and further tests of knowledge and competency.

Nonprofessionals may assume this is the end of the torment, but no—it has barely begun. Now the physician, having acquired a professional status, must maintain it. This entails continually reading medical journals to keep up with advances in research and attending conferences to be instructed on the most recent medical interventions. In addition to this, he or she will be under scrutiny by other physicians. They will evaluate his or her competence to determine if he or she is qualified to receive hospital privileges and/or be referred patients. None of this is a matter of indifference to most doctors. Having endured years of arduous labor to attain their standing, few are prepared to throw it away. In having undergone what is essentially a rite of passage, their self-identity has been modified such that being regarded as a competent doctor is essential to maintaining ego-integrity. In other words, they care about what other MDs think and will work hard to sustain a good reputation.

All this adds up to the core of professionalism. To put the crux of the matter simply: professionals must be *self-motivated experts*. They must be very good at doing something very important, something few others are comparably equipped to accomplish. Moreover, they must be personally motivated to do this well. Physicians should not seek to cure patients because they are trying to please a boss. Rather, they must value accurate diagnoses and effective prescriptions because these are in accord with their self-images. This motivation needs to be part of who they are. There is, of course, a less beneficial corollary to this attitude. Doctors have been accused of having a "God complex." They are purported to think of themselves as superior to other humans and therefore worthy of the prestige they obtain. Most physicians are indeed proud of their intelligence, proud of their knowledge, and proud of their effectiveness. They do not wish to squander any of these; hence, most dedicate themselves to doing the best they can.

Here, then, is the utility of the professional model. Professionals are persons who can be allowed to engage in self-supervision. They do not require bosses to tell them how to perform their work. To the contrary, they can be delegated responsibility for their activities because they routinely discharge these with competence and devotion. Nowadays, physicians do not dedicate themselves to preserving health because they are committed to achieving God's will but because they have become the sort of person who cares about this goal. As such, they do not need to be controlled within a bureaucratic hierarchy of authority. Their professional role is usually sufficient to keep them doing what is expected. In fact, their bosses, who may not be trained in medicine, often have neither the expertise nor the personal commitment to make superior decisions. They must, therefore, frequently yield authority to organizational subordinates who are medical experts.

Professionalized organizations are, as a consequence, decentralized and democratized. They neither stress nor benefit from the strict controls of classical bureaucracies. In the Weberian and Taylorite models, supervisors select and enforce the appropriate rules and procedures, whereas in the professional model, lower-level role players often make independent decisions. More likely to choose wisely in the areas where they are more expert than their superiors, they are, as a result, ceded control. This reduces the ability of the larger organization to coordinate complex activities or to impose uniformity. Nonetheless, while the coordination provided by professional collegiality may be looser, it provides compensatory advantages suitable for the activities characteristic of techno-commercial societies.

Professionalized organizations, in being decentralized, are liable to be more flexible. They are much better able to make adjustments at the local level, the need for which may not be visible to faraway executives. Thus, instead of everyone being shoehorned into the same Procrustean bed, the players are allowed to do things differently; that is, if the circumstances warrant. One of the chief complaints about bureaucracies has been their rigidity. The professional model overcomes this drawback by allowing self-directed experts to make exceptions that may be further modified as events dictate.

Closely related to this increased flexibility is increased responsiveness. If individuals who are closer to the scene of action are allowed to make changes on the spot, they can adjust to what they directly perceive as necessary. This enables them to fine-tune their activities to suit the demands of the moment and/or those of their clients. Consequently, when things go wrong, they can compensate for unanticipated problems. Or if an unexpected opportunity arises, they can likewise take advantage of it. They do not have to await orders from above but can act on information that they appreciate better than their managers. The old Soviet Union fell apart, in large measure, because five-year plans devised in Moscow could never account for the vicissitudes of manufacturing in Siberia. Their unanticipated irrationalities demonstrated that when those implementing a task are trusted to make decisions in line with organizational goals, these determinations, rather than those made miles away, are apt to be more efficient.

Ritzer says that McDonald's-style bureaucracies increase efficiency, calculability, and predictability, but this is from the perspective of managers who are only looking at the big picture. These arrangements may not do so when seen from below. In fact, in complex organizations, because a multitude of discrepancies at the local level can add up to enormous deviations at the upper one, too much centralization can be deadly. When excess bureaucratization prevents those qualified to exercise discretion from doing so, merely because they are lower in the chain of command, disastrous consequences can arise. In addition, an over-concentration of authority typically squelches creative impulses. If only good ideas are allowed to come from the top, the rich intellectual resources of an organization are needlessly wasted. As a result, instead of innovation flourishing, it is smothered in the crib.

It follows that rigid centralization is not in the interests of modern universities or of their students. Techno-commercial societies, in which multitudes of strangers not only rub shoulders but are dependent upon many invisible others for survival, cannot afford to be inflexible or unresponsive. They must adjust to unexpected events because these occur with great regularity. Nor can they afford to ignore talent or ingenuity when the challenges they face are so massive. To the contrary, they require that many millions of people aspire to positions where they can make decisions that affect millions of other persons. In such a society, leadership roles have to be widely dispersed. The same also applies to higher education—perhaps more so.

Since universities are the primary locus for the socialization of professionalized persons, they too must be professionalized. Not just doctors but lawyers, business managers, engineers, biochemists, bankers, social workers, and politicians get their training in institutions of higher learning; hence, these schools must be geared to inculcating the self-motivated expertise that is required (Vollmer and Mills, 1968). In theory, universities do not have to follow the professional model in order to achieve this, but as a practical matter, they do. Unless they themselves are decentralized, flexible, responsive, and creative, they are unlikely to pass along these characteristics to their students. More precisely, if their professors and curricula do not reflect a self-directed professionalism, they can scarcely model or recommend what they refuse to implement.

The problem with the professional model—and it is significant—is that in many cases, it is embedded within the bureaucratic model. Independent professionals are nowadays the exception rather than the rule. Most operate within bureaucratic organizations; hence, most are subject to the imperatives baked into the DNA of centralized arrangements. As will soon become apparent, this leads to incessant conflicts between professionals and those who administer them.

Professionalization

The numbers of professionals in our society have rapidly increased (Fein, 2011), but these persons do not come close to representing the majority of our friends, neighbors, and colleagues. How, then, can a professional model be said to be appropriate for most social institutions and especially for universities? If only a fraction of those upon whom we depend are professionals, wouldn't this be like asking the tail to wag the dog?

This question requires a good answer. While it is true that doctors, lawyers, and engineers represent a fraction of our workforce, they constitute an important and expanding fraction (Fein, 2012). Nonetheless, no society can function solely on the basis of the services these people provide. No, the growing import of the professional model lies in its relevance to the many jobs in the process of "professionalizing." These occupations are not wholly professional in the sense of requiring the same levels of knowledge and dedication as full professionals. Still, they are headed in that direction, and hence their occupants must also be able to coordinate activities, motivate effort, distribute scarce resources, and provide internal and external protections. Moreover, they too must do this well.

As our society becomes more complex and technical, the tasks people perform also become more complex and technical. Instead of working with things—as our farmer ancestors did—more individuals are required to work with people and data. This means that they need to know more about their specialties and to exercise greater discretion with respect to these. While not everyone becomes a high-level social leader, more people than previously are delegated to make independent hierarchical-style decisions. This is true whether they are social workers, accountants, or air conditioning technicians.

It is also true that better-educated people desire greater control over their lives and work. On the job, they resent being lorded over by managers who are only marginally more proficient than they are. No longer do they consider these higher-ups as belonging to a different sphere of humanity. While they are prepared to show some deference, they are unwilling to toady to anyone. As a result, they wish to emulate the traditional professionals. They too want to know more than non-specialists and to be respected for this knowledge. They also want to be trusted because they are worthy of trust. If this means that they must personally commit to doing a good job, most are prepared to make this sacrifice. The freedom they gain by not being subjected to close supervision is deemed worth the extra effort.

Emblematic of jobs currently undergoing professionalization are those of nurses and police officers (US Dept. of Labor, 2001). Both were historically working-class jobs—but no longer. Those who occupy these positions consider themselves middle class, albeit not upper middle class. What is more, members of both groups are liable to be college educated, especially registered nurses and the supervisory personnel in criminal justice systems. This, of course, is in response the more complex and responsible positions they now hold.

As remarked upon previously, nurses were once confined to emptying bedpans and changing bandages. Currently, these tasks are left to lower-level staff. Nurses themselves are much too accomplished to waste their talents on overly-routine activities. While in college, they may not accumulate as much knowledge as physicians, but they can take justifiable pride in how much they do learn. They realize this is far more than laypersons know about health matters and that it prepares them to make responsible decisions when working with patients. While they do not exercise the ultimate responsibility, they are able to make recommendations to physicians that are often acted upon because they (the nurses) interact more intimately with patients than do their superiors.

The upshot is that nurses must undergo a strenuous period of socialization that also acts as a rite of passage. Consequently, once they become RNs, their self-image is altered, such that they feel responsible for the work they do. As with physicians, albeit to a lesser degree, they are therefore capable of being delegated significant authority. They know, for instance, that in moments of crisis, they may need to intervene in order to save a life. While they are not as respected as the physicians to whom they report, neither are they as deferential as they once were. Moreover, they too adhere to rigorous ethical principles; hence, they too press for greater power. Simply put, because they exemplify many of the characteristics of the traditional professions, they believe they are due the esteem commensurate with their achievements. Having come to perceive themselves as possessing the equivalent of a "calling," they wish others to acknowledge this as well.

Police officers are in a similar situation. They, however, do not report directly to other professionals (lawyers sometimes constituting an exception) but are embedded in a quasi-military chain of command. This might seem to make them fit the bureaucratic model, yet they have a great deal of latitude, especially when out on patrol. Moreover, since (like nurses) they must often make life-or-death decisions outside the direct supervision of their superiors, they need to do so responsibly. Far from being the bullyboys from whom they are descended, they must exercise restraint and intelligence on the job. Indeed, a failure to do so could lead to tragic consequences.

Obviously, police officers do not know as much about the law as attorneys, but they must know enough about it to make arrests that stand up in court. Nor do they know as much about the human psyche as psychologists, but they must understand enough to cope with a broad array of irate citizens. Neither are they as socially sophisticated as most sociologists, but they must be knowledgeable enough to deal with diverse constituencies. Consequently, nowadays much of what they must comprehend is derived from a college education. And as with higher education in general, this often serves as a rite of passage. College-trained police officers tend not to be intellectuals; nevertheless, many are quite astute about the matters within their purview. They are not empty-headed fools or unfeeling "pigs," as is sometimes alleged.

Here, then, is another pathway toward professionalization. It too entails the acquisition of considerable knowledge, although most of this is not theoretical. A rigorous indoctrination into the ethical standards of policing also modifies the attitudes that candidates hold toward criminals and the public. In the process, they too become the sorts of persons who can be delegated authority. While they do not control their work to the same extent as full professionals, they too take justifiable pride in their competence—and yes, professionalism. Few consider themselves mere ciphers or cogs in a bureaucratic machine.

Another group that is professionalizing and might therefore consider themselves professional are the middle managers who run huge corporations. Once, they too rarely went to college, whereas today an MBA is mandatory in many precincts. It used to be assumed that executives would automatically identify with the owners of their companies, but that was when most entrepreneurs supervised their own businesses. It is likewise assumed that most managers are motivated by a desire to make money—which many are. Even so, it has become normal for administrators to take pleasure in their managerial skills. Some people—usually those not in positions of power—believe that being a "boss" is merely a matter of issuing orders. They do not recognize that making good decisions or coordinating complex efforts entails considerable expertise. Those occupying these slots do not share this mistake. They know that knowledge and personal adroitness can make the difference between success and failure.

As a result, potential executives are flocking to college (Hardy and Everett, 2013). Many imagine that once they graduate, they will be whisked to the top of the executive suite, but they soon learn that the academic information they imbibe must be supplemented by experience and that genuine competence needs to be demonstrated in action. Nonetheless, what they learn in school helps them make appropriate decisions, and a degree burnishes their subsequent authority. In other words, they too are changed by a college education, such that they become more like traditional professionals.

Were they to look at the Bureau of Labor Statistics (BLS) surveys of American jobs, many people would be surprised. Some seem to believe that manufacturing—and hence, manufacturing jobs—makes the economy go round. They further imagine that because the bureaucratic model is associated with these enterprises, it must be the dominant mode of social organization. Yet manufacturing jobs constitute less than 10 percent of the labor market. And of these, many entail working with complex automated devices that require expertise to operate.

In fact, most American jobs are located in employment sectors such as management, finance, health, education, engineering, science, and legal affairs. Clearly, a great many of these positions demand an advanced education that prepares their occupants to exercise discretion and authority. While it is true that many traditional manufacturing jobs have migrated abroad, that does not mean rampant unemployment followed in their wake. To the contrary, the jobs left behind tend to be more complex and therefore less routine.

But professionalization extends beyond occupational endeavors. In a democratic, market-oriented society, it spills over into politics and family life. A democracy depends on the enlightened participation of a significant proportion of its citizens. Unless voters intelligently choose their leaders and then wisely monitor their activities, they cannot be well governed. Demagoguery flourishes when people have neither the knowledge nor the inclination to participate in political pursuits. Moreover, many ordinary persons must be prepared to run for office if they are to avoid being indentured to a hereditary ruling class.

A democratic professionalism thus involves an ability to judge character, an awareness of when one is being covertly controlled, and an acquaintance with government policies. In a representative democracy, the electorate selects between multiple candidates. If voters cannot tell which are honest and competent, they are doomed to be misgoverned. Similarly, if they are so easily swayed that they fall for agreeable lies, they will be lied to both regularly and egregiously. Thus, an effective democracy requires an informed electorate. Voters must know what is at stake and make choices based on likely outcomes. To this extent, they must be experts in government operations who are personally motivated to make good choices.

Family life too must be professionalized in a society where nuclear families are responsible for guarding their own well-being and for raising children who can perform the economic and political tasks later demanded of them (Fein, 2005). In this case, the requisite self-direction applies to living together in harmonious intimacy and competently socializing their young to assume adult responsibilities. The wealth and flexibility of contemporary civilizations place a huge burden of choice on the shoulders of ordinary people. The abundance of resources upon which they draw, provides countless alternatives. These options are so numerous that if individuals cannot distinguish what fulfills their needs, they are bound to suffer. This especially applies to personal relationships.

Once upon a time, individuals had few potential mates from whom to select. For many, there was no selection but an arranged marriage. Parents decided on a suitable partner and then made sure the union was consummated. Today, of course, this responsibility is placed on the marital partners (Pines, 2005). When they come of age, they enter a matrimonial marketplace where the possibilities—including cohabitation, same-sex unions, and remaining single—abound. Making a good choice is imperative; nonetheless, doing so wisely can be difficult. This too requires an expertise and the internal motivation to undergo the rigors of courtship.

To begin with, those seeking a mate must know what they want and what will meet their needs. This entails considerable self-knowledge. Then there is the problem of knowing what sort of person a potential partner is. People don't change after marriage; hence, it is critical to be accurate in assessing a possible match. This takes time and necessitates a learning curve. It is why dating and courting take so long. In any event, the challenges are not over once the parties pledge their troth. Learning to live in partnership with another person also requires learning. It is essential that a couple know how to work out their differences—because there are always many of these. This entails negotiation skills that also take time to acquire. These undertakings thus benefit from personal professionalization and therefore a college education. Divorce has become a problem in contemporary society, but it happens that the divorce rate among college graduates is less than half that of those who do not attend college (Murray, 2012). Evidently, a higher education has something to do with personal maturation.

Nor does competent childrearing come naturally. While some people may be temperamentally suited to the task, effectively providing children with the needed support and guidance takes knowledge and dedication. Here, too, research shows that upper middle-class parents (i.e., those likely to have gone to college) are far more successful (Lareau, 2003). The maturity attained consequent to a higher education evidently has an impact on parenting styles. If nothing else, well-educated parents are apt to be better role models for their children.

Bureaucracy versus Professionalization

The professional model of organization may be necessary to supplement the bureaucratic model in our complex techno-commercial world, but that does not imply that the two always operate in harmony. It certainly indicates no such thing with respect to how universities are run. The clashes between their bureaucrats and professionals can be of epic proportions. This follows the experience of hospitals, where the conflicts between physicians and administrators are also legendary.

To state the obvious, universities need administrators. These are the people who organize, coordinate, and schedule routine activities. They also adjudicate disputes, pay the bills, and see to it that the garbage is picked up. Meanwhile, universities just as obviously need faculties. These are the people who teach the classes, do the research, and generate creative products that require great discretion. The question is to what degree should the former supervise the latter? Since administrators tend to believe, as per the bureaucratic model, that their central responsibility is to control what happens on the campus, while professors, as per the professional model, believe that they should control their classrooms and disciplinary endeavors, who is to come out on top? As of the moment, this conflict remains unresolved.

Professor Benjamin Ginsberg (2011) of Johns Hopkins University has captured what is at stake. In *The Fall of the Faculty: The Rise of the All-Administrative University and Why It Matters*, he documents a host of administrative abuses. Thus, he argues that although enrollments have rapidly increased, faculties have remained nearly static. Meanwhile the number of administrators has risen dramatically. Thus, from 1975 to 2005, the number of managers at public colleges rose 66 percent, while those at private colleges rose 135 percent. To make matters worse, administrators are often paid several times more than professors. For this, they spend much of their time writing mission statements no one reads, attending meetings and conferences that produce few viable programs, and engaging in image polishing and fund-raising that do little to improve classroom outcomes.

Nonetheless, administrators, including legions of vice presidents and disciplinary coordinators, insist that classroom results are their principal concern. They contend that they are there to make sure that faculty shirkers have their feet held to the fire. To this end, the watchword is "accountability." Professors, it is said, must be held accountable to make sure that students learn what they are supposed to learn. Never mind that the faculty is asked to teach more students, with lesser resources and for fewer dollars. The public wants to know it is getting its money's worth; hence, administrators demand performance.

To this end, there are incessant calls for standardization. How, it is asked, can effectiveness be measured if there is no uniformity? Hence, professors are required to implement "the best practices." As per the bureaucratic model, those in authority assert that they (i.e., the administrators) must develop the most efficient rules and procedures and then make sure these are adopted. This includes syllabi that have a standard format specifying measurable learning objectives. This also entails standardized teaching rubrics and pretested classroom materials. Furthermore, faculty members are obliged to document their success. They are asked to evaluate what has been learned so that objective outsiders can be sure their claimed achievements are real.

As might be expected, faculty members bridle at these impositions. They counter that they are the experts in what they teach and therefore on how it should be taught. According to them, classroom flexibility is essential. Moreover, they claim that they cannot meet the needs of students if they are not allowed to be responsive. Besides, how can the university be creative if creativity is stifled? Likewise, how are students to benefit from the unique expertise of professors who not allowed to organize what they teach?

Here, then, lie the seeds of a contentious relationship. At first glance, administrators seem to have the upper hand. They, after all, are the hierarchical superiors. Moreover, because exercising control is their central duty, they have the time and motivation to impose their will. On the other hand, professors are in the classroom. They teach behind closed doors. Were their morale to be grievously damaged, the quality of their work would suffer. Consequently, we have a stalemate.

At this point, we must also take cognizance of the different tiers to which colleges and universities belong. Elite schools, because their faculties are elite, allow them greater professional control. Their professors possess an eminence that makes them difficult to replace, thereby affording them substantial leverage. Academics teaching at a lower level are, however, more vulnerable. Neither as accomplished in research nor as prestigious, they bring less power to bear in confrontations with superiors. They consequently face greater pressures to standardize. As Ginsberg testifies, these forces are not absent at the upper reaches of academe, but they are more muted. It is at schools nearer the bottom of the pecking order where faculty members are more likely to feel they are treated like high school teachers. It is there that their role expertise is least respected.

To add to this disparity, the students at mid- and lower-level colleges and universities are themselves less elite. Almost by definition, elite schools are more selective. They cream the best high school graduates and leave the leftovers for the rest. Therefore, the lower down one goes in the educational pecking order the smaller the number of students who desire—or are capable of—a fully professionalized career. Not surprisingly, few of these learners perceive themselves as capable of the sort of leadership expected of Ivy League or flagship state-university graduates. As a result, they make fewer demands for complex subject matter. In this, albeit not by design, they make it more difficult for their professors to insist on greater flexibility. Because what these academics are called upon to teach is often less professionally oriented, they cannot use this to argue that they require greater professional discretion.

Nonetheless, even lower-level schools (i.e., precisely where the greatest bubble-related stresses are found) are professionalizing at a breakneck pace. Schools like Princeton University boast that they are in the business of producing tomorrow's leaders, and in this they are correct. For generations, Princeton and similar institutions provided the personnel for Wall Street law firms and congressional staffs. But there has been a sea change. Our economy and government require so many skilled managers and technicians that businesses and agencies have been forced to reach further down to the lower-ranking schools in their recruitment efforts (Sander and Taylor, 2012). Nowadays, while the elite schools still produce a disproportionate number of our nation's leaders, it is remarkable how many successful people have begun their careers elsewhere. Nor is it irrelevant that the lower-level schools must often expend greater resources in promoting social mobility. Although many of their students may start lower in the social pecking order, this increases rather than decreases their need to provide opportunities for professionalized success.

Nor should it be forgotten that nurses, police officers, and their equivalent are also professionalizing. These college graduates may not need to acquire the same degree of discretion as the CEOs of major corporations, but they must still be capable of making independent decisions. Indeed, it may be argued that the less prestigious colleges are extremely important in fostering this competence—an important consideration in a democracy (Duncan, 1965). If advantaged students are more likely to obtain an advantaged education, those who are less advantaged also deserve institutions that can place them on the ladder to significant, albeit less elevated, achievements. Thus, if these institutions are to prepare semi-professionals for greater professionalization, they must be organized to do so.

The bottom line is that the central mission of institutions of higher education must be professionalization. They may not all engage in this to the same degree—indeed, they do not—but virtually all must facilitate the ultimate exercise of professionalized leadership. How they achieve this differs according to the needs of their student bodies, but that at which they aim is not wholly different. Ergo, research universities will continue to remain distinct from regional colleges, and these will differ from community colleges. Nevertheless, all must make instilling self-direction a major concern.

Conclusions

Higher education must emphasize the professional, as opposed to the bureaucratic, model of organization. If greater professionalization is required by an increasingly complex techno-commercial society—as it is—then our colleges and universities must reflect this development. History demonstrates that mass societies, in which millions of strangers are interdependent, must cultivate self-motivated expertise if they are to thrive. Higher education must therefore be organized so as to facilitate the ability of students to exercise this discretion. Only this can produce the flexible and responsive leadership required in a Gesellschaft society.

Colleges and universities should also be decentralized. Critical decision making needs to be delegated downward toward the professoriate, as opposed to being concentrated in the hands of administrators. If the self-motivated intellectual expertise of academics is to be brought to bear in teaching and research, professors must be allowed greater control over their work. They cannot be treated as cogs in a bureaucratic machine but need to be regarded as semi-autonomous decision makers.

As will later be discussed, self-direction is best developed in students within organizations that themselves respect self-direction. An iron cage that restricts professional discretion teaches the lesson that independent decision making is neither desired nor desirable. Students are unlikely to develop authentic decision-making abilities in an atmosphere that discourages anyone, including the faculty, from doing so. In this case, professors can scarcely model self-direction.

As we will also soon discuss, the curricula, extracurricular activities, and ambience of colleges and universities can encourage independent thinking. Self-direction is best promoted by actively furnishing students the opportunity to engage in self-direction. How lessons are taught, as well as the means whereby students interact, ought, therefore, be designed to facilitate independent thought. This should include the development of emotional maturity and an ability to disagree with authority. Most important, however, is an ability to exercise leadership that coordinates, motivates, distributes scarce resources, and protects society from within and without. This is the sort of elite that will be most needed in the mass techno-commercial world upon which we are embarking.

5

Self-Direction

What Is Self-Direction?

What does self-direction have to do with professionalization? And why should anyone who wishes to be successful value it? Furthermore, why should colleges and universities promote self-direction? How can this help them deal with the tangle of bubble-related problems they face? The answers to these questions lie in the fact that the United States has become a middle-class society and that our middle class is becoming increasingly professionalized (Fussell, 1983). In earlier chapters we explored the details of both hierarchy and professionalism. This was necessary if we were to discover the sort of leadership our society requires. Only understanding this can enable us to provide the appropriate preparation for the appropriate aspirants. Moreover, only this can tell us which types of education are relevant or furnish the standards against which to judge when they are of suitable quality.

As should be evident, ours is no longer a family-based society. It is not governed by ruling families that hand power down from one generation to the next. Nor does it follow an estate or patrimonial model. We do not believe in impermeable social boundaries that force people to remain in the same status into which they were born. Our ideal is social mobility wherein merit and effort are afforded an opportunity to advance a person's standing. And while we continue to engage in social networking, we do not favor rigid pseudo-families. Mentoring is encouraged, whereas patronage chains grounded in a semi-aristocratic inequality are not.

Our society is not even wholly bureaucratic. While virtually all large-scale organizations endorse a bureaucratic model, this is usually supplemented by efforts at decentralization. With larger numbers of leadership positions filled by professionals and semi-professionals, for many Americans this is the most promising route to enhanced social status.

It enables them to become self-motivated experts who, on the basis of their abilities, exercise greater discretion both at work and at home.

But what is self-direction? What does it mean to describe someone as exercising this capacity? Clearly, if we do not understand this, we will have difficulty promoting it. Moreover, how can self-direction be cultivated in higher education per se? What sorts of programs and attitudes enable these institutions to prepare their students to exert skilled discretion? Unless we are clear about what they can and cannot do and have a good idea about how best to implement what they can, we are unlikely to devise effective reforms.

Self-direction may be defined as an ability to make competent decisions and to make them independently—even in an environment of uncertainty. Self-directed people do not need to be told what to do. They can initiate appropriate actions without being directed to do so by a superior. These individuals may not always make optimum choices, but they generally make reasonable ones—that is, given the data at their disposal. In other words, they are capable of "satisficing"—in Herbert Simon's (1947) sense of the word.

Professionals, it must be remembered, are self-motivated experts. As such, they possess knowledge and skills that few others enjoy. They can, as a consequence, convert these into unique accomplishments. To do so, however, they must be proficient at selecting the "best" of multiple options and then of putting these into action. This, then, is "self-direction." Professionalization without it is a contradiction in terms. The sort of person who cannot or will not make good independent choices is a follower, not a leader. He or she is not someone who can sensibly be delegated authority.

In a complex techno-commercial society, where decentralization is an advantage, self-direction is as well. It underwrites effective discretion. Nonetheless, independent decision making is not easy. Given the complexity of Gesellschaft societies, superior alternatives can be difficult to identify. Indeed, the uncertainties and limited information with which people must cope often make it impossible to ascertain the optimum course. Still, decisions must be made and actions taken.

Self-direction is challenging for several reasons. First, the effort needed to master advanced technical knowledge is substantial. With economic and political specialization having reached undreamt of levels of sophistication, what must be learned, therefore, needs to be intentionally acquired. Watching one's parents go about their business generally does not result in picking it up. Rigorous instruction is typically a minimum. Moreover, no matter how detailed this training, it cannot incorporate all that must be known. A person must therefore engage in independent learning. When the time comes to apply information not previously assimilated, he or she must know where to look.

But technical information is not enough. Self-directed professionals need to understand other people. Because they do not work only with things, they have to recognize the motivations and abilities of others. Whether these are colleagues, superiors, subordinates, or customers, competent decisions are often contingent on accurate projections of how they will act. Individuals for whom others are black boxes require guidance. They are like blindfolded children playing pin the tail on the donkey, except that if they stick the pin in sensitive parts, they may have to cope with more than howls of displeasure.

Closely related to this is a need to understand social structures and cultures. People are not like Leibnizian monads (Weiner, 1951) that never come into contact with each other. They are more like pool balls on a table with elastic sideboards. As a result, they regularly bang into each other within this semi-confined space. Consequently, if they do not know the rules of the game or where the other balls are located, they hardly ever score points. Such persons are unable to work with allies, or defend against enemies, or devise winning policies. Ignorant of the constraints and opportunities provided by the structures and cultures in which they operate, they blunder about, breaking a lot of china.

All of this brings up the necessity of self-knowledge. People who do not understand themselves cannot be competently self-directed because their plans leave out an essential element. Unable to perceive their own strengths and weaknesses, they do not appreciate what they are capable of achieving. Confined to a world of fantasies and self-delusions, they frequently initiate projects they are ill-equipped to complete. Nor do they understand their own motivations. Unsure of their values and needs, they pursue objectives that, if attained, are unsatisfying. Furthermore, because they are out of touch with their interiors, they are rarely able to identify what is occurring in the interiors of others. For them, the world is an out-of-focus mystery. A lot is happening around them, but they cannot distinguish which pathways to follow. As a result, they falter when pitted against others whose vision is more accurate.

All of this can be disconcerting. Not only are errors liable to made, but these can be very damaging. This is frightening, especially for people who do not know how to fix what is broken. Aware that they might not be able to recover from a serious blunder, they often do nothing. Thus, instead of making their best calculations and then forging ahead, they remain frozen in place. In fact, it takes courage to deal with uncertainties. Self-directed individuals must therefore possess the confidence to take chances. Although they too may be frightened, they must be able to keep their wits about them. Rather than run away, they have to gauge the circumstances and take the plunge. Then if things don't work out, they must be honest and flexible enough to recognize what went wrong and how it might be remedied. Those who cannot do this must depend on others to rescue them. Accordingly, people who hide from reality cannot be delegated authority. Everyone makes mistakes, but those who make them too frequently ought not be leaders.

Nor are those who are afraid of independent decisions apt to be creative. Because doing something new inevitably entails uncertainties, insecure people tend to be conservative. Thus, they do what is predicable rather than innovative. Yet because discretion is most necessary in just those areas where the tried-and-true is least available, people who are risk-averse are rarely pioneers. Since one of the constants of our techno-commercial society is change, this means such folks are less capable of managing progress. In short, given their inflexibility in an environment that demands flexibility, they too are rarely deserving of authority.

Competent self-direction is vital to achieving higher status in our society. Those who aspire to social mobility, therefore, do well to strive for it. They must, to be blunt, become the kinds of persons others trust to make crucial decisions. This means they need to seek the technical, interpersonal, social, and personal knowledge that lend themselves to making reasonable choices. They must similarly become the kinds of person comfortable making bold decisions in an environment of uncertainty. Despite their misgivings, they must hold body and soul together, even when events conspire against them. Although it is true that some people are born more courageous than others, most of us are capable of achieving the requisite daring. It is a matter of grasping what is necessary and taking the steps to get there, albeit sometimes with assistance.

This is where higher education is helpful. If its mission is to groom an elite capable of meeting the challenges of a mass techno-commercial society, it ought to facilitate the acquisition of the relevant abilities. Whether the objective is economic, political, or personal competence, the sorts of knowledge and personal attitudes that further these must be successfully inculcated. Instead of blindly following tradition or just as blindly following the latest fad, academic reformers must keep their eye on the ball. They have to be clear about what is needed and the best ways to accomplish this.

Self-Direction in Context

The social scientist who first brought the importance of self-direction to our attention was Melvin Kohn (1969). Almost a half-century ago he began studies in what at first glance might seem fallow ground. He asked if there were differences in the values parents of different social classes held for their children. Did they desire dissimilar outcomes in what their offspring became? And sure enough, there were. Upper middle-class and working-class parents consistently favored opposing end points. For the most part, middle-class parents wanted their children to be considerate of others, to show an interest in how and why things happen, to be responsible, and to exercise self-control. Working-class parents, in contrast, emphasized good manners, being neat and clean, and obeying their parents. Kohn then bundled these attitudes together and concluded that middle-class parents favored self-direction, whereas working-class parents preferred conformity.

But Kohn did not stop there. He investigated why this difference existed. And here too he found a consistent pattern. The correlation turned out to be with the nature of parental occupations (Kohn and Schooler, 1983; Kohn and Slomczynski, 1990). Members of the upper middle class tended to have more professionalized jobs (i.e., ones where they were required to be self-directed). As professionals, middle managers, and successful entrepreneurs, they exercised discretion. Often engaged in supervising themselves and others, they understood the importance of making good choices, even in an environment of uncertainty. They therefore sought to prepare their children for similar challenges.

Meanwhile, members of the working class held jobs where others supervised their activities. They might, for instance, work in a factory where a foreman instructed them on the tasks they were to perform, while executives and engineers developed the procedures they were to follow. As a result, they did not control their workplace but were obliged to obey the mandates of others. They might not enjoy this—few did—but they had little choice. Consequently, they demanded obedience at home. If they were forced to knuckle under to authority on the job, they were determined not to do so in the bosom of their families.

Hence, although they did not intentionally decide to teach conformity, this was the effect of the attitudes they brought home.

The upshot was that middle-class parents, because they wanted their children to understand how and why things worked, patiently answered the questions of their offspring. They likewise treated their young with consideration and behaved responsibly toward them so as to model the behaviors they desired and personally exemplified. By the same token, because they were self-controlled on the job, they were unlikely to lose control at home. Not for them, corporal punishment or unpredictable tirades. Having internalized the standards needed to be occupational leaders, these became a natural extension of who they were. Accordingly, their children knew that their parents believed in what they asked them to do. These adults were, to use the psychological jargon, congruent human beings.

Working-class parents, on the other hand, did not always live by the maxims they preached. They might, for instance, demand that their children have good manners but then fail to exercise the same when events put them out of sorts. They also wanted their children to be neat and clean because they were apt to have jobs where cleanliness was impossible. These demands were, in essence, an endorsement of white-collar rather than blue-collar work. Nonetheless, what counted most for them was obedience. They would not truck insolence. Talking back was not allowed. The parent was the boss and the child the child, and that must never be forgotten. This, obviously, aroused antagonisms. The young too resented being pushed around; hence, they were often rebellious. The outcome was that they refused to learn the lessons that might have enabled them to engage in social mobility. For instance, rather than pay attention at school—as their parents demanded—their interests generally lay elsewhere.

The upshot was middle-class children who engaged in self-direction and working-class children who repudiated this objective. This was not consciously intended—certainly not by working class parents—but it was what occurred. As a result, social class blueprints tended to be replicated. This violated the canons of social justice, yet it was customary. Thus, if higher education is to disrupt this pattern, it must be aware of the handicaps under which lower-class children labor, and it must provide antidotes to attitudes that inhibit mobility. Wringing one's hands about the unfairness of it all is worse than useless; it creates unsatisfied expectations.

The anthropologist Oscar Lewis (1966) furnished further insights as to what thwarts self-direction among the lower classes. His observations about a so-called "culture of poverty" have been controversial; nevertheless, they augment those of Kohn. Lewis's field work in Mexico, New York, and Puerto Rico convinced him that poverty creates mindsets that perpetuate poverty. Thus, he postulated that growing up in a disorganized social setting inculcated habits of disorganization. Instead of developing routines that enabled a person to coordinate activities efficiently, a haphazard spontaneity resulted from a lifestyle where systematic pursuits were absent. Individuals who did not have regular jobs did not have a schedule to meet and, therefore, neither did their children. In the end, this produced a lack of punctuality and of responsibility that made it difficult to hold down a normal job.

A second postulated attribute of the culture of poverty was a present-orientation. People who had been disappointed by life did not want to be disappointed again. They therefore developed the attitude that one should "get while the getting is good." If one waited for something better, the odds were that one would get nothing. Yet the trouble with this strategy is that it is self-defeating. People who will not delay their gratification do not do what is necessary to obtain future rewards. Since many of the most agreeable prizes take time to come to fruition, they thereby deny themselves these benefits. Disinclined to plan, they are unprepared when opportunities come their way. Nor do they put in efforts today that pay off the day after tomorrow. This makes it unlikely that they will go to college or that having gone to one that they will take the time to do praiseworthy work. This lack of preparation also handicaps them as potential leaders. Absent advance calculations about what their subordinates should do, the odds of supervising effective coordination are not good.

A third attribute of the culture of poverty is a local orientation. People who are both disorganized and present-oriented are not apt to be terribly successful. As a result, they avoid unflattering comparisons. This makes it sensible to stick close to home where one knows what to expect and where most others are at a level comparable to one's own. But this means that one will not discover opportunities outside the neighborhood. If, for instance, the factory where one's relatives are employed closes down, it may be emotionally difficult to look elsewhere for a job. This also means one's learning opportunities are limited. While a person may know a great deal about his or her friends and neighbors, outsiders remain a mystery. This too robs a person of flexibility and makes it difficult to work in conjunction with diverse coworkers.

Lastly, Lewis reported that people trapped in a culture of poverty tend to be fatalistic. Having experienced countless failures, they become convinced that failure is inevitable. In this case, it makes no sense to seek control over one's destiny. Since success is a matter of luck, there is nothing a person can do to improve his or her lot. Why, then, tempt fate and endure additional disappointments. It is better to hunker down to fend off the slings and arrows of what really seems to be an outrageous fortune. While it is, of course, true that many of the best-laid human plans go awry, it is also true that people who never attempt to succeed almost never do. Those who acquire a "learned helplessness" are indeed helpless. They do not even try to do what they might be able to achieve. As a consequence, they are caught in a self-fulfilling prophecy. What they believe to be the case becomes the case because they do not challenge what they assume is unavoidable.

When these attributes are added up, they create a barrier to developing self-direction. Instead of calculating the best choices, individuals trapped in poverty may refuse to calculate at all. Moreover, they may hate learning because this entails the acquisition of knowledge believed to be useless. Similarly, rather than adopt routines that conserve time and energy, they aimlessly spin their wheels. Not exactly "know-nothings," they usually know very little about what facilitates upward mobility in a techno-commercial society. Nor are they risk-takers. Although they are envious of the leaders to whom they must defer, they fear mistakes and hence avoid areas of uncertainty. Motivated largely by a desire for safety, they eschew professionalization.

Individuals who do desire professionalization, however, can take a cue from this. They must shun these pitfalls. If they wish to become self-directed, they need to esteem what most poor people do not. Thus, they must become organized, look toward the future, survey the world outside their ordinary experience, and defy the fates. Where others are apathetic, they must be enthused. They have to care about doing better and must try to do better. These aspirations too point to what a worthwhile higher education should provide.

But there is more. The urban planner Joseph Howell (1973), in his version of the culture of poverty, stressed the chaos of lower-class marriages. His observations indicated that these were worse than disorganized; they were hotbeds of conflict and betrayal. Spouses, both of whom felt disillusioned, looked to their mates to provide what fate would not. When this wasn't forthcoming—as it almost never was—they felt cheated. This produced anger, and such unresolved anger fomented additional disappointments. A downward cycle ensued from which escape was nearly impossible. Subsequently, some people stayed put to endure their misery, while others opted out. It should therefore come as no surprise that the divorce rate among the poor is more than double that of the middle classes (Murray, 2012). Nor should it be a shock that cohabitation and unwed parenthood are rampant among them (Edin and Kefalas, 2005). The resultant strife and lack of social support make self-direction difficult, in that people in the midst of emotional turmoil usually do not have clear heads. Nor do they employ what knowledge they possess to calculate what is best. Generally self-absorbed; their immediate goal is survival, not upward mobility.

Worst of all, the belligerence and emotional immaturity that accompany marital problems are devastating for children. Parents in the midst of what feels like life-threatening battles rarely have time to worry about raising children to be self-directed (Whitehead, 1998). Unable to provide them with clear guidance or sustained emotional support, their young find it difficult to acquire a self-motivated expertise. These children, who are also oriented toward survival, find that their knowledge base and personal maturity sustain a direct hit. They may aspire to something better, but the resulting inner turmoil takes its toll.

Charles Murray (2012) has also documented just how devastating these circumstances can be. In his book *Coming Apart,* he details how widely the upper middle classes and the poor have diverged. As a result, he too makes it plain that their marital situations are diametrically opposed. But to this he adds the additional problem that their values have moved in opposite directions. For example, he presents evidence that the lower classes are less concerned with honesty than their more successful peers. Because they live in a world where a great many people are untrustworthy, they learn to be wary. This, unfortunately, is problematic because trust is essential in a techno-commercial society where most people are strangers to one another (Fukuyama, 1995). Conventional wisdom has it that business people are largely dishonest; that they attempt to get away with whatever they can. This, however, discounts the degree to which economic transactions depend on the parties carrying out their commitments. Those in responsible economic positions know this; therefore, they are alert as to whom they can trust and whom they cannot. While they understand that dishonesty exists, they tend to place confidence in those who have demonstrated their integrity.

Honesty is also fundamental to depending on the expertise of others. How many of us would choose a doctor who tells untruths about our condition? Or what of a lawyer who is secretly in league with our adversaries? Or an engineer who provides false figures about the tensile strength of a bridge? Could we trust these people? Would we do business with them? Whatever their purported expertise, if it were not genuine and they were not motivated to apply it honorably, our society would soon collapse. No one would know where to turn for help or for reliable products.

The poor, who do not trust, are therefore at a disadvantage when compared with the middle classes. But that too is not all. Murray's data reveals that members of the lower classes are less industrious than previously. Having developed a sense of entitlement, many see no sense in doing dead-end jobs that earn them little more than they can get from the government for doing nothing. Why, after all, put in effort for little return? On the face of it, this is a rational attitude, whereas in the long term the effects are devastating. Once again, people who do not try to do better are condemned to wallow in failure. Hard work can be draining, but when it is compensated by success it is invigorating. Achievement is one of the most satisfying experiences a person can have yet one many poor people are denied.

In sum, poverty is debilitating. It discourages a quest for self-direction and professionalization because it questions the validity of the attitudes that promote these. Cynicism, whether with regard to honesty or industry, discourages initiative or effort. Why, to repeat myself, seek a demanding expertise or attempt to apply it if there is no evident benefit. If upper-class loafers have stacked the deck against you, why provide them with the opportunity to make a fool of you one more time?

Once more, however, fatalism is itself fatal. A constructive higher education must therefore inoculate against such pessimism. But it must do so honestly. A stars-in-the-eyes idealism is not calculated to produce effective self-direction. People who make decisions based on fantasies are hell-bent for ruin. They may assume that they are dedicated to making a better world, whereas numerous disappointments await them around the bend. Perhaps they will recover from these, but why foist imaginary facts on them in the first place?

As it happens the sorts of socialization to which children are exposed in their families of origin can make a huge difference in their ability to cope with life's demands. Melvin Kohn, with his inventory of parental values, started us on the road to appreciating these disparities. Annette Lareau (2003) has moved us further along this path. In her ethnographic studies about how parents raise their children, she has revealed crucial social-class dissimilarities. According to her, upper middle-class parents engage in "concerted cultivation," whereas working-class parents believe in "natural growth." Moreover, these philosophies have different outcomes. As indicated by Kohn, they are connected with the occupational experience of the parents and go beyond these in how they foster self-direction.

Let us begin with concerted cultivation. Middle-class parents do not intend to leave their children's futures to chance. They actively attempt to shape them so as to improve their prospects. Consciously determined to implement strategies designed to produce academic results, they believe that knowledge and interpersonal skills are essential to success. And so they talk to their children. They tell them what they think they need to know and ask questions about what they are doing. This way they share important lessons while simultaneously encouraging their children to think for themselves. This sends the message that independent thought is valued, as is an ability to engage in it competently. Youngsters so raised are usually confident in their talents—because they are genuine.

Middle-class parents also encourage their children to participate in extra-curricular activities. These structured endeavors, be they Little League, gymnastics, dance lessons, or language classes, may require time or money, but their parents are prepared to provide these, including chauffeuring services. This frequently entails complicated scheduling wherein a multitude of commitments must be dovetailed to meet the desires of several parties. In many cases, lengthy negotiations precede a decision to honor one or another obligation.

This might be assumed to obviate self-direction in that it repudiates personal impulses. Yet this is misleading. First, in requiring the young to interact with a variety of outsiders, it sharpens their interpersonal skills. Second, in demanding personal responsibility, it turns them into reliable role partners. Third, in calling for complex planning, it promotes a future-looking attitude. Fourth, when different activities collide, it necessitates making choices. Fifth, in honoring the desires of the young, it helps them understand what will meet their needs and to prioritize these. Sixth, it encourages self-reliance, in that many of these activities are competitive; hence, the young discover that how well they do depends on the effort put in. Seventh, they have an opportunity to learn from failure. Provided that they have parental support and good coaching, they discover that "crashing and burning" is not fatal and may even provide the key to doing better the next time.

Some concerted cultivation entails direct advice (e.g., the best way to apply to a college), but much depends on modeling (Lareau and Conley, 2008). Parents who are emotionally mature and effectively control their own anger are able to pass along this skill. They demonstrate that self-control is possible, as well as how this can be achieved. They also provide lessons on the benefits of doing so. If, for example, a parent controls his own anger so as to hear out a child's complaint, the child discovers that better choices derive from cool-headed listening. Parents can also model skills such as reading. Those who read to their children when they are young send the message that reading is important. Likewise, parents who read for their own edification send the message that vital knowledge can be acquired this way. Intentionally or not, they indicate that no one knows everything and that filling in the gaps is nothing to be ashamed of.

Working-class parents, on the other hand, provide very different lessons. In fact, according to Lareau, they largely abjure offering lessons. They tend instead to assume that children learn what they need on their own. As long as parents provide them with food to eat, clothes on their backs, and a roof overhead, the rest is up to them. Thus, working-class parents are not prone to answering questions. Caught up in their own problems and often inexpert in what their children want to know, they brush off inquiries as inconsequential. They may even angrily growl at youngsters who interrupt parental activities.

It is therefore expected that when children come home from school, they will simply go out to play with their friends. Parental supervision is absent as they choose for themselves which games to play and what rules to enforce. While this, on the face of it, would seem excellent practice in self-direction, it is not. Jean-Jacques Rousseau (1979) is celebrated (in some quarters) for recommending that students choose what to learn. He feared that adult demands would corrupt them and extinguish their inborn innocence. Nevertheless, a child left exclusively to his or her own devices remains an ignorant savage. Children do not know what they need, nor do they come equipped with the discipline to pursue difficult subjects. Neither are the young born with strong emotional controls. All this must be learned. Moreover, generally speaking, it is best learned with the support and guidance of knowledgeable and concerned adults. To assume otherwise is to imagine that children wandering about alone in a forest would somehow discover how to build a modern city.

It is the same with children playing entirely on their own. They may enjoy themselves and will probably learn lessons about participating in a group, but these developments will be modest compared with children under the proper supervision. Nor will they learn that they are important persons whose wishes deserve recognition. Yes, they will make independent decisions, but these may not be good ones. And if they are not, the lesson learned may be that they should desist from them in the future. They will certainly not make expert decisions; hence, they are unlikely to inspire confidence in strangers.

Nor is natural growth the only sort of preparation in which universities and colleges should specialize. True, they are not dealing with young children. But neither are they dealing with finished products. Young adults do not always know what they need to know. Nor do they always have the personal controls required to become self-directed experts. The question, therefore, is what sorts of cultivation should institutions of higher education provide? The answer is not obvious. What is required, of course, will differ with the sorts of students in which they specialize. More selective schools are apt to attract learners who possess a good grounding in self-direction. On the other hand, mid- and lower-level institutions may have to deal with the more knotty problems of preparing enrollees for social mobility. Given that many of their learners come from working- and lower-class backgrounds, they may need to compensate for gaps in their earlier socialization. It is to the how's and why's of these questions to which we must now turn.

Knowledge

Technical Knowledge

No one doubts that our colleges are capable of providing excellent opportunities to acquire technical knowledge. A complex techno-commercial society requires expertise in many specialized fields, and these are largely available in contemporary American universities. Moreover, it is widely understood that these competences are a ticket to social mobility. As a result, higher education has become the port of entry to most professionalized occupations. Indeed, colleges have become the gatekeepers for many highly respected occupations. Without a credential from one of these schools, it is virtually impossible to be hired for some jobs or to obtain licenses and/or certification for others. In other words, a college education can be a *sine qua non* to occupational placement.

Among the specialties currently taught on college campuses are medicine, law, nursing, radiology, physical therapy, accounting, mathematics, statistics, marketing, finance, systems analysis, computer programming, teaching, mechanical engineering, electronic engineering, civil engineering, architecture, biology, genetics, pharmacology, chemistry, physics, geology, geography, oceanography, meteorology, social work, psychology, economics, police science, political science, anthropology, foreign languages, history, literature, journalism, art, music, and sociology. There are many others, including a host of newly hatched disciplines that have yet to win their spurs. (Among these I include women's studies, black studies, and environmentalism.)

Also featured on some campuses are subjects that should not make the cut. These do not demand the intellectual horsepower historically associated with professionalism nor require much in the way of the self-direction or interpersonal leadership. Among these are carpentry, culinary arts, pipefitting, and auto mechanics. As important as these skills are, they require no more than a community college education and often no more than a high school degree. The competences learned are real and worthy of respect but are not as demanding as professionalized ones. Many, in fact, are best learned on the job or through an apprenticeship. Chiefly concerned with neither people nor data, they are thing-oriented and therefore benefit from hands-on practice.

As impolitic as it is to say, these non-college specialties are not intellectual in nature. As a consequence, most do not require the intelligence needed to master professionalized skills. Some reformers believe that IQ it totally malleable. They assume that with the proper upbringing, they can cultivate above average intellectual abilities in anyone. This is a pipe dream. The "g" factor that was once assumed to be heritable and therefore the font of all intelligence has not been definitively established, but that intellectual aptitudes include a genetic component has been (Herrnstein and Murray, 1994). The simple truth is that many people do not possess the intelligence to become proficient at the materials colleges teach. This is not a moral failing, but it should be a disqualification for higher education. Just as people with poor eye/hand coordination should not expect to make the first team in baseball, so those with weak intellectual abilities should look elsewhere than college for a promising career. It must always be remembered that no matter how robust their educational ambitions, they will have to compete with rivals who bring more candlepower to the enterprise.

Nor does the acquisition of a self-directed, technical expertise end with obtaining the appropriate degree. Nowadays it has become a cliché to say that a college commencement is a beginning. This is tediously repeated precisely because it is true. That which is learned on college campuses is never fully sufficient to instill professional prowess. It can provide a foundation, but this must be built upon. Individuals who have truly become self-directed use this orientation to keep on learning. They understand that competent decisions require both judgment and information. They further understand that neither of these has reached its apex upon college graduation. Both must be continually refined if a person is to be worthy of authority.

This is why it has also become a cliché to recommend lifelong learning. Individuals who are motivated to be the best they can be need to remain open to new knowledge and improved skills. To do less is to fall behind the competition. In the long run, it is the equivalent of inferior intellectual capacities. Consequently, colleges must not only impart information; they must inculcate the techniques needed to keep learning. Their graduates have to become intellectuals in the broadest sense of the term or they will not be able to develop shared strategies worthy of deference. Having fallen behind their peers, they will not be able to adjust in a world where knowledge is expanding at an exponential rate.

So how can lifelong learning be instilled? The most fundamental skill is reading. It is not for nothing that college entrance exams stress reading comprehension. In an environment of uncertainty, by far the largest reservoir of relevant knowledge can be found in written form. Colleagues who possess the necessary know-how can be helpful, but they are not always available or sufficiently well versed in the relevant details. Likewise, clients, friends and family members may assist—but then again, they may not. Books, journals, and the Internet can compensate for these deficiencies. These can tap into information developed by prominent experts, both living and dead. As such, they provide answers or at least clues to potential answers. It is a matter of knowing where to look and how to take advantage of what is found.

A university education can be invaluable in developing these abilities. If it encourages reading, it helps pierce a barrier non-readers may never penetrate. When reading comes easily, the utility of consulting references does not seem as daunting. More than this, college courses that mandate reading heavy-duty materials provide practice in "deep reading" (Carr, 2010). Nowadays, the omnipresence of the Internet has fostered a culture of "grazing." Facebook, Twitter, and Google have encouraged habits of flitting from one sound bite to another. Short attention spans promote a hunger for scintillating factoids that are forgotten almost as quickly as they are scanned. Research has demonstrated that disconnected pieces of information enter the short-term memory, but if they are not consolidated, they never make it to the long-term memory. As a result, it is as if they had never been examined. Worse still, because they are unavailable for further processing, they cannot help solve problems for which their significance has never been established.

Deep reading is different. A book, for instance, can be read at leisure and assimilated step by step. A person can think about new ideas as they come forward and conjure with their connections to old ideas. This establishes networks of memories that can be called upon when new associations suggest they might be useful. Such an ability is vital for competent problem solving. In its absence, decisions are made without consulting what should be readily available data. Colleges can help would-be professionals avoid this pitfall by requiring that books and journals be read—and read carefully. As might be expected, this is often a challenge at mid- and lower-level schools. Because many of their students find reading uncomfortable, tangible efforts must be made to inculcate the habit.

Also crucial to professionalization and self-direction is communication—both oral and written. Decisions that cannot be effectively communicated might as well not be made. If others cannot determine what is desired, they can scarcely benefit from the most competent instructions. To motivate others, a person must connect with clarity and verve. A university education can enhance this ability by stressing assignments in writing and speaking. When employers come to college campuses to recruit talent, they frequently complain that graduates are not proficient writers. The grammar and spelling of these alumni are atrocious, and their capacity to convey complex ideas is minimal. Since a great deal of commercial activity is nowadays memo and communiqué driven, this can be a serious deficit. A proposal, for instance, that is not articulately written may have difficulty being persuasive. Neither one's customers nor subordinates are liable to be impressed with what is intended but not clarified. Worse still, they may not care. This is bad for business, bad for the bottom line, and bad for the prospects of a promotion.

It is also bad politics, and since political skills can make the difference between success and failure in business, government, and nonprofits, those who hope to be social leaders cannot afford to neglect their writing skills. Once more the elite universities generally have less difficulty with this. Fortunately, college courses that insist upon original papers can remedy potential deficiencies for working- and lower-class students. Because good writing derives from practice, they must be provided the opportunity to practice. This will help them overcome fears of the written word, thereby enhancing their interpersonal competence.

Fears of public speaking can also be addressed. It is often said that one of the most terrifying moments for many people occurs when they must stand up and talk before a group of strangers. Before they begin, they imagine how badly they will stumble and how badly they will be judged. In their mind's ear, they hear the unspoken ridicule directed their way, and the gales of silent laughter at their expense. Hence, with knees trembling, they proceed to make fools of themselves. Whether mumbling inaudibly or mangling their logic, they do not communicate what they desire. Here too the remedy is practice. Classrooms that encourage a dialogue between students and professors, as well as periodic presentations, take the sting out of public speaking. Not everyone will become a skilled orator but then again, few have to. All that is necessary is to improve the ability to share technical expertise when the need arises.

Self-Knowledge

Apart from technical knowledge, self-directed professionals benefit from social skills. Because they must work with others, they must be able to coordinate activities. A capacity to write and speak provides the beginnings of what is needed. Also of value is an awareness of how others are likely to react. To communicate clearly that which does not have the intended effect is comparable to having communicated ineptly. As a result, those who mistake the nature of their audiences are not likely to be effective leaders. Their leadership is not usually acted upon because their initiatives are not internally accepted. This was Chester Barnard's (1938) conclusion in the *Functions of the Executive,* and it is a true today as when he wrote about it more than half a century ago.

Consequently, those intent on joining a democratic elite must know what makes others tick. They must understand what these persons can do and why they might choose to do it. But first they must understand themselves. We, all of us, have abilities and limitations. Furthermore, we, all of us, have some things we desire and things we do not. To assume that we are interchangeable with other people is thus a profound mistake. We humans are unique and therefore what we accomplish is shaped by who we are. Would-be leaders, whose choices are not influenced by this awareness, are not building on their strengths. In the end, however expert they may be technically, their leadership is unlikely to be effective.

As already noted, self-knowledge is likewise crucial to understanding others. We humans differ, but we are also alike in crucial dimensions. Our basic equipment is remarkably similar. Thus, we all have comparable emotional and cognitive faculties. And we all make choices utilizing parallel techniques. This means that when we face an identical environment, we tend to have analogous responses. We do not, of course, respond in exactly the same way, partly because our circumstances differ and partly because our temperaments and intellects do as well. Nevertheless, when we imaginatively place ourselves in the shoes of others, we can often come up with a reasonably close approximation of what they are experiencing. This procedure, which George Herbert Mead (1934) called role-taking, is essential to competent social functioning. Without it, we are unable to estimate how others will act. Thus, what we choose to do commonly derives—and should derive—in large part from what we predict they will do. We would not, for instance, force a public dance upon a person who has just lost a beloved parent.

Role-taking, however, begins with accurate self-knowledge. Individuals who are not in touch with their own responses have difficulty assessing those of others. Self-knowledge, in turn, begins with introspection. To be accurately self-aware, a person must be able to look inside with reasonable clarity. Those who cannot—or will not—are condemned to remain ignorant of essential information. What they have been told about themselves by others may or may not be true. These others, it must be remembered, often have ulterior motives. Nor are outsiders always in the best position to perceive what can be known about one's self by oneself. This is particularly so with regard to unconscious feelings and beliefs. An individual is far better situated to know about these than is any external observer. Still, this knowledge can only be ascertained by those who seek it.

It also turns out that there is a social class difference in the proclivity to engage in introspection. The upper middle classes are far more likely to examine their interiors than are the lower classes. Persons who have experienced a great many failures in life usually do not want to see what they fear is present. They suspect that their difficulties derive from personal defects; hence, they would rather not confirm these. Those who possess a sense of control are, in contrast, less anxious about what they may find. This provides them with the additional benefit of being able to peer into the psyches of others. In the end, because they have a better comprehension of the lay of the land, they usually make better decisions.

Colleges can foster self-knowledge by encouraging students to look inward. They should not, however, engage in classroom psychotherapy. This is not the reason students attend college, nor is it fair to expose their personal secrets to strangers, even if they agree to do so. No one can know beforehand if what is revealed might be damaging to the analysand (Fein, 2011a). Besides, college professors are not trained to be therapists. Most have neither the knowledge nor the temperament for the job. Worse yet, they do not have the time or support services to protect people from their internal conflicts. To imply that they will and then to fall short could inflict grave psychic damage.

Nonetheless, introspection can be promoted. Questions can be asked and subjects can be taught that demonstrate the importance of knowing oneself. Papers can likewise be assigned and books read that endorse self-examination. Moreover, what takes place outside the classroom often involves self-analysis. Placing a group of young adults in close proximity and introducing them to a host of new ideas is an invitation for them to speak to each other about how these are affecting them. Because they are at a stage in their life where they are exploring their identities, most can scarcely be persuaded to desist from such probing. They will want to know about themselves; hence, they use one another as sounding boards for their private investigations.

When all goes well, this will be accompanied by a surge in independent thinking. Having been cut loose from their families of origin, they will ask themselves what *they* believe, rather than what their parents and siblings want them to believe. Universities have boasted of how they promote "critical thinking," but this is neither always honest nor their highest priority (Sowell, 2009, 2013b). Too often, what professors mean by critical thinking is being critical of the ideas and values they oppose. Nowadays, this is apt to mean a critique of capitalism and American exceptionalism (Lipset, 1996; Wood and Toscano, 2013). What should be occurring instead are efforts to get students to think for themselves. Much as middle class parents encourage self-direction by asking their children what they believe, college professors can foster the same in the classroom. Students who are presented with conflicting ideas can be asked to use facts and logic to come to their own conclusions. Indeed, faculty members intent on cultivating entourages of disciples are frequently frustrated by students who change their minds once their grades are posted. Nor is this a bad thing. Authority has its virtues, but if it cannot be trumped by personal reevaluations, self-direction has been thwarted.

Knowledge of Others

One of the hallmarks of middle-class status is cosmopolitanism. Rather than the local orientation of the lower classes, higher-ranking folks are open to peoples and ideas that differ from the ones they encountered when growing up. As inhabitants of a larger world, they expand their horizons to include others they had not previously known. A university education can assist in this process. Both in the classroom and outside of it, it can introduce a revolving cast of unexpected characters.

In recent years, colleges have bragged about fostering diversity. In defense of affirmative action, they have argued that bringing students with different backgrounds to campus provides a benefit for all. Majorities get to know minorities, thereby discovering that they are all human and that even odd cultures have validity. This, however, is only partly true. Efforts at forced desegregation, whether in schools or housing, have demonstrated that learning occurs when mixing is voluntary (Deutsch and Collins, 1951). Those forcibly compelled to interact with others often erect barriers that inhibit insights. Indeed, the effect is frequently to increase antagonisms.

This can, however, be avoided. Providing opportunities, rather than insisting upon them, can make all the difference. For instance, by encouraging study abroad, as opposed to enforcing sensitivity training, schools can open eyes that had previously been closed. In particular, by allowing students to discover one another on their own terms, learners can carefully and at their own pace exchange notes about who they are and why they are that way. Most students are actually quite curious about the differences they encounter. Thus, if allowed the space to explore, they make useful discoveries.

Members of the upper middle class also tend to be cultural omnivores. It is almost impossible to tell in advance what music they will like or which foods they will favor. Because they are open to many options, they have multiple possibilities from which to choose. Also, because they are less threatened by differences, they can go in unexpected directions. Happily, this too improves their chances of understanding how others differ. It means that they are not afraid to take classes about unfamiliar peoples and do not reflexively reject their lifestyles (McWhorter, 2003). This in turn improves their ability to understand the social and psychological dynamics of strangers.

Social Knowledge

The world in which we live is composed of more than individuals and things. Potential leaders must also be aware of the social structures and disparate cultures that illuminate how people behave. We humans do not treat others in the same ways. We make distinctions in how we relate to individuals because we are immersed in ways of life that encourage some forms of interaction while forbidding others. Persons who cannot tell the difference between what is allowed and what is not are bound to suffer. Their decisions are not respected. To the contrary, they elicit antipathy.

Social structures are enduring patterns of interpersonal behavior. They include things like our economic, political, and familial arrangements. To consider the last of these, we do not regard spouses as interchangeable. Unlike sardines, we distinguish between individuals and hence, if we have a binding attachment to one, we do not throw this connection overboard without a jot of inner turmoil. Similarly, we do not regard children as transposable. Few parents would entertain a proposal to swap their children for those of their neighbors. For better or worse, emotional ties and social constraints bind us all. Individuals who fail to understand this cannot maintain stable family relationships. They may desire love, but an inability to honor interpersonal commitments precludes attaining it. Nor can they respect the bonds holding others together if these are invisible to them.

Similarly, people who do not understand how commercial markets work find themselves at a disadvantage if they seek economic success. If they, for instance, have no idea about how supply and demand are connected through price, they may invest in unsalable items or purchase goods at inflated rates. In other words, they are unlikely to make a profit. They may also endorse social policies that lead to a ruinous inflation or a protracted depression. In short, people who elect to remain economic illiterates are apt to inflict suffering on themselves and others.

Political illiterates can be just as dangerous. Bored to tears by current events and innocent of the differences between political systems, they provide fertile ground for demagogues and mountebanks. Large-scale democracies are dependent upon an informed electorate. But more than this, they require participation, even if at a distance, by unelected leaders. If those who are responsible for important social decisions do not make their views known, they—and others—are liable to be handicapped by government policies that harm their respective interests.

Higher education can address these issues by introducing students to the rudiments of economics, political science, and personal relationships. Because we have learned a great deal about these, ignorance is unnecessary. The same can be said about cultures. The various ways of life people adopt have also been studied in great detail. Thus, divergent norms and values, as well as belief systems and rituals, have been and can be deciphered. The same goes for technologies, symbolic practices, and aesthetic productions. In fact, once these are appreciated, peoples who initially seemed very different come into sharper focus. Now they appear human, and it becomes possible to do business with them in ways that benefit all concerned. In this case, it is the social sciences and the humanities that are able to provide the key to informed decisions. They can open windows to otherwise unforeseen options.

Motivation

Professionals, it must again be recalled, are self-motivated experts. Their knowledge—whether technical, personal, interpersonal, or social—is therefore only half the equation. They must also be personally disposed to making competent choices without external pressure. Supposedly self-directed persons who cannot do so are not self-directed. They may be academic experts, but if others habitually impose their determinations upon them, they are followers, not leaders. Consequently, those who intend to become professionalized must cultivate the disposition to make good choices.

EQ

Daniel Goleman (1995, 2006) popularized an interesting—if misleading—concept. He called it the emotional quotient (EQ) in emulation of the IQ (intelligence quotient). Unfortunately, neither he nor anyone else had a good way to measure or define this capacity. In any event, the IQ, despite its methodological limitations, exhibits a face validity. Most people believe that some individuals are more intelligent than others and that this difference is at least partially heritable. They further believe that disparities in intelligence are correlated with disparities in social success. EQ, on the other hand, does not imply heritable differences. It does, however, contend that emotional abilities are associated with interpersonal success. The claim is often expressed thus: while a high IQ can get you a job, a high EQ enables you to keep it.

Given the difficulties in defining EQ and/or demonstrating a genetic linkage, a slightly different concept, one that the preserves its fundamental meaning, may prove more useful. "Emotional maturity" (Fein, 2011a) comes close to what Goleman intended yet emphasizes socialization rather than biology. We humans are all born with roughly the same emotional equipment. Thus, we are all capable of getting angry or becoming frightened. Correspondingly, we all have a capacity for love and, when we experience a loss, we all grow sad. What differs is how these effects are expressed and/or implemented. The primitive emotions with which we are born must be tamed before we become adults. Simply growing angry as an infant might (e.g., by biting one's mother's breast) is unacceptable, even for adolescents. To the contrary, we are expected to learn controlled ways of getting irritated; ways appropriate to the circumstances in which we find ourselves.

Self-directed persons are particularly in need of socialized emotions. If they cannot, for instance, deal with their fears, they may be too frightened to make competent decisions. Primitive emotions (i.e., unsocialized ones) tend to go overboard. Especially when they are intense, they can be expressed dangerously and irrationally. Fears become terrors, and people run away from perceived dangers with such blind haste that they stumble into greater dangers. Likewise, anger becomes so extreme that it is transformed into rage and commits savage murders. It is therefore crucial that self-directed people master strong feelings. A failure to do so could make their decisions worse than unreliable; they would likely be stupid and unstable.

Most successful people develop emotional maturity within their families of origin. Were this not so, it is doubtful they would acquire the academic credentials for admission into a decent university. Their parents, especially if they are middle class, probably modeled the appropriate behaviors and instructed them on techniques for remaining in control. Nonetheless, some hard edges usually persist. It is these a college education can smooth out.

It must again be emphasized, however, that this does not entail "in class" psychotherapy. Formal mechanisms of education are remarkably inept in dealing with intense emotions. The classroom, with its emphasis on cognitive achievement, does not offer a suitable venue, nor do untrained professors, who do not have deep or enduring relationships with their students, possess the means of taming their unconscious passions. Therapy, if it is necessary, is best left to the experts. As a result, many universities offer counseling services, and it is to these that unstable students should resort.

Meanwhile, there is a form of emotional maturation where higher education can be effectual. Because most college students are transitioning from teenager to adult, they can be assisted in weathering the tempests of this period. Resocialization is the process whereby individuals relinquish social roles that have lost their ability to satisfy personal needs so that they can replace these with better ones (Fein, 2011a). Clearly, younger college students are in the process of doing precisely this. This is what the wild gyrations witnessed on college campuses are usually about. The tempestuous parties, the binge-drinking, the sexual experimentation, the sports enthusiasms, and the inconsistent classroom performances are of a piece. So too are the anxiety and depression that frequently punctuate this changeover. These are all aspects of letting go of what was in preparation for embracing what is to come.

Erik Erikson (1968) wrote of the frequent need for a psychosocial moratorium on the journey to self-discovery. People often require a time-out, during which the demands of family and work slack off, so that they can focus on the self. This egoism, which in normal circumstances can be disruptive, when found in the midst of a personal transition can provide the room to make dramatic changes. Much like a caterpillar enters a chrysalis eventually to emerge as a butterfly, college students afforded the room to transform their identities can make strides toward emotional maturity. In large part, all that is needed to facilitate this makeover is tolerance. If instead of carping on the inconsistencies of this interlude, the young are allowed to develop according to their personal schedules, the outcomes can be positive.

Nonetheless, college professors really are not psychotherapists. Though some are tempted to behave as if they were, they cannot coach students on how to attain emotional maturity. Unable to commit the time or emotional resources to the job, even those who know how must stand back and permit events to unfold as they will. Faculty members can, however, serve as models for how to handle strong emotions. They can also present classroom materials that address these issues. Even so, they must not engage in unconscious interpretations as a Freudian (Freud, 1953–1974) might or in emotional reflection as Rogerians do

(Rogers, 1951, 1961). Sometimes refraining from doing harm is the best that can be managed.

In the meantime, persons even less equipped to engage in professional interventions than are professors can assist in furthering the necessary work. I am speaking of the peers of those undergoing personal growth. Fellow students, often themselves engaged in emotional maturation, can join in a community of self-exploration. Much of what mature adults look upon as jejune posturings are part of this process. Ethereal philosophical speculations, spirited debates about the meaning of life, and visions of personal grandeur may seem like intellectual naval-gazing, whereas they are better understood as emotional adventures. They are about coming to terms with one's fears, loves, rages, and sadness.

Self-Discipline

Closely related to developing emotional control is self-discipline. When we are young, much of what we do is at the behest of adults. Parents, teachers, and ministers tell us what they expect, and we have little choice but to comply. The directions we follow and the sanctions we endure are therefore often external in nature. To become self-directed, however, these controls must be internalized. An individual must decide what needs doing and then apply the necessary effort to get it done.

The first step in this process is determining a suitable goal. Since there are so many potential options, this requires a clear head. A person must take the time to think things through and to make comparisons grounded in facts and logic. Jumping to conclusions or embracing an impetuous spontaneity are rarely productive. Those, for example, who get carried away by strong emotions, generally come to grief on the shoals of their own zeal. It is therefore necessary to achieve the emotional maturity to hold strong feelings in abeyance while making important decisions. To do less is to place oneself at the mercy of fate.

But this is not all that is required. Good decisions must be implemented. Effort must be exerted to convert possibilities into actualities. This, however, is not always fun. The work needed can be arduous, even dangerous. Some educators maintain that learning should always be enjoyable. This is nonsense. While pleasure can motivate people to engage in important endeavors, many vital activities are distasteful. Life is not composed of all desserts; there is broccoli to be consumed as well. Thus, those who cannot discipline themselves to do what is unpleasant usually fall behind those who can. Unwilling to work hard, they have little to show at the end of the day.

We who inhabit a wealthy techno-commercial society sometimes forget that this good fortune did not materialize out of thin air. A rampant sense of entitlement has convinced many people that they should receive the necessities of life—and many of its frills—for free. As we shall see, this attitude is widespread on college campuses. Yet it is self-defeating. Few people who do not work to get good grades obtain them. Fewer still achieve success after they graduate. Individuals who cannot motivate themselves to serious exertion normally get little done. They are human grasshoppers who feed off the labors of others.

Then again, most students do not find a college education to be like a sprint. It is more like a marathon, where effort must be applied over several years. Often, it takes personal discipline to keep coming to classes, many of which are dull. It also takes effort to research and write respectable papers. Similarly, it takes stick-to-itiveness to read and comprehend technical books and treatises. In fact, it has been claimed that the primary function of a college education is to establish that a graduate has the discipline to complete arduous tasks. Employers take this as evidence that he or she has the character to put up with the nonsense sure to exist on the job.

Ambition and Initiative

Why go to college when it can be so grueling? Yes, it takes discipline and emotional maturity, but why subject oneself to so much misery? For most people, the answer is ambition. They hope to do better than others in the race to the top of the greasy pole. A desire for social mobility is our legacy as a hierarchical species (Fein, 2012a). Virtually all of us are motivated to rank above at least some others. We realize this may take effort, but we fervently want to be winners rather than losers. A university education is pursued precisely because it is perceived as a means toward this end.

We also know that many of our rivals are equally ambitious. They too want to move ahead, and if they can, they will do it at our expense. If some students do not realize this before entering college, they will discover it on campus. Not everyone gets good grades; not everyone receives glowing recommendations upon graduation. Many hope to reach the apex of the academic pyramid, yet relatively few do. There is a vigorous *competition* to come out best. Individuals are pitted against each other to determine who will excel. If they are not prepared for this contest; if they are not internally motivated to engage in it, their prospects are dim. Both in school and afterwards, go-getters are more apt to achieve leadership positions. Both self-motivated and tutored in the rigors of competition, they better endure the struggles for economic and political success.

Once more, social status makes a difference and therefore a disparity in what colleges must instill. Students from deprived backgrounds are frequently intimidated by the need to compete. As a consequence, the less elite schools they are more likely to attend must be alert this problem. They need to realize that many poor and working-class students fear that they do not have what it takes to keep up with their middle-class peers. These learners must thus be disabused of this concern. Ironically, if schools stress cooperation over disciplined competition, they may further erode the confidence of these nervous learners. Instead, they need to match students with tasks at which they can excel, thereby confirming their abilities. At the same time, substantial demands must be made, lest undergraduates acquire a phony self-assurance that later crumbles under real-world pressures.

Students should also find that a university education prepares them to exercise initiative. They may, for instance, be asked to write papers or make presentations where what is required is not spelled out. It will therefore be up to them to determine how to proceed. To achieve this, they may need both ingenuity and a willingness to take risks. Rather than wait to be guided toward a predetermined goal, they must figure things out for themselves. Of course, they might be wrong—or they could be right. This is the essence of self-direction.

This challenge is also a precursor of creativity. As has been indicated, self-directed people often make decisions in an environment of uncertainty. Not only may they not know what is best; they may not know where to get started. Indeed, they may have to generate directions from scratch. Where others have not tread, they may be called upon to be pathfinders. Perhaps they will have to make unexpected discoveries or invent new technologies. This, when it occurs, is leadership at its best. Clearly, colleges cannot automatically cultivate genius, but they can encourage originality. Instead of demanding that students follow in the exact footsteps of their mentors, they can reward innovation.

Then there is the issue of personal responsibility. Self-directed people must be prepared to shoulder this burden. When they are authorized to make choices, they must do their best to make competent ones. And when they make mistakes, they must be willing to accept the blame.

As important, they must be ready to fix what is broken. If not, then others would be foolish to entrust them with power. Here too university training can be of use. Few students make it through four or more years without major missteps. The question then becomes, how do they handle these? Do they correct their errors, or do they perseverate in their foolishness? If it is the former, they gain experience in dealing with difficulties similar to those that are sure to arise later on.

Values

Individuals delegated to make important choices must possess internalized standards of behavior. If they are to make good decisions without consulting higher authorities, they must be committed to socially acceptable objectives. These must be built into their psyches such that they are pursued without being externally enforced. Leaders who do not have good moral compasses are apt to fly off in dangerous directions. Still, the crucial guideposts do not derive chiefly from higher education. Although many educators claim this is their central mission, theirs is a secondary role. These values too originate primarily from one's family of origin.

Once more, however, professors can serve as important role models. They can exemplify what it means to be fair and honest and diligent. Many students do, in fact, pattern their conduct after admired mentors. But professors cannot—and should not—enforce a predetermined set of virtues, save for maintaining standards directly related to the educational process, such as rules against cheating and plagiarism. They may personally believe in the value of merit, expertise, and responsibility, but the best they can manage is live by these and to reward their expression. Furthermore, while they can apply self-directed values in the classroom and recommend their emulation, they cannot ensure that they will be honored elsewhere. To attempt moral indoctrination is not only unfair; it is impractical. Research has shown, for instance, that sensitivity training does not inculcate habits of tolerance (Dobbin, 2009). Individuals can, to be sure, be coerced into expounding what is demanded, whereas their actual attitudes remain largely unaffected. Nor is it the place of professors to impose social commitments. This is not why students take their classes; hence, it is unreasonable to burden them with the personal hobbyhorses of their instructors.

Nowadays with the conflict between liberals and conservatives having generated more heat than light, surreptitious efforts to impose one side or the other are shameful. Too often professors imply that what they believe is true and therefore must be learned as factual. This is dishonest. It confuses disciplinary achievements with personal loyalties. And while professors are allowed to be moral activists on their own time, this is not their classroom role. At the very least, they must inform students of the difference between what they have faith in and what they professionally know.

One major exception applies to religious institutions. Because these schools openly advertise their value orientations, students and parents know what to expect. Secular institutions, however, have no such mandate (French, Lukianoff, and Silverglate, 2005). Therefore, to the extent that they provide a values education, it must be based on neutral evaluations. To illustrate, they can provide courses on particular religious and/or ideological perspectives without endorsing these. They can also review surveys of socially held values.

Beyond this, schools can develop cultures that reinforce values, such as honesty and fairness. They may also develop reputations for supporting particular ideological orientations. Hence, overtly liberal institutions can underline their allegiance to greater equality, while overtly conservative ones can emphasize freedom. In any event, students will most likely develop their own belief systems that they pass along to entering freshmen, irrespective of what the college authorities desire.

Last, an introduction to the middle-class virtues may be most useful to non-middle-class students. Elite universities can usually assume that most enrollees are familiar with these, whereas mid- and lower-level institutions need to be more explicit in encouraging them. Thus, while some degree of cheating is virtually universal among students (upwards of 80 percent admit to it), the temptation to crib papers off the Internet is especially intense among students with poor writing skills. Particularly with so much research being done by consulting Wikipedia, norms regarding plagiarism need to be rigorously reinforced.

Conclusions

If higher educational institutions are to be constructed with an eye to promoting professionalization, their programs should encourage self-direction. More specifically, the courses made available and how these are taught ought to advance independent thinking and the personal motivation to apply the skills and knowledge inculcated. Too rigid an insistence on "the one best way," however, ought to be avoided. Whatever is intended with respect to quality by insisting on uniformity, this attitude squelches the individuality needed for students to become competent decision makers.

Ancillary programs should also encourage self-direction. As will soon become evident, learning does not always take place in the classroom and therefore, self-direction should be promoted by living arrangements and non-curricular activities as well. Too restricted a focus on academic criteria can actually interfere with developing the personal characteristics needed to become intellectually independent. The ideal should therefore be "a community of learners" where faculty and students participate, both within the classroom and without, in encouraging autonomous thought.

Colleges and universities must likewise return to the ideal of "a marketplace of ideas." The truth is most likely to emerge when competing ideas are allowed to contend, so as to determine which are valid. Enforcing intellectual orthodoxies is thus a prescription for ignorance and conformity. If our knowledge were complete, we might profitably demand that only it be taught. But it is not absolute. We humans are fallible. Furthermore, because our biases can interfere with our judgments, it is imperative that we allow critiques of even widely held beliefs. It is this that encourages genuinely "critical" thinking.

Colleges and universities must therefore tolerate dissent. Genuine debate cannot occur if out-groups are ostracized or punished. Too often nowadays, majorities pose as beleaguered minorities and use this as an excuse to suppress the opposition. Thus, articles go unpublished and tenure is denied to professors, while students get bad grades and/or inferior recommendations. This atmosphere is not conducive to new ideas or an honest evaluation of merit. Nor does it encourage independent reasoning.

One way to achieve this is for schools to sponsor regular and honest debate. Controversial subjects should be vetted on campus. One of the best formats for doing so is open discussion regarding social, political, and intellectual questions. If this is held between committed partisans who are free to be candid, self-directed ideas can be stimulated. Failing this, neither technical, nor self, nor other, nor social knowledge can be effectively inculcated. A self-satisfied conventionality that places blinders over students' eyes may promulgate the prevailing wisdom but not legitimate learning.

Nor must it be forgotten that self-direction depends as much on attitude as a store of information. Personal maturity, self-discipline, creativity, responsibility, and professionalized values are all more difficult to transmit than are facts or technical skills. This, however, does not diminish their importance. Institutions of higher education that do not make these a priority are therefore deficient in what they seek. Nevertheless, it must be admitted that these goals are amorphous and emotional. As a consequence, intentional efforts must be kept in mind when designing and implementing academic improvements. Here too what counts is what colleges and universities are, as opposed to what they say they are.

The above qualities and abilities are, in fact, in line with what many employers say they desire (Stratford, 2013). For years, surveys have indicated that business persons want employees who are capable of innovation and who have demonstrated "an ability to think critically, communicate clearly, and solve complex problems . . ." (AAC&U, 2013). More than nine of ten also seek new hires who exhibit ethical judgment, integrity, intercultural skills, and an ability to engage in lifelong learning. Moreover, even when the jobs in question are technical, exposure to the liberal arts is favored. Put together, these dispositions indicate that those operating in the midst of our mass techno-commercial society clearly prefer employees who are flexible thinkers and trustworthy decision makers. What, then, is this other than self-direction?

6

A Self-Directed Curriculum

The Core Curriculum

Assuming that promoting professionalization and self-direction are at the heart of what a higher education should be about, we must now enter the realm of specifics. We need to examine what should be taught and, to some extent, how it should be taught. Here is where we get to scrutinize what has been done, what reformers insist needs to be done, and what, in fact, is most conducive to imparting a self-motivated expertise to those who can best apply it. Moreover, because we are finally getting down to brass tacks, much of the following will be controversial. Generalizations can be stretched to cover contradictory approaches, whereas particulars tend to be more difficult to reconcile. The question is, therefore, which academic policies genuinely promote self-direction? Which are, in fact, suitable for the techno-commercial world we inhabit?

Most universities require students to take an assortment of mandatory courses. These are usually presented as a minimum of what every educated person should know. For the most part, they are actually the lowest common denominator of what every self-directed person should know. The goal is thus to provide students with a broad overview of the world and of the societies in which they are about to participate. However parochial their individual upbringings, diverse undergraduates are to be introduced to a larger slice of reality than they have previously encountered.

Whether consciously intended or not, this usually exposes young learners to the beginning elements of self-direction. In addition to the technical skills they will need, they are introduced to the social understandings demanded of democratic leaders. To this end, they are encouraged to acquire knowledge of themselves, of others, and of the social structures and cultures in which they will eventually operate. They are also asked to engage in studies that uncover their personal motives. As self-directed professionals in the making, they are likewise expected to benefit from the emotional maturity, self-discipline, initiative, responsibility, and moral values they will hopefully internalize in the process of becoming more cosmopolitan and self-assured (Durkheim, 1961).

Many colleges expedite this process by requiring students to take a prescribed set of core courses. These are presumably selected because they have demonstrated broad utility. In fact, they have largely accumulated through accretion. Both history and self-interested lobbying efforts have conspired to mold the basic prerequisites of most universities. Moreover, despite recurring efforts to modernize these, their outlines tend to remain stable. This is because, as participants in a common culture, those responsible for improving them generally come to similar conclusions. These administrators, faculty members, and interested laypersons usually have been inspired by equivalent sources; hence, they see things the same way (Fain, 2012a).

Nonetheless, what has emerged generally does achieve many social needs. Self-direction and professionalization may not have been consciously sought, but they are usually promoted by these courses. There are, regrettably, notable exceptions and a troubling drift away from implanting valuable aptitudes. Even so, the standard approach retains much merit. As such, the prevailing core does not need to be jettisoned as much as refined. Its impact did not cause the college bubble, although it has sometimes accelerated it (D'Souza, 1991).

So let us look at what most colleges require. To begin with, they ask students to take courses in the humanities (Sarton, 1962; Nussbaum, 1997; Durden, 2012). These subjects, the lineage of which traces back many centuries, center on literature and history. Their goal is to teach fundamental language skills and to place the students' experience in historical context (Davies, 1997; Duchesne, 2011). With respect to English studies, communication skills are considered essential. Likewise, with respect to history, an awareness of why others behave as they do is believed vital. To these are usually added courses in the social sciences. Economics and political science generally have first call, although one or the other of psychology, sociology, and anthropology is also likely to be mandated. Here too the objective is to understand the social structures in which graduates will eventually operate. Fortunately, self-knowledge and internalized motivation are often a side effect of these courses—in part because they are concerned with appreciating individual differences.

The hard sciences, to which mathematics is usually appended, similarly make the cut. One or the other of physics, chemistry, and biology and sometimes geology is characteristically required. Some schools, however, offer a watered-down course on science. Given the technological sophistication of contemporary societies, this is deemed crucial to appreciating the ideas upon which this bounty is founded. While it is not expected that most students will make science a career, it is assumed that knowledge of science will make them more supportive of those who do.

Once foreign languages and classical studies were a regular part of this mix, but many universities have dropped these. Perceived as outdated, they are sometimes replaced by computer studies. This last is also declining in popularity, mostly because students now enter college with extensive computer skills. Less widely required are courses in communication that purport to teach how to speak and/or write. There has also been a tendency to include courses in study skills, yet these are judged as boondoggles by many students.

The next question is, how well do these efforts succeed at inculcating a critical minimum of knowledge? Do they, in fact, improve the self-direction habits of students? If not, should we modify what is taught or how it is taught? Let us begin by looking at the humanities.

The Humanities

By common consensus, the humanities are in trouble (Anderson, 1992). Subjects that were once the unquestioned soul of a college education have been reduced to hangers-on. Currently liable to be regarded as irrelevant, many fewer students major in English literature or history. Nor do most who are forced to take introductory courses in them rave about their worth. Generally considered dull and uninformative, they are endured rather than celebrated. This lack of enthusiasm also extends to those who teach these subjects. They too seem to have lost their conviction that these disciplines are valuable. Despite countless defenses of the necessity of restoring them to their former glory, the energy has gone out of these arguments.

This does not, however, mean that the study of literature and history are doomed to extinction. Nor does it indicate that they have nothing to offer in terms of self-direction. Quite the contrary, their contributions are indispensable. Let us start with English literature. If reading and writing are important, then courses that instill these are as well (Fitzhugh, 2011). Although other disciplines require language skills, they do not concentrate so completely on developing them. Literature courses that, by their very nature, mandate reading books and writing cogent reviews are well situated to impart symbolic skills. They can teach how to read, as well as how to communicate ideas. Thus, within their precincts, the art of reading and interpreting what is read are discussed for their own sake. Similarly, writing is critiqued in terms of style and cogency, not merely validity.

Reading books, essays, and poems and then writing about them (Zorn, 2013) is also infused with an emotional intensity. Formal classrooms, because they concentrate on cognitive truths, frequently shortchange our affective nature. They do not directly deal with personal motives because they emphasize value-neutral realities. Nor is the classroom equipped to deal with emotional outbursts. These are usually disruptive; hence discouraged. Indeed, some professors find it useful to pretend that we humans are fully rational—as opposed to passionate— animals.

Courses in English literature tend to be different. Because much reading is done independently and because much is saturated in emotion, students can be personally moved by their assignments. We humans are instinctive storytellers and story consumers (Gottschall, 2012). It is via narratives that we commonly understand both ourselves and others. We think in terms of plots and interpersonal motivations. As social animals, this is how our minds and viscera operate. It is the way we remember things and the way we learn to deal with distressing challenges. Much of this, it must be admitted, is vicarious, yet this too can be beneficial in that it helps us to keep otherwise overwhelming stimuli under reasonable control.

This mode of coping with emotional realities provides those who teach literature a window of opportunity. They can foster intro- and extro-spection in a manner few other disciplines can emulate. Thus, by utilizing narratives that stimulate self-examination, they can assist students in understanding themselves and others. Moreover, they can do so by arousing emotional reactions that bring these analyses to life. This makes it likely that what is discovered will stick. Having been exposed to three-dimensional experiences that are largely absent in other classes, students are better able to identify with what they observe. In the end, they learn more about themselves and others than at the beginning. But isn't this exactly the kind of knowledge that fosters self-direction? Isn't this what brings crucial choices into focus?

It might be supposed that given this advantage, English lit would be in great demand. True, students worry about the sorts of career these courses make available; nevertheless, their potential for personal growth should turn them into a valued adjunct to other studies. This, unfortunately, is often no longer the case, in part, because of what the discipline has become. Along with sociology and anthropology, its practitioners have been transformed into political radicals. Perhaps the best way to describe them is as "nihilistic idealists." On a certain level, they do not believe anything matters. Even so, they are committed to making the world a more humane place. Although many have lost their faith in what they teach, they remain devoted to improving the lot of humankind (Graybar, 2013).

The dilemma these professors face arises from their academic role. As scholars, they are expected to add to our knowledge. For some, this entails creative endeavors, but for most it centers on interpreting the works of others. They are to analyze the novels, plays, poems, and essays of significant authors and provide the public with novel insights. The trouble is that there are only so many works to be analyzed and many tens of thousands of faculty members who need to produce discerning analyses. Where, then, are individual professors to acquire the ideas that enable them to identify truths that others have not? This is more difficult than it might seem.

When I was an undergraduate, Freudianism reigned supreme. All sorts of works were reinterpreted to fit the psychoanalytic model. This was supposed to reveal emotional dynamics that, while not immediately apparent, were, in fact, the driving force behind what had been written. Eventually, however, Freud became passé. His obsolescence was accelerated by a surfeit of increasingly tedious reviews and by the emergence of feminism. With larger numbers of women attracted to the study of literature, they resented Freud's purported male chauvinism (Freud, 1953–1974). This business about "penis envy" and a "phallic stage" of development were obviously the result of a hegemonic conspiracy against women.

To the rescue soon rode the twin saviors of neo-Marxism and post-modernism. They explained why women had been disrespected and why the opinions of those doing the disrespecting did not matter. Nonetheless, these critiques were achieved at a price. To begin with, the Marxists claimed to elucidate the nature of social conflicts (Marx, 1967; Gramsci, 1977). They ostensibly demonstrated how competing social classes fought for dominance and how the victors exploited the losers. On the economic level, this entailed capitalists submerging proletarians; while on the gender level, men did the same to women. It was therefore incumbent upon decent human beings to promote a revolution whereby equality became the norm. Anything less was unjust. Moreover, literature, because it had been created under the dominance of the capitalists, needed to be "deconstructed" to rid it of its oppressive characteristics. This was essential if the underdogs—including women—were to attain their rightful status.

To this amalgam were added the nihilistic doctrines of the post-modernists (Derrida, 1997; Foucault, 1979). These thinkers argued that truth was unknowable. All any person had at his or her disposal were opinions. As a result, human interactions consisted primarily of narratives intended to influence. People sought to persuade others by way of the stories they told. This, of course, placed literature at the center of human endeavors and in so doing, appealed to the vanity of English professors. The problem was that it also removed the touchstone by which one could determine who was correct. If there were no absolute truths, then whose opinions were to prevail? In any event, for many academics, this quandary was of little concern. Dedicated to social justice, as promulgated by the neo-Marxists, they knew which objectives needed to be endorsed and they believed themselves courageous enough to endorse them.

All this made enough sense for this mishmash to emerge as the dominant literary perspective. Unfortunately, it was thoroughly incoherent. Asking a simple question can expose the difficulty. When post-modernists say that there is no truth, is what they say true? If it is true, then their statement is false. But if it is not true, then why does what they say matter? Why, if everything is a matter of persuasion, should the opinions of the post-modernists, or for that matter the neo-Marxists, be taken more seriously than those who disagree with them?

Just how disorienting this dilemma can be was unmasked in the case of Rigoberta Menchu (Menchu and Burgos-Debray, 1984; Patai, 2012). A Guatemalan peasant, she rose to prominence with the publication of an alleged memoir of surviving the revolution in her country. Her testament to the violence and injustice perpetrated against a supposedly peaceful indigenous people aroused worldwide sympathy. Indeed, so great did her celebrity become that she was awarded a Nobel Peace Prize. In the meantime, English professors made her book *I, Rigoberta Menchu*, a campus favorite. Students avidly read it as evidence of how

vicious elites could be and therefore as proof that they needed to be overthrown.

Even when the anthropologist David Stoll (2008) did research to demonstrate that what much of what Menchu claimed was untrue, a bevy of enthusiasts rushed to her defense. At first, they contended that Stoll was both dishonest and biased, but when most of what he wrote was vindicated, they changed their tack. The new justification was that the memoir was a "narrative" and therefore was not open to criticism based on its literal accuracy. It was emotionally true, as well as respectful of a disrespected minority; hence, it deserved to be honored. In other words, here were professors insisting that factual truth was irrelevant. What then were they teaching their students? If they objected to Stoll's bias, what of their own?

And so personal prejudices were elevated to preeminence. Political correctness and social justice triumphed over other considerations. What then was a college education for? If that which students read was selected on the basis of the moral commitments of their instructors, what happened to the pursuit of knowledge? What was to be the fate of a quality education, as opposed to a purely emotional one? Clearly, this trend undermined the credibility of English departments. If all they imparted were the idiosyncratic musings of left-wing eccentrics, why spend time with them? As a consequence, not completely gone yet definitely in eclipse were the writings of Shakespeare, Austen, and Dickens. The glimpses into the workings of the human heart provided by these "dead white males" (and a few women) were replaced by the hip-hop rantings of "street poets" and the diatribes of ideological pied pipers. All this made for an intellectual irrelevance directly opposed to the proclaimed desires of New-Wave professors. More and more, the only persons who cared about what they said were those who already believed in them.

History has not yet fallen into such disrepute, but it is not far behind. The proportion of radical activists in its ranks is not as large and therefore not as dominant. Nonetheless, the leftward skew is striking (Hoffer, 2004). The twin notions that capitalism and the American democratic system were responsible for corrupting the world seeped into the discipline's mainstream. What is often taught is consequently determined by political considerations. These interpretations influence what makes it into the classroom and what gets left out. Generally speaking, where previous generations were exposed to a narrative of American exceptionalism and its triumphant march to world

leadership, contemporary students learn of their country's shabby history of oppression and inequality.

Symptomatic of this development has been the popularity of Howard Zinn's (2010) *A People's History of the United States.* Zinn sought to correct the previous academic tendency to concentrate on political heroes and military adventures. Instead of celebrating the achievements of a few great men (and a handful of women), he focused on ordinary people. Their lives and experiences, rather than those of the tyrants who subjugated them, were at the center of his story. And yes, this was a "story." Incidents were selected and presented so as to further his goal (i.e., to demonstrate how elites systematically hold ordinary people in bondage). Blacks, women, and the poor were all portrayed as victimized. The establishment had rigged the game in its favor and then, just as the Marxists alleged, used their power to fool those whom they wronged into believing they had been helped. Zinn and those who agreed with him would see to it that this villainy was exposed (Loewen, 1995). They would tell the truth so that ordinary students were no longer hoodwinked.

Of course, the truth being told was the truth as these activists saw it. This meant that Sojourner Truth made it into their revised canon, while Thomas Edison was set aside. It also meant that Joseph McCarthy sometimes got more ink than George Washington. The point was to highlight virtually every injustice that could be found, while minimizing the accomplishments of what was regarded as the enemy camp. If called out on their biases, these scholars responded much as the literary people did. They too talked about the importance of "deeper" truths. According to them, the inevitable march of history, rather than a few transient events, deserved intellectual attention. Besides, value neutrality was grossly overrated. What counted was helping people, not being confined in the protracted examination of obscure facts.

As a consequence, political correctness became the order of the day. While some traditionalists held out, a majority in the discipline saw no difficulty in infusing their lessons with parables intended to have a desired effect. Where once history was considered dull because it demanded that students memorize incomprehensible names and dates, it retained a reputation for being tiresome because it was now predictably tendentious. Moreover, that which did not fit the preferred narrative slid to the cutting room floor. Evidently, it was essential that academics plow the ground for social reforms but not be so bold as to arouse public wrath. They could deceive, but this had to be more by

omission than commission. Thus, what was taught needed to be left wing, but this could be disguised by intellectually sounding rhetoric.

And so history, as an effort to put the present into perspective, languished. Rather than help students understand why the world had moved in the directions it did, an eccentric interpretation of events became ascendant. Not a marketplace of ideas but an arrogant left-wing hegemony took hold. Where self-direction could have benefited from both a balanced perspective and an honest discussion of historical dynamics, a new catechism arose. History did not come to life but was frozen in an ideological time warp. That which happened long ago was not seen in terms of human beings like ourselves who were struggling to deal with conditions unlike our own. To the contrary, individuals were presented as cardboard characters intended to convey a moral message. As a result, few students cared about them, because few could identify with them. To make matters worse, many academics insisted on interpreting the past in terms of the present. Because their political aims overshadowed their historical objectives, they did not help students understand why their ancestors thought as they did. This made bygone figures unsympathetic. They did not seem real; hence, they did not stimulate interest.

A parallel trend resulted in downplaying Western civilization. Because many academics were ashamed of the depredations produced by colonialism, they sought to resurrect the reputations of non-Western societies. As card-carrying relativists, these professors believed all cultures are of equal merit (Norris, 1997). None deserved greater attention because none was inherently superior. This meant that Africa, China, and India rated as much time as Europe or the United States. It did not matter that American students were the product of Western cultures. Nor was it important that Western standards had altered international conditions. This conviction was ethnocentric and therefore illegitimate. While it was true that a nativistic myopia had previously produced an unbalanced worldview, correctives prejudiced in other directions were no improvement. They made it difficult for students to understand the world in which they would later operate and hence the kinds of decisions they would eventually be required to make.

Assuming that much of what has just been said is true, then the decline of the humanities has, to a significant extent, been self-imposed. A jaded idealism that neglects and distorts what self-directed professionals need to know begs to be pushed aside. In eschewing honest scholarship and an evenhanded exposition of reality, it makes itself beside the point. If what is taught does not promote competent decision making, why bother? And so students have voted with their feet. They elected to look elsewhere for the information they needed and they will continue to do so unless reforms are effected.

The Social Sciences

In the interests of full disclosure, I must underline the fact that I am a sociologist. I must also make it plain that I stand with a minority of my discipline. In an academic specialty where the ratio of liberals to conservatives is at least thirty to one, I am utterly outnumbered (Adams, 2004; Jaschik, 2012c, 2012d; Grabar, 2013). Moreover, as a victim of this disparity, I cannot claim to be completely neutral. Yet I love sociology and believe it is essential to understanding our social environment. Hence, I begin this section by doing what I believe is incumbent upon an honest scholar. Those intellectuals who tell us that total neutrality is impossible are partially correct (Damasio, 1994). We all have biases, including me. But I am convinced that academic progress depends on taming these. Unless we recognize our prejudices and filter them out of our judgments, we cannot get closer to the truth. Unlike the postmodernists, I believe this is possible but only if we honor the integrity of the attempt. Indeed, I believe that disputing our conclusions with others who disagree with us is essential to weeding out errors. Those with differing perspectives can point out that which we do not see because of the motes in our own eyes. In remaining open, these criticisms enable us to get beyond where we are. This said, I hope it is in this spirit that the following will be received.

We humans are social beings; hence, in order to understand our situation we must be socially aware. To this end, we have evolved a number of social sciences that include sociology, psychology, economics, political science, and anthropology. Each of these specializes in a different aspect of our inter- and intra-personal lives. As such, all throw light on what professionalized decision makers need to know. They can therefore assist in developing the requisite self-knowledge, other-knowledge, and structural/cultural knowledge vital to competent choices. In this sense, they merit inclusion in a core curriculum. Nevertheless, time constraints preclude incorporating them all. Triage is therefore required.

Even as a sociologist, I must place economics and political science at the head of the list with respect to creating a core curriculum. These are so central to understanding our techno-commercial society that any educated person dare not overlook them (Heilbroner, 1980). Living, as we do, in a Gesellschaft society, the food on our tables and the clothes on our backs arrive by way of an impersonal marketplace. Furthermore, depending as we do on democratic governments to defend our rights and well-being, these too are basic to our survival. Those who would join the ranks of the democratic elites that keep these institutions functioning must consequently be well versed in their fundamentals. An ignorance of them could expose all of us to death and destruction.

Meanwhile, sociology, psychology, and anthropology have a more private import. These are capable of providing insights that enable us to deal more effectively with other human beings. Sociology, for example, can provide information about how families are organized and how social change occurs. Psychology, in its turn, can help people understand how they and others think, as well what can go cognitively and emotionally wrong. Lastly, anthropology deals with the diversity of the human experience, thereby enabling us to perceive the vast possibilities at our disposal. Some observers have argued that anything is conceivable for creatures as plastic as ourselves, but the social sciences demonstrate otherwise. They reveal that while our limits are broad, they are circumscribed by the nature of who we are and how we live together.

How, then, should we decide which of the latter social sciences should be part of the core? What usually happens is that schools allow students to choose in which of these to enroll. While as a sociologist, I would love every student to take sociology; I believe this policy is reasonable. What remains to be discussed is how these courses should be taught so as to promote self-direction. The sad fact is that while a great deal of good work is currently being done in these fields, as with the humanities, much of what is made available to students is not relevant to their needs (Ellis, 1998).

We may begin with economics where the siren song of political correctness has garnered the fewest disciples. In a subject dedicated to what happens in the marketplace, a significant number of practitioners are sympathetic to its operation. Some have neo-Marxist orientations, but those who don't need not disguise a conservative or libertarian bent. Unlike in other social sciences, many economists believe it is morally acceptable to make money. They therefore have no objections to teaching about supply-and-demand or the banking system. As such, they enable students to understand the impact of public policies on the marketplace.

Nonetheless, there are glitches in what takes place in the classroom. Thomas Sowell (2009) has bemoaned the fact that some academic economists are so fascinated by mathematical modeling that they conduct their introductory courses around this technique. Instead of recognizing that most students will not become professional economists, they emphasize methods suited for advanced research. What is needed instead is uncomplicated instruction in the basics of the discipline. Meanwhile, other academics make the opposite mistake. They want students to understand economic transactions from a personal perspective; hence, they resort to the "discovery" method. Analogous to the Socratic method, this is geared to pulling the relevant information out of students. They are to be led step-by-step to discerning facts that required centuries for economists to master. Obviously, this can be both time-consuming and an excellent way of putting learners to sleep. Far more effective are lucid explanations of what students need to know.

Turning to political science, it has become more liberal than economics in a society where many young people are encouraged to enter politics as a vocation. Furthermore, given that the young tend to be idealistic, many are drawn to ideological stances that purport to be principled (Fein, 1999). This has produced a host of introductory courses that pander to idealism. Instead of neutral explications of how political institutions operate, professors, who have strong political predilections, present these as objective. Many, in the hopes of advancing particular political movements, fail to distinguish their own commitments from more impartial analyses. This, however, discourages students from thinking for themselves. To the contrary, it substitutes indoctrination for education, thereby making it difficult to develop habits of independent judgment.

Next, let us examine some of the foibles of contemporary anthropology. This is useful in its own regard, but it can also serve as an object lesson in explicating many sociological quirks (Gouldner, 1970; Horowitz, 1994; Lopreato and Crippen, 1999; Cole, 2001; Best, 2003). Years ago, the father of American anthropology, Franz Boaz, sent one of his disciples, Margret Mead, to study Samoan culture (Mead, 1928). He had heard that teenagers in the South Seas did not experience the Sturm und Drang American adolescents did, and he wanted to know why. Mead, who was only twenty-two at the time and did not speak Samoan, had been an anthropology student for a scant two years. Thus prepared, she traveled to and from a Samoan village for several months, utilizing a group of preteens as her primary informants. Then, when she returned to the States, she wrote a book called *Coming of Age in Samoa*. In this best-seller, she explained that there was no need for teenage rebellion in Samoa, because their youngsters were allowed to engage in sex totally free of moral censure. During the Roaring Twenties, when academics and poets alike were advocating free love (Russell, 1929), this came as welcome news, and she became the most celebrated anthropologist in the country.

Fast forward several decades, and an Australian anthropologist named Derek Freeman (1983) decided to check up on Mead's research. He too traveled to Samoa and, using his linguistic skills, sought out the persons from whom Mead obtained her information. One he found who was now elderly told him how she and her friends pulled the wool over Mead's eyes. They laughed at her gullibility as they spun yarns that had only a passing resemblance to the truth. Yet Mead had no idea she was being snookered. Freeman was also able to confirm that the idea of teenage free love was a fairy tale and that the Samoans, far from being peaceful, had a long history of violence. Naturally, he took what he learned and wrote a book to expose the limitations of this anthropological icon.

Freeman may have expected acclaim for revealing these facts, but like Stoll, he was seriously disappointed. In fact, the American Anthropological Association voted to censure him for the temerity of criticizing so exalted a personage. Even afterwards, when most of his revelations were substantiated, textbooks continued to cite Mead's work as if it were gospel. Here, then, is a capsule of what has gone wrong in contemporary American social scholarship. Instead of a careful quest for knowledge, a series of headlong stampedes intended to advance favored moral positions have taken precedence. Whether or not these deserve exclusive patronage, they have shouldered aside what has traditionally been considered science. Their devotees call themselves anthropologists and sociologists, but they are actually moral activists. While this is their right, when they teach courses based on their personal allegiances, they engage in misrepresentation. As such, they are not offering information in a manner that encourages independent thought. What, then, is the message transmitted? Is it that honest investigations lead to legitimate advances in knowledge, or that knowledge can be held hostage to political objectives? If it is the latter, how does this foster the self-direction?

Which brings us to sociology. The erstwhile queen of the social sciences (Lenzer, 1975) has also lost its way. Instead of schooling introductory students in the rudiments of social structure and culture, the emphasis has been on demonstrating the pervasive nature of social inequality. Once so-called "critical theorists" captured the discipline's citadel, they moved to institutionalize a neo-Marxist agenda. Students were taught that illegitimate elites, whether rich capitalists, arrogant males, or heterosexual chauvinists, exploited those over whom they had power and that, in the interests of social justice, they had to be overthrown (Salerno, 2013). Only then could economic equality, androgyny, or minority rights flourish. Only then could society be reorganized along collectivist lines. To this end, sociology professors considered it their duty to make sure no student left their classrooms without acknowledging that oppression was wrong and that social equality was a fundamental right.

How thoroughly sociology had been politicized is demonstrated by the proliferation of courses in "race, class, and gender." Not usually part of the core, these classes are nonetheless aimed at non-majors. Somehow, for many sociologists, it has become an article of faith that the relationship between husbands and wives is parallel to that between capitalist employers and their proletarian employees. In both cases, it is supposedly self-evident that the dominant group is, for its own benefit, suppressing the weaker. Scientific proof of a shared mechanism may be lacking; nevertheless, its existence is not to be questioned.

This sort of tactic came to suffuse introductory courses in sociology. Their textbooks became anthologies devoted to demonstrating the pervasiveness of inequality (Kornblum, 2011). Belittled as of lesser importance were lessons in how families operate, why bureaucracies are constructed as they are, and the mechanisms whereby social class differences are established. Younger college students were struggling with how to enter viable intimate relationships, how to cope with bureaucratic rigidities, and how to engage in social mobility, but information that threw light on these was snubbed in favor of a politicized agenda. Was it any wonder that many students found these courses boring? Sadly, many came to consider sociology a joke best taken if one were in search of an easy A.

Psychology, in recent years, has sidestepped the worst of this trap. Although most of its practitioners are liberal, they have reinvigorated its scholarly aspirations. With enormous progress achieved in understanding how the brain operates, there is a diminished emphasis on less rigorous materials. The problem with respect to psychology as part of a core is that what is taught does not match student expectations. Whereas students imagine that an introductory course will provide them with invaluable insights into how people think and feel, they are more likely to receive lessons on how the eye is wired. As with sociology, what is presented is chosen in accord with faculty interests, not student needs. This too is a shame because psychology has unearthed numerous facts that can facilitate self-direction. It can, for instance, explain why people often make non-rational choices. An awareness of this might help students avoid mistakes, as well as recognize when others make them.

The Hard Sciences

Almost everyone agrees that some of the hard sciences, along with mathematics, deserve to be part of the core. It is frequently alleged that the technical advances to which we have become accustomed require sophisticated customers, as well as a deep pool of scientists and engineers. Members of a democratic elite must, at minimum, appreciate the contributions the sciences have made to our joint welfare. Were they not to, they might not support the research needed to produce breakthroughs in solving longstanding social and technical problems. Sadly, in so doing, they would sacrifice their own wealth, health, and personal safety.

As to teaching these subjects to lower-division students, the selection of relevant materials should remain in the hands of faculty members proficient in these areas. One caveat, however, is that many universities have delegated these courses to international professors and/or graduate students. Because American students have shied away from these intellectually demanding subjects, non-Americans have frequently filled the void. This is unobjectionable (except in cases where national security is involved), but it has an unhappy side effect. Instructors who are not fluent in English must often teach introductory courses. The result is that difficult materials become more so as students struggle to understand what has been said.

Another caveat is that scientists are also open to politicization (Money and Ehrhardt, 1972; Bonevac, 2012). They too participate in our larger culture and therefore are influenced by campus trends (Gardner, 1957). Although less ideological than their peers in the humanities and social scientists, they are not immune to appeals for social justice. One area in which this has inserted itself is environmentalism. In fact, some biologists and chemists have jumped on the bandwagon in an attempt to be socially relevant. Detached science, it appears, has lost some of its former allure.

Majors and Electives

Almost all universities require students to select a major. Learners are obliged to identify a discipline in which to specialize. Here too there may be a list of prescribed courses within each major, but there is also latitude in choosing additional courses. The rationale is that this fosters the development of an expertise. With the boundaries of our collective knowledge having grown beyond the ability of any individual to master, the emphasis has turned to becoming proficient in a narrower sphere. This makes sense in terms of what is possible but also with respect to occupational demands. Persons versed in valued specialties make profitable employees, who, because they are professionalized, require less supervision.

This logic once seemed beyond reproach; nevertheless, universities have been inching away from traditional majors. Many reformers argue that the customary disciplinary borders are outdated. The social sciences, in particular, are chastised for being restrictive. Thus, it is alleged that scholars indoctrinated in one field habitually refuse to look outside it to recognize connections with other fields. As a consequence, progress is stymied due to academics who stubbornly defend their turf against encroachments (Mead, 2011, 2012). More concerned with their careers than with advancing knowledge, they do themselves, their students, their universities, and society a huge disservice.

In recent years, it has become conventional to lament the existence of what are described as disciplinary "silos." This metaphor is supposed to underline the restricted and impervious barriers that professors erect to keep outsiders at bay. Instead of coordinating their studies with other disciplines, they become parochial and in-bred. If, however, interdisciplinary studies are fostered, channels of communication will be opened so as to spark new avenues of approach. In the end, everyone will learn more. Students, society, and professors will all benefit from smashing artificial obstacles to new knowledge.

At first blush, this seems to make sense. It sounds like a reasonable antidote to academic rigidity. Unfortunately, it has significant drawbacks. First, as any good farmer knows, silos serve a useful purpose. They protect the harvest from destruction. In the same way, a committed cadre of academics can defend the integrity of a subject. Because their professional identity is at stake, they are motivated to preserve the best of what has been achieved, as well as to add to this legacy. By the same token, they can imbue students with a similar disciplinary loyalty. Unfortunately, were these neophytes too expansive in their interests, most would not sufficiently apply themselves to become truly expert.

But the problem goes deeper. If interdisciplinary studies are to encourage productive communication between disciplines, which disciplines should these be? Consider sociology—should it be linked to psychology, as was once unsuccessfully attempted at Harvard? Or should the partner be anthropology, economics, or perhaps political science? How about biology or business management? Even nursing might be conjoined with medical sociology. Then, too, what about compelling professors to coordinate their work with particular others? What if their interests did not match? What if one changed direction? Wouldn't efforts to channel scholarly activities along predetermined lines interfere with personal initiatives? If it did, this could well discourage the intellectual breakthroughs being sought (Gardner, 1957). Isn't this what happened when Stalin demanded that his social scientists adjust their scholarship to accord with the biological theories of Trofim Lysenko (Montefiore, 2004)? Didn't this foreclose advances in genetic studies in the old Soviet Union?

As it happens, no impermeable boundaries currently separate academic disciplines. To the degree that their practitioners are free to pursue individual projects, they are also free to engage in these with colleagues of their choosing. This has happened in the past and continues to take place today. Why, then, disparage the traditional fields of study? Wouldn't this reduce their stature? Wouldn't it also rob them of necessary resources? Ultimately, we might all learn less, including the students denied a solid grounding in a coherent sphere of knowledge.

Closely associated with the assault on traditional disciplines has been the rise of "boutique" majors. Where once the number of university departments was relatively small, these have proliferated at an astounding rate. Nowadays most decent-size schools offer well over a hundred potential majors. Many of these were once subsidiary parts of other specialties that in recent years gained independence. Consider several of the breakaways from sociology. One of these is women's studies. Not long ago, courses in gender were the exclusive preserve of sociologists. But then women in other fields decided they wanted a piece of the action. Nearly always committed feminists, their credentials for teaching the subject consisted almost entirely of a dedication to the cause (Whittier, 1995). Even a cursory review of the syllabi they produce discloses the neo-Marxist origins of their teachings. In other words, the enterprise, as practiced by them, is essentially an ideological, not an academic, one. Worse still, students (usually women) who choose this major foreclose occupational opportunities. It may not be politically correct to say so, but most employers know that if they hire these women, they may be signing up for a lawsuit.

Comparable considerations apply to black and Latino studies. Social activists intent on advancing left-wing political goals, as opposed to expanding specialized areas of knowledge, also established these. Likewise, they generally attract students intent on furthering the cause. Many choose these majors because they believe they are expert in the subject matter, often because they belong to a particular minority. Unfortunately, if they learn nothing new from a college education, what value will it have? Moreover, as with women's studies, graduates in these specialties pose a danger to employers. They cannot say so out loud, lest they be sued, but business people have reason to believe that social activists may have other objectives than performing the jobs for which they are hired. Why then would an intelligent employer delegate responsibility to such persons?

Perhaps an even stranger boutique major is peace studies (Chatfield, 1992). It too is a stronghold of left-wing activists. Here also the central qualification for teaching the subject is an allegiance to well-defined political views. Proudly proclaiming that they seek peace, whereas those who disagree with them are evidently warmongers, they are distinguished by their self-righteousness. Once more, legitimate knowledge is not at stake. Were this the case, instructors in this area would be analyzing the failures of historic peace movements—an exercise they vigorously eschew. Where, then, is the contribution to a neutral professionalized expertise?

If universities are to prepare students to exercise a self-direction, this trend is a dead-end. It is little more than an egoistic effort to disguise a lack of scholarly rigor. That institutions of higher education have not been able to defend themselves from this onslaught is an ominous sign regarding their ability to preserve their reputations as bastions of advanced knowledge. Worse yet is coupling this trend with a greater emphasis on quirky electives.

The elective system grew to prominence because it promised to allow students to tailor their studies to their personal needs (Thelin, 2011). If but a few prescribed courses were required, the remainder could be flexible. This made sense when most electives were exacting. When, however, courses in the movies of John Wayne or the writings of Millard Fillmore pervade college catalogs, the selections made by immature undergraduates come to resemble undisciplined recreation in an academic sandbox. Each year, a host of fly-by-night courses that represent the current work of enterprising professors pander to the imagination of students seeking non-demanding credits. How these add up to a professionalized competence is of little concern to the parties; ergo, they do not.

Electives doubtless are a good idea. They serve a useful purpose. But they can be abused; hence, colleges make efforts to rein them in. Most have curriculum committees designed to do precisely this. Nevertheless, an "I'll scratch your back if you'll scratch mine" mentality, especially among faculty members, has often obviated this safeguard. A sense of order must consequently be restored.

Finally, some popular majors must be rethought. Many are either too undemanding or impractical to fit into a university program geared toward fostering self-direction. On the undemanding side of the ledger are majors in elementary education (Kramer, 1991). Once the preserve of "teacher's colleges," deemed a rung below actual colleges, they today attract untalented students looking for a job—and an intellectually laidback schedule. Communication majors are also among the least intellectually inquisitive students and have the misfortune of entering a field that promises difficulty in providing employment. Few will become newsreaders or hotshot journalists. The competition is too fierce and the job opportunities too limited.

As to the most popular of all majors, a degree in business is less practical than is generally thought (Hardy and Everett, 2013). To the extent that its students acquire an expertise in marketing, accounting, or finance, they are ahead of the game, but to the extent they do not become self-directed, they fall behind. Unhappily, many lag behind because the courses they take are simplistic. They are not challenged to think and, therefore, they do not rise to become CEOs. The fact is that many never acquire the curiosity or broad knowledge needed to exercise discretion in an environment of uncertainty; hence, they do not possess the credentials to move up. As to the law, which has emerged as a favorite field of graduate study, it is wildly overpopulated. The nation has far too many attorneys for most to be gainfully employed in their area of expertise. They must therefore look elsewhere upon graduation.

Extracurricular and Supplementary Activities

It would be a serious mistake to suppose that all of the personal development that takes place on college campuses occurs in the classroom (Wrong, 1961). Much is stimulated by other college-sponsored activities. Some of these are extracurricular; some take place in conjunction with course activities. These programs go well beyond traditional classroom practices; well beyond learning names and dates or memorizing chemical formulae. In the next chapter, the focus will be on contributions that student culture and student choices make to the evolution of self-direction. Nevertheless, the current picture would be incomplete without a bow to the social environment provided by universities. It too sets the stage for the emotional and intellectual independence.

Here, we can begin with university-sponsored athletics. At the end of the nineteenth century, Harvard and Yale gained fame not through scholarship but via their football programs (Horowitz, 1987). Millions of Americans who never aspired to a higher education nonetheless followed the gridiron heroics of their athletes. By the twentieth century, the frenzy had grown greater. Knute Rockne and his fighting Irish from Notre Dame democratized the sport, as did motion pictures that celebrated the raccoon-coat–wearing, fight-song–singing, football-rooting college students of the day. All of this was considered exciting and glamorous and in the process, elevated universities to iconic status.

Yet voices of dissent were heard even then. Where was the seriousness of a higher education if students cared more about attending football rallies than reading books? If all they did was engage in the hijinks depicted in Marx Brothers films or get drunk while drag racing in souped-up jalopies, weren't their intellects going to waste? Today, serious-minded critics still lament the resources squandered on immense stadiums and even more immense coaching salaries. Couldn't these be better spent on state-of-the-art laboratories or well-stocked libraries?

This said, the staying power of college athletics has been impressive. There must thus be a reason why they have endured despite the withering attacks. Some argue that they provide a welcome diversion from academic studies, but this is not altogether bad. Uninterrupted studies can lead to burnout, as well as insufficient time to consolidate lessons initiated elsewhere. All work and no play has long been disparaged as a recipe for producing uninspired drudges—and not without cause.

Nevertheless, there are more positive reasons for endorsing athletics, both at the varsity and club levels. Sports mirror the challenges of life (Wooden and Jamison, 2010). They enable us to rehearse skills that have application outside the playing field, and they do so without our having to endure failures that have a lasting impact. Sports enable us to engage in fabricated competitions and to practice temporary cooperation. As hierarchical animals, we all want to be winners, yet while we are in school our opportunities for major achievements are limited. Yes, we can do well in the classroom, but athletic activities allow students to win as part of a team and/or in structured tournaments, where emotional toughness is forged and mettle tested. Psychologists distinguish between distress and eustress. The former can be debilitating, whereas the latter strengthens one's character and tempers one's resolve. Athletics specialize in this latter.

Participant sports, whether of the varsity or club variety, teach players how to endure the rigors of competition without giving up or running a way. Losing is part of life, not just athletics; hence, those who learn to survive defeat and come back to play another day also learn to keep their options open. They may not win today, but tomorrow might be different. Similarly, if they do win, they can learn to be good winners. Sportsmanship has gone out of style in some professional sports, but on the college level, it is alive and well. In this, competitors learn to treat their rivals with respect, for just as losses can be temporary, so can victories. By the same token, not all successes are of the individual variety. Many depend on coordination with teammates. This too is an essential life lesson that promotes competent self-direction by teaching players how to make good choices in conjunction with allies. Enemies likewise need to be dealt with in ways that make it possible to become friends later on.

Spectatorship also provides substantial benefits. People who identify with teams and/or players learn vicarious lessons. The personal strengths that are acquired, whether with respect to enduring defeat or cooperating with allies, are not as robust, but they are real. With respect to universities per se, identification with teams and/or their players builds school spirit. This contributes to a sense of community that can be emotionally sustaining. To submerge oneself in the "we feeling" of a particular school might seem to hinder self-direction, but this ignores the importance of social support to developing a community of learners. Making decisions in environments of uncertainty can be especially harrowing if one feels alone in the world, whereas being part of a larger community can infuse the necessary courage to take intellectual chances.

Next, universities sponsor a variety of theme clubs and activities. These facilitate students coming together to pursue common interests. Perhaps as reviled as big-time college sports, have been fraternities and sororities. These are often characterized as antagonistic to higher education. Frat boys and sorority sisters are depicted as beer-guzzling, sex-crazed, muddle-brained party animals who would rather engage in dangerous hazing than crack a book. Nor is this image completely misplaced (Horowitz, 1987). Few self-styled nerds are attracted to the social swirl of the fraternity scene. They would rather spend time in the library or laboratory. But for others, for whom interpersonal relationships are more important, these organizations are relevant. No doubt, not all fraternity types become social leaders, but many do. In fact, for some of them, the lessons learned navigating the political minefields of these associations are invaluable. Just as Robert Putnam (1993, 2000) and Alexis de Tocqueville (1996) argued, joining groups and participating in their governance is excellent training in how democracy works. This is true on the governmental but also on the commercial level.

Then, too, there is all of that socializing. Research shows that students are less likely to find future mates on college campuses than in previous years; nonetheless, acquiring social skills in interacting with members of the opposite sex (and sometimes the same sex) can pay off down the road (Pines, 2005). There is a great deal to be learned about oneself and others from these encounters. This is why Facebook has become so popular but also why it must be supplemented by face-to-face interactions with live human beings. Fraternities and sororities arrange such meetings. They also encourage the informal gossip and bull sessions that help clarify the thinking of relatively immature students.

Other more academically oriented organizations also foster the similar sorts of growth. These include the clubs most academic disciplines support, the honor societies they underwrite, the interest groups universities organize, and the service associations of which they boast. They too provide practice in self-governance and opportunities for social interaction. They likewise reinforce desirable motives. In some cases, these are overtly academic, as when students are honored for their intellectual achievements. In many cases, they are eleemosynary, as when they support worthy causes. In still others, they provide emotional sustenance for identity groups with similar concerns or problems—for example, minority groups or religious communities. Whatever the glue holding them together, they provide a sense of belonging that furthers personal objectives.

In addition to these ongoing groups, most schools sponsor one-shot activities that can offer comparable benefits. Among these are debates, political speakers, movies, concerts, art festivals, radio stations, newspapers, magazines, and charitable events. Many schools also have dormitories where students interact informally and food courts where they compare notes about professors or argue over current events. Some schools also organize orientation sessions for incoming students and ice-breakers where they meet others in the same situation. A large majority sponsor advising facilities to help students make course selections or address personal problems. In other words, students are not left exclusively on their own. Many venues are made available as they struggle to discover who they are or what they want to become.

Nor is this the end to the supplementary amenities available to university students. There are also health services and at some colleges, religious services. Today, large numbers of universities encourage service learning. They urge students to get involved with charitable organizations and good causes. The idea is to build bridges to the larger community and instill an orientation toward giving, not just receiving. Also geared toward developing connections with reality are internship programs. Rather than allow students to wall themselves up in the ivory tower, they are asked to work and learn in community organizations, some of which are commercial, others of which are governmental, and still others of which are private service associations. Rather than depend on strictly intellectual lessons, these external activities are employed to forestall reality shock upon graduation by introducing a dose of reality much earlier.

Likewise becoming prevalent is foreign study. Whether in the form of university-organized tours or courses taught abroad, the goal is to widen student horizons. If diversity has emerged as a campus watchword, how much more broadening is interacting with different peoples on their home territory. Even students from privileged backgrounds tend not to have dealt with non-Americans on an adult-to-adult basis. They too are inclined to be parochial, and hence, living in a different culture, even temporarily, can promote a more cosmopolitan orientation. Here self-direction is advanced by competent role taking. In this, students frequently discover that seeing things from the perspective of others can be liberating.

Online Learning

Currently among the most consistently recommended of higher educational reforms is a dramatic expansion of online learning.

As we saw in chapter two, perhaps the most extravagant claims made on behalf of any major innovation have been put forward to tout the value of electronic modes of education (Wildavsky, Kelly and Carey, 2011; Christensen, and Eyring, 2011). These are said to be cheaper, more flexible, more convenient, more stimulating, and all in all of superior quality. As a consequence, a bandwagon effect has seen virtually every institution of higher education add these offerings to its catalog. There are, however, very good reasons to doubt the hyperbole and to question the wisdom of moving more fully in this direction (Lederman and Laschik, 2013; Verene, 2013). The partisans of distance learning can be quite enthusiastic; nevertheless, the benefits of which they rave have yet to be conclusively demonstrated.

As computer technology became more sophisticated and skill in navigating the Internet more widespread, it was quite natural that its devotees should argue that it made common sense to take advantage of this incredible innovation (Anderson et al., 2012). Just a few short decades ago, who could have imagined the sophisticated things currently done with electronic devices? No wonder that college professors have been chided for resisting this advance. They are therefore told, time and again, that just as manufacturing and commerce gained from adopting the computer, so can colleges and universities.

Thus, we are assured that this modality enables more to be taught—and taught well. Students, it is claimed, can pick and choose what, when, and where to absorb the data they need and have it delivered by the very best professors our universities can offer. Moreover, universities will be spared the need of additional brick-and-mortar facilities, as well as for additional high-priced academics. Furthermore, even less well-prepared instructors will be able to take advantage of prepackaged rubrics that meet the highest scholastic standards.

This sounds so good—so incredibly modern—that those who have not experienced online learning assume it may well be the wave of the future. Why, they agree, should universities be trapped in a technology first devised in ancient Greece? As it turns out, there is a reason. These new electronic approaches are far less satisfactory than advertised (Shapiro, 2011; Fain, 2013b). Far from improving the quality of what is taught or lowering costs, these advantages are largely chimera. While some computer-based learning makes sense, much has been a huge disappointment. The advocates of distance learning ballyhoo its effectiveness, yet those who talk to its consumers hear a very different story. Although many students are pleased with online convenience, few, especially the best students, praise its quality.

Recent research (Xu and Jaggers, 2013) suggests that online students learn less than those who attend traditional classes. Indeed, they are more likely to fail subjects and to drop out altogether. The attrition rates are especially high for "massive open online courses (MOOC's) (Rivard, 2013). These have seen up to 90 percent of enrollees fail to complete what they start (Kolowich S, 2011, 2013). Worse still, the students who tend to do the most badly are precisely the ones most in need of a solid education. African Americans, men, and older students are all reported to learn the least. In other words, just those learners who may require assistance in becoming self-directed are the ones least likely to obtain it.

Supporters of the Internet admit there are problems, but they assure us these will be overcome as experience and improved technologies enable computer-based learning to approach and exceed what can be accomplished face-to-face. No doubt there will be improvements, but how far these can go is questionable. One area where upgrades are clearly necessary is cheating. By most accounts, online cheating is rampant. With students home alone, they can farm out exams and reading assignments to others. While classroom cheating is also a problem, the temptations brought about by a lack of direct supervision are substantial. Perhaps new hardware or software, such as integrated computer cameras, will rectify the situation, but this awaits future developments.

There are, however, more serious flaws that may prove very resistant to correctives. First among these is quality. In order to ensure first-rate teaching by instructors who are less closely monitored than their students and many of whom are less academically prepared than the professors they replace, universities have instituted "best practices" programs. Most schools demand that the syllabi for these courses conform to precise formats that are reviewed and approved by academic experts—albeit often from other disciplines. This admittedly produces a great deal of rigidity, but it is also thought to impose higher standards. This, unfortunately, ignores human nature. It dismisses how both instructors and students respond to technologically imposed constraints.

The foremost reality of distance learning is isolation. Both the students and instructors operate apart from other human beings. If conscientious, they are planted in front of computer screens where human feedback is virtually nonexistent. For the students, this means they must be strongly motivated to engage in independent studies. They have to do the readings and to participate in the exercises. In fact, few are so powerfully motivated. Those who are self-starters, which normally means they are older and nontraditional, could, if they chose, learn on their own. Younger, less well-motivated students, however, are unlikely to gain this dedication just from being online. Since most of these classes are deadly dull and devoid of human stimulation, these students get little more than they put in. No wonder many slack off.

Consider the ambiance of computer-based chat rooms. Because cross-talk must be typed in, it tends to be tedious and superficial. Furthermore, because face-to-face interactions are absent, insults are exchanged that would usually be suppressed in person. This is just the opposite of what was expected but is a big turn-off for sensitive learners (Jaschik, 2013b). The result can be a great deal of effort in return for very little nuance. Perhaps this is acceptable in math or science courses, whereas in the humanities and social sciences, it is poisonous. People do not learn about people by being isolated from them. Maybe they can pass simpleminded tests, but this is not the same as dealing with flesh-and-blood humans (Edmundsen, 2013). Without other students present to provide encouragement or competition, they miss the niceties of interpersonal interaction. There are no smiles or grimaces that might get them to rethink a position. They are, in this sense, stuck in a solipsistic world. Online intellectual relationships are about as capable of consummation as online love affairs. Thoroughly drained of emotional content, they can come to life only when the players actually get together. This too is why businesspersons continue to travel, despite the possibility of computer-based meetings. They know there is no substitute for eye contact.

Nor are these learners apt to be inspired by the most expert professors. Charisma rarely makes it through the electronic filters, nor does enthusiasm translate well into binary codes. Worse yet, with adjuncts and dead-enders filling the ranks of online teachers, instructors who truly care about what they are doing are in short supply. Most of the best people know that they do their best when they receive direct feedback; hence, they opt for traditional classrooms, even when these pay them less.

Then there are the other obstacles to learning thrown up from the instructor's side of the transaction. If online courses are boring for students, they are more so for those who teach them. Once the challenge of creating a class has worn off, the day-to-day routine of sitting before a computer is most rewarding to persons who are uncomfortable with human contact. Others generally feel disengaged. Without human signals to let them know they are making a difference, they drift into mechanical communiqués. Good teaching is responsive teaching. It is about using one's expertise and making adjustments in order to get a message across. Distance learning, in contrast, is nonresponsive. Nor does it elicit instructor enthusiasm. Because it takes more time to impart less, while simultaneously providing little reinforcement at either end of the arrangement, less gets accomplished.

Even an electronic aid as ostensibly innocuous as PowerPoint can interfere with good teaching. Thus, Christopher Conway (2013), an associate professor of modern languages at the University of Texas at Arlington, complains that "teaching with PowerPoint has been an exercise in frustration. . . . I find that my course preparation takes twice as long, and that the results more often than not are unsatisfying." Yes, course materials reduced to simplified outlines and dazzling graphics can catch one's attention, but students confronted with reams of projected data typically spend more time watching this than listening to their instructor. Meanwhile, the teacher feels constrained by the organization built into a set of slides. Instead of following classroom interaction where it may lead, prepackaged materials are thus slavishly adhered to, despite their inadequacies. By the same token, as much as reading from a paper can drive students into paroxysms of boredom, so can reading on-screen quotes intended to provide legitimacy to a lesson. When these same techniques are transferred to online courses, the misery is merely compounded.

Nor is online learning cheap. It has been sold as an efficient mode of educating in that it presumably requires less infrastructure. But this too is misleading. Because it is so time-consuming for professors, classes are smaller and therefore more instructors are necessary. Even though many are adjuncts, it has also become conventional to award them bonuses for taking on a task few find rewarding—except, that is, if they need to work out of town or prefer to direct their energies to completing dissertations. This too has resulted in less experienced instructors filling many slots. The upshot is more dollars are expended on lower quality.

For-Profit Schools

For-profit schools and distance learning are not new ideas. They have been around in the form of business colleges and correspondence schools for generations. Nonetheless, during this lengthy apprenticeship, they have earned a justifiable reputation for being third-rate (Fain, 2011; 2012). Now, however, we are told they are the wave of the future and the answer to the higher education bubble (Jaschik, 2012b). For-profits, in particular, with their explosive growth and presumed lack of cost to taxpayers, seem attractive. Their need to be profitable, we are assured, forces them to be efficient. Unless they meet the needs of their customers and do this economically, they will presumably go out of business. Since most have not, they must therefore possess a formula that deserves to be copied.

A key part of the not-so-secret for-profit formula turns out to be accepting any applicants who can breathe. Academic qualifications are deemed irrelevant. What matters is, can a given student get a government-backed loan? Ergo, the aggressive television advertising aimed at the lower classes. What takes place after signing these folks up is of no concern as long as additional enrollees remain available. This translates into abysmal quality. That which is taught is rarely taught well, nor does it impart the skills needed for high-quality jobs. Furthermore, what well-qualified teacher would choose one of these operations in preference to a traditional university? After all, the pay is nothing to write home about and the students are unlikely to be Rhodes scholars.

As for prospective students, they are routinely promised simulating work in law enforcement or medicine. But then—if they are lucky—they find employment as security guards or medical assistants. Since until recently these jobs did not even require a high-school degree, this is no great bargain. Yet what do they expect? With so many unchallenging courses taught by uninspired teachers about lower-level subjects, what else would be available? Consequently, it is primarily the scholastically unsophisticated who are fooled.

But the situation is much worse than this. Most of the people who sign up with the for-profits drop out. They never complete the programs for which they are recruited but wind up with huge student loans upon which they are bound to default. This does not matter to the schools, but it should to taxpayers when it adds a trillion dollars to the national deficit. Who, then, is benefited?

The Fundamentals

If the above is considered in its entirety, college curricula do not demand dramatic change (Bok, 2013). The programs of most colleges and universities are not in need of major revision. While these schools may not consciously aim at preparing students to become self-directed, many of their offerings achieve precisely this. Yes, they can be tweaked in order to make them more effective, but they do not need to be thrown overboard in favor of bold new innovations. Quite the contrary, many proposed substitutes offer less. Whether these recommend emulating the for-profits or radically expanding online education, their benefits are illusory. The justifications for them may sound legitimate, whereas they are bogus.

David Little, chancellor of the University of Michigan's Dearborn campus and a philosopher by training, put what is needed in perspective in, of all places, an editorial in the *Huffington Post* (2012). He wrote, "The most basic justification for a liberal education is the idea that these disciplines help students gain important qualities of mind that lay the foundations they will need for productive and innovative lives—rigor, critical reasoning, creativity, communications skills, ethical capacities, respect for human diversity, and the like." This is not an endorsement of self-direction or of professionalization per se, but it is a ratification of many of their components. Nor should these be unfamiliar to most academics. They are the building blocks upon which they have erected their careers and virtues they share with their students on a daily basis.

As expounded upon in chapter three, the content of contemporary university curricula evolved over the course of millennia. Most of this occurred blindly—nonetheless, it was shaped by social needs. The key word here is that these offerings *evolved*. Many innovations have been added over the years, while many errors have been weeded out. This is a process that continues, even as this is being written. Moreover, it is one to which millions of persons have contributed. No single brilliant mind devised what is being done, nor confirmed its validity.

These are the fundamentals. They are basic categories of knowledge that have been found broadly useful. Over the years, they have provided countless graduates with a platform upon which to build their careers and lives. While it is true that too much respect for tradition can be stifling, too little refuses to learn from the experience and insights of our predecessors. We did not create the world from scratch, nor will we discover all of its secrets by ourselves. This is what education is about. It is essentially a collaboration between the old and the new that ultimately passes the torch to the next generation so it can surpass its forebears.

Too much innovative boldness ought therefore be suspected. We must, of course, continue to make modifications in what we do, yet wholesale change is perilous. One is reminded of the promises of the neo-Marxists. They regularly swore that if their revolution came to fruition, universal love, full equality, and unimagined prosperity would be the order of the day. Clearly, this did not happen. In the real world, collectivist regimes produced tyranny and poverty (Montefiore, 2004). Would the equivalent be the case were higher education completely overhauled so as to match the promises of any given theory? Or does it make more sense to allow piecemeal experiments to unearth that which works best? As long as we keep our eyes on what our society requires, we will probably not go too far wrong. It is the premise of this book that this will turn out to be in accord with the demands of self-directed professionalism.

If there is, however, an area in which significant adjustments are necessary, it is probably in facilitating social mobility. The elite schools are doing fairly well with their elite students, whereas learners who possess more modest skills and derive from less promising backgrounds may require a more focused approach to cultivating self-direction. The mid- and lower-level institutions that most of these students currently attend may have to adjust their offerings so that they better promote the personal and technical skills needed to make professionalized decisions. The question is, what do these students need?

Last, if the fundamentals are to live up to their promise, they must not be corrupted. An excess of moralism must not lead colleges and professors to choose indoctrination over education. In their zeal to produce a better world, these educators must never underrate the knowledge they have accumulated or abandon their ability to inspire. Self-direction is best cultivated in a vibrant community of learners that remains dedicated to maintaining an open marketplace of ideas. This may sound old-fashioned, but when it is realized, it can have a potent impact.

Conclusions

First and foremost, colleges and universities must protect their core. This means protecting the traditional academic disciplines. These evolved over many years, during which they demonstrated substantial utility. To dismiss them as "silos" discourages the accumulation of the knowledge upon which higher education depends. Additions to the roster of disciplines can be made—but with caution. Trendy and/or politically correct supplements dilute efforts to increase our erudition. Likewise, elevating the status of "interdisciplinary" studies in an effort to encourage coordination is artificial. Nothing currently prevents diverse professors from working together if they wish.

Second, the core cannot be maintained if its funding is not safeguarded. Diverting scarce resources away from the courses in which all students should be proficient undermines the foundation upon which even esoteric courses depend. If schools cannot offer a sufficient number of well-taught sections in the basics, their graduates cannot develop into the cultivated individuals they should become.

Third, general education requirements should continue to be encouraged. Students, especially traditional students, do not have the experience to know what they need to know; therefore, colleges and universities should require a set of basic courses designed to assist in their explorations. Subjects such as English literature, history, mathematics, economics, social science, and basic hard science need to be included in this core, but they must also be strengthened. Thus, special attention should be paid to reading and writing. Reading and writing are the foundation of competent self-direction. Essential for professionalization in both technical and commercial occupations, no college graduate should be without facility in these. Consequently, reading and writing assignments ought be numerous. Schools might also incorporate programs such as "reading across the curricula," so as to underscore the importance of literacy. This approach is especially important for non-elite schools, many of whose students lack an academic orientation.

Fourth, colleges should limit the use of online courses. These must not be allowed to drain scarce resources from the traditional classroom. Making more of them available at the expense of the traditional courses is, in fact, self-defeating. Even if online courses are as effective as their proponents claim, stripping the best of what presently exists so as to experiment with what is theoretically expedient reduces the quality of the tried and true. Moreover, if, as the evidence suggests, many online courses are not as effective as traditional ones, this reduction in quality will cast doubt on the soundness of the established degrees. This means that if employers and laypersons cannot distinguish graduates who have learned online from those who have not, the reputation of historically recognized credentials will be impaired. Thus, when schools offer dedicated online programs, these should be identified as such by awarding e-degrees.

Fifth, there is a place for online learning; nevertheless, these offerings frequently constitute niche courses. They can be useful in providing flexibility, but they are not equally good at teaching every subject. In disciplines such as mathematics, they have demonstrated their utility; whereas in the humanities and social sciences, they have not. For the latter, face-to-face contacts are invaluable in inspiring learning. Research has also demonstrated that unrestrained Internet grazing is no substitute for reading and thinking. Resources such as Google provide ease in accessing data, but when they take over from traditional forms of study, they stifle learning. Important information is no longer retained in long-term memory. Instead, it enters the short-term memory, only to be lost within minutes.

Sixth, the for-profits must be reined in. They must also be distinguished from traditional colleges and universities. Because the quality of these proprietary schools is uniformly lower than genuine colleges and universities, to label them the same is therefore misleading. Perhaps they should be called "institutes" or "trade schools." Indeed, it may be necessary to legislate these distinctions. Clearer categories might also codify the differences between colleges, universities, community colleges, and research institutions. This would allow students to better judge where they ought to go. Furthermore, accreditation agencies have apparently been politicized. Thus, they too must be scrutinized to improve their performances. When they fail to distinguish diploma mills from legitimate colleges and universities, their procedures must be rectified.

Seventh, government funding of the for-profits should be curtailed. Government grants and student loans for them must be brought under control. Because these schools rarely live up to their advertising, their graduates rarely obtain robust jobs. Moreover, their dropout rates are enormous. The result is massive loan defaults. Unless this trend is reversed, another financial bubble is indeed in the offing.

Finally, colleges and universities must themselves be aware of the temptations to become moralistic. Most professors and administrators are good people. They genuinely want to make a difference in the lives of their students and for society in general. But they are often carried away with their ideals to such an extent that they undermine the strengths they could pass along to their students. The fundamentals must not be neglected. The academic specialties over which professors preside—be they in the humanities, the social sciences, or the hard sciences—are potent tools in imparting the knowledge and motivation that self-directed professionals require. These must, therefore, not be weakened by efforts to redo our communities along revolutionary lines. When this occurs, it breaks the contract that higher education has with its enrollees. Worse still, it provides the impetus for parents and students to look elsewhere for assistance in achieving social success.

7

Self-Directed Students

The Entitlement Culture

When does a person become an independent adult? There was a time when teenagers entered the world of work, laboring side-by-side with their elders. As a result, they dressed as adults and to some extent thought as adults. But then the Industrial Revolution changed the nature of employment (Ashton, 1965; Doty, 1969). In due time, it also demanded more schooling; hence, a grammar-school education was supplanted by a high-school education. With this came the advent of a teenage culture. Adolescents who now attended school together developed a stand-alone lifestyle. At this point, intent on distinguishing themselves from their seniors, they collaborated in creating values, norms, and beliefs of their own (Kurtines and Gewirtz, 1987).

Eventually, of course, college replaced high school. At first, this was the preserve of the offspring of the social elite and a smattering of intellectuals. Then, as enrollments grew, the rah-rah playing grounds of the Roaring Twenties thundered into existence. Football cheers and hip flasks came to characterize even prestigious universities. After World War II, of course, the middle-class revolution changed this (Fein, 2005). The percentage of young people going to college rose precipitously. So routine did college-attendance become that it was assumed everyone should go. Just as a high-school degree had evolved into a universal expectation, so now did a college degree. To be without one became the mark of Cain (i.e., a stigma to be avoided if at all possible).

And so the college culture evolved into something it had not been. With so many students pursuing a higher education, the concentration of young adults in one place reached a critical mass. It now seemed normal for both men and women in their early twenties to be absent from the workforce. Many perhaps had part-time jobs to meet expenses, whereas full-time responsibilities lay in their future. In the meantime, college students were still considered "children" (West, 2007). They remained on their parents' medical insurance and returned "home" to get their laundry done. They had, in short, been infantilized (Lasch, 1979). Their parents and even complete strangers did not regard them as having entered the adult world but thought of them as youngsters who were a notch or two beyond grammar school. Moreover, this is how many students wanted things. "Growing up" had become anathema, something thrust upon one without one's consent. If a person were lucky, the fun might continue for decades, with adult tasks indefinitely postponed.

Indeed, colleges conspired in this transformation. They may have renounced the *in loco parentis* policies of the past, but they still held students' hands and spoon-fed them in the classroom. Because these "young" people were clearly not old enough to manage their own affairs, someone else had to. Consequently, university life became a far cry from what it had been when the GI Bill introduced millions of sober-minded scholars to the campus. For many contemporary students, school is party-central, with institutions rated in terms of their festival ambiance. Why study? Why opt out of the movable feast? This was for the mentally and/or socially impaired. In the meantime, a little alcoholic lubrication could go a long way to keeping time from slipping away.

College thus morphed into another social entitlement (Samuelson, 1996). Obviously, everyone deserved not just an opportunity to attend a university but a degree. This was their "right" (Glendon, 1991)! In a democratic society, where a college education provides the ticket to social mobility, to exclude anyone was tantamount to discrimination (Howard, 2001). It was to condemn them to eating table scraps, while everyone else supped at a reserved seat at the banquet. This was grossly unfair and palpably unacceptable (Hughes, 1993). No one should be left behind! The results had to be the same for everyone. An egalitarian society demanded no less (Huntington, 2004).

How did this new attitude come about? Why have so many people come to believe everyone deserves to be equally successful and that a college education is obligatory? And what does this development mean for the development of self-direction and professionalism? Many of these changes in outlook can be laid at the feet of our techno-commercial success (Galbraith, 1958). No large-scale society—in the history of the world—has been as wealthy and free as our own. Despite neo-Marxist predictions of doom and gloom, more people are living more comfortably than ever before. Even the poorest among us own automobiles, television sets, and cell phones. Few go hungry or walk the streets unshod.

Yet most people want more. They glimpse the lifestyles of the rich and famous in films, and they are envious. They too want the good life! And why should they be denied it? In a democracy, no one should be better off than anyone else. If some achieve more, this violates the premises of social justice. Or at least that is what some people contend. In the past, this sort of extreme covetousness was destined to frustration. The standard was self-reliance; hence, those who sought a free lunch were dismissed as deadbeats. People who did not pull their weight and were left behind may have felt cheated, yet few tears were shed about their fate.

There have been other changes as well. With prosperity has come a population explosion. Today, hundreds of millions reside within our borders. Nonetheless, most remain strangers to one another (Diamond, 2013). Although we are interdependent, we do not know each other personally. Consequently, we cannot depend on close emotional attachments to elicit help in moments of need. Where once families, friends, neighbors, and even churches might come to our rescue, more often than previously, we are today on our own. Where, then, can we turn for assistance? As it happens, we have acquired a rich uncle. So wealthy has our society become, that the government is able to appropriate the resources to protect most of us from adversity.

But more than this, the government, thanks to the universality of the bureaucratic model, has developed the means to organize our collective welfare. It has established reliable channels for transferring monies from some persons to others. Thus, the rich can be forced to disgorge significant chunks of their assets so that the poor may live more comfortably. In addition, because we have a democratic government, the poor can elect representatives willing to pay them off so that they (the politicians) can get reelected. This grand bargain has come to include universities, which now receive a large proportion of their financing from public sources. Whether via government-run colleges or student-loan programs, nearly everyone is provided an opportunity to go to college.

Recently, however, the pressures toward universality have escalated. The government is increasingly asked to ensure that all students graduate and obtain degrees of equal value. Remember, no one is to be left behind. George Bush said so; Barack Obama (2006) says so (Kloppenberg, 2011). All are to be successful. This is an American birthright. It is what citizens are entitled to. The schools know it, and the students know it, and they behave accordingly. Courses are therefore organized so that attendees can pass without too much difficulty. Meanwhile, if they cannot, many engage in self-righteous protests, which are, in turn, treated as legitimate by their professors.

One can scarcely go to an academic conference these days where professors do not compare notes and complain about the decline in student standards. They grumble about how students keep their laptop computers on in class, not to take notes, but to engage in social activities. One might call this the Facebook Generation. Many students are far more interested in exchanging information with acquaintances than with learning new materials. This enables them to feel like media stars in a world where everyone deserves to be famous. Although they have accomplished nothing of note, having been told since they were toddlers that they are special, they believe it. Why then would anyone want to puncture their self-esteem by suggesting otherwise. Certainly, most college professors and administrators do not. They could be sued if they did.

And so an academic culture based upon excuses and "unconditional positive regard" has arisen (Rogers, 1961). No one is at fault for what goes wrong (Fiamengo, 2013). Everyone is a victim of circumstances. Whether a person is poor or rich, old or young, a minority or in the majority, a believer or a non-believer, gay or straight, handicapped or able-bodied, smart or dim, depressed or high-spirited, a good reader or dyslexic, and a male or a female, there are valid reasons why he or she cannot perform as required. Furthermore, if none of these conditions gets you off the hook, you can always complain that a bad grade would ruin your life; that if you are not granted a passing average, you will never be able to get a good job, which will be on the head of the professor—or the administrator—who did not give you the break you deserve (Johnson, 2002).

This orientation—this sense of entitlement—flies in the face of professionalization. Its premise is that a self-motivated expertise is superfluous. We are presumably so wealthy and our economic and political institutions are so vibrant, that difficult skills are superfluous. The machinery that keeps us supplied in goods of every sort evidently operates so smoothly that any given person can be delegated to keep any aspect of it humming. Likewise, everyone deserves to be successful, just because of who they are. Competent performances are unnecessary. Each of us, merely as a condition of being human, is worthy of respect. Those who judge us harshly are consequently immoral oppressors. They rob us of our heritage—manifestly out of spite and meanness. Were they decent people, they would assist us in moving forward. And isn't that what a higher education is supposed to do?

To describe this attitude as self-indulgent is to invite a charge of being racist, sexist, ageist, homophobic, or elitist. The notion that university training is intended to prepare people to join a democratic elite is regarded as abhorrent. Indeed, it is dismissed as anti-democratic. Many believe that just because some people are less gifted than others, this should not condemn them to social inferiority (Vonnegut, 1998). Besides, if they were treated with the respect they deserve, they would perform as effectively as everyone else. That others have held them back is not their fault; hence, they should not be asked to pay the price for the sins of their detractors. If anything, they should be provided with assistance in making good, perhaps via special programs dedicated to their needs.

As for self-direction, should immature children be asked to make competent decisions in an environment of uncertainty? Aren't they supposed to be protected by leaders, who although their equals, are charged with keeping them safe? Anyway, why this allusion to uncertainty? Don't the experts always know what is best? Hasn't technology advanced to such a degree that it can go on automatic pilot? Those who suggest otherwise are probably in search of positions of power to which they are not entitled.

Self-direction is, in fact, for adults (Fein, 2011a). Social stations that require discretion are likewise for adults. To make choices that affect the destiny of other human beings takes the courage to recognize that consequences are contingent and that errors are inevitable. Persons with an overdeveloped sense of entitlement are therefore not suited to leadership niches. All of this is by way of again saying that not everyone can benefit from a college education. Individuals who are emotionally, biologically, or temperamentally unsuited ought not be shoehorned in. To put the matter baldly, when too many people who are not college material flood onto college campuses, these institutions cease offering a higher education. Clearly, this problem is greatest at mid- and lower-level institutions. They are the ones asked take all (or most) comers. They are thus the ones that have to decide where to draw the line.

Numbers

Perhaps the single greatest cause for the college bubble is the notion that everyone deserves a college education. This goal has fostered an enormous waste of resources, for which the payoff has been miniscule, if not negative. What reformers like Bill Gates push for cannot come to pass (Rogers, 2013). His software companies may profit from an expanded customer base, but this does not mean their products are benefiting society (Fain, 2013). Based as the target of universality is on false premises, it is a blind alley; a chimera that makes some people feel good about their humanitarian impulses, while condemning millions of others to frustration and disillusionment.

Most bubbles derive from an oversupply of optimism. The housing bubble would not have occurred if politicians and laypersons had not been seduced into believing everyone could afford a house (Sowell, 2009). Similarly, the dot-com bubble would not have burst if investors realized that not everyone would get rich on the Internet. In general, bubbles occur because people overestimate what is possible. Classically, business people who are making a good profit extrapolate sales upward toward infinity, only to be disappointed when they discover the ceiling was lower than expected. Either they miscalculated the potential demand or they misjudged the potential supply. In both cases, the supply and demand did not match, and the anticipated profits never materialized.

Something analogous happened with respect to a college education. Either the demand for a college education was grossly overestimated or the supply of appropriate students was as wildly misjudged. In both cases, what was predicted could not happen; hence, efforts to stoke up the impossible prepared the way for disillusionment. Much of this miscalculation can be attributed to the propaganda of the neo-Marxists. These activists not only believe in total equality, but they intend to produce it (Norris, 1997). Their two-pronged assumption has been that everyone can benefit from college, and when they do, money and power will be uniformly distributed. This way, everyone can get rich and everyone can be his or her own boss.

The sad fact is that this is overly idealistic. It ignores social realities and the limitations of the human condition (Fein, 2012a, 2012b). Neither individually nor collectively can we humans "have it all." Choices must be made. Moreover, if these are to be good ones, they must be consistent with what is possible. Disregarding how people interact can provide a modicum of comfort, but when based on fantasy, it generates its own comeuppance. Reality—as educated folks should know—is a hard taskmaster.

So to begin with, the demand for college-educated employees is not unlimited. It is not the case that our society needs or can absorb every person who obtains a traditional university degree into a college-level job. For over a decade, college advocates have cited the statistic that graduates earn about a million more dollars over the course of a lifetime than non-graduates. This, however, is verbal sleight of hand. It assumes that the disparity between the educated and uneducated will continue, even when the ratio between them is radically altered. Yes, current college graduates earn more. But that is partly because there are fewer of them. Once everyone joins their ranks, this advantage will disappear. Indeed, we are watching it vanish before our eyes. The competition for jobs has grown so fierce that many with inferior degrees are falling by the wayside. The promises made them have not been redeemed—nor can they be (Bennett and Wilezel, 2013). There are simply not enough appropriate positions to satisfy all of their ambitions. Worse yet, the situation can only grow more dismal as the number of persons who join the fray increases.

Ours may be a professionalizing society, but that does not mean every job will be equally professionalized. Physicians will remain close to the top of the heap, whereas retail sales persons will remain further down. The tasks they perform simply differ in complexity. This is a fact that cannot be canceled out merely by adding to the ranks of college graduates. If this is the situation, then not everyone needs to be comparably self-directed. Some people will continue to exercise more discretion—and therefore, leadership—than others. This is not fair, but it is life. Increasing the pool of those capable of self-direction may offer political and familial advantages; nonetheless, suitable economic niches cannot accommodate all. Why, then, are people snookered into expecting what they cannot have?

As to the supply side of the equation, it too has been oversold. Not everyone is college material. Not everyone has the intelligence or the diligence to assimilate challenging forms of knowledge. To pretend they have the same brainpower or motivation is absurd (Jaschik, 2013a). Anyone who has lived in the real world knows this. Certainly, college professors know it—as do their students. The advocates of universal higher education should know it too. These reformers assume that they themselves are among the "best and brightest" (i.e., that they are smarter and more altruistic than most others). But if they are, then their premise that everyone is equally equipped for college must be wrong. Once again, this is not fair. It dictates that some people will be more successful than others. On the other hand, efforts to force everyone, irrespective of their abilities or desires, to perform at the same level is both exasperating and impossible. If fully implemented, it would only foist incompetence upon us all.

It turns out that only way to enforce college for all is to dumb-down our universities and convert them into something else. Many faculty members, especially at mid- and lower-level schools, argue that this process is well along the way. They often express displeasure in how high school-like their institutions have become. Some therefore demand that actual high schools live up to their responsibilities and turn out college-ready graduates. But this merely passes the buck. These secondary schools are faced with similar problems. They too are enjoined to teach students with neither the ability nor the desire for an academic education.

In any event, we have witnessed ever-climbing rates of grade inflation and the multiplication of unchallenging courses. The only way for everyone to do well in school is for them to be asked to do less, yet be treated as if they had done more. The mentality is much the same as Little Leagues that fail to keep score but provide trophies for every player at the end of the season. Reformers know that not everyone can be a winner; nonetheless, they pretend that they can for the sake of social harmony. Well, that is not exactly true. Some losers convince themselves they are winners, because, after all, they got good grades. The trouble is that after they graduate, they feel entitled to jobs commensurate with their inflated self-images. They may not be self-directed experts, yet they assume that they must be because they were treated as such. The proliferation of dumbed-down online courses and even more dumbed-down for-profits has merely exacerbated this problem.

The only way to correct this situation is to restrict a university education to those who can benefit from it. Admission standards must be elevated if graduation standards are to be raised. Quality is not possible if quality is not demanded. This said, the *opportunity* for a college education must remain universal (Fonte, 2011). People must be allowed to prove themselves, even if they start out disadvantaged. Talent can be found in unexpected quarters; hence, it should be cultivated wherever it turns up.

I teach at a regional university. While it has aspirations to become more research-oriented, it remains dedicated to quality teaching. As it happens, many of our students are non-traditional or transfers. For one reason or another, they did not go to college after graduating from high school. Or if they did, they were terrible students. Nonetheless, having decided to try higher education once again (or maybe two or three times), it is surprising how well many do. Now dedicated to learning, they learn. Perhaps they no longer feel oppressed by family circumstances, or maybe the school of hard knocks instilled unwelcome lessons. In any event, they are ready to apply themselves. This sort of flexibility must not be foregone for the sake of preserving quality college education. The motivation to study and apply oneself should not be confined to a single point in time. Things can change, and when they do, universities must be prepared to make adjustments.

Flexibility and quality are key to maintaining our democratic aspirations and to taking advantage of talent. By the same token, false hopes and dishonest evaluations are not. College is not for everyone, because not everyone is capable of becoming self-directed. This should never be forgotten. But neither should the door be closed to those prepared to put their shoulders to the wheel (Turner, 1960). Although all schools are not for everybody, a pathway for self-improvement should remain available to those ready for it. As long as they demonstrate progress as they move forward, they should be allowed to keep moving.

Explorations

Some psychologists are fascinated with the concept of self-actualization (Maslow, 1954; Rogers, 1961). They imply that we are born with a "self" destined to grow to its full potential if appropriately cultivated. No doubt we are born with a spectrum of diverse attributes, but to assume what we will later become is already present in an inchoate form is deceptive. Our genetic legacy may shape what is possible, but we are sufficiently plastic to succeed in many different areas. What we do depends partly on who we are and partly on the opportunities fortune makes available. From the beginning, we must therefore explore our prospects before setting out to grab the gold ring. This is true when we crawl out of the crib; it is true when we matriculate on a college campus.

If self-direction is to be nurtured, students must be encouraged to explore the directions available to them. They must become aware of the niches from which they must choose, the strengths and weaknesses they personally possess, and how these two match up. This is because if they are to win the tests of strength that allow them to exercise hierarchical leadership, they must understand the field on which they will compete and the relatives strengths of the competition (Fein, 2012a). Otherwise they will have a difficult time winning and becoming successfully professionalized.

Our techno-commercial society offers a wealth of options. So do college curricula. But which pursuits are suitable for specific individuals cannot be known in advance. The possibilities must therefore be tested before the most promising are decided upon. As children, our worlds do not extend beyond our homes, whereas college students find a vast universe of opportunities arranged before them. It is consequently up to our colleges and their students to take advantage of these.

Clearly, to be self-directed, a person must have some idea about the directions in which to proceed. This entails understanding the sorts of pathways that are accessible and the probable outcomes of choosing one rather than another. Yet this is often more difficult than is imagined. Most of us, by the time we reach college age, are chock-full of "supposed to's." Our parents, friends, and teachers have filled our heads with what they think we *should* do. When the time comes to choose, however, we are the ones who must determine what works best for us. Nonetheless, freeing ourselves to consider these options can take some doing.

Sigmund Freud (1953–1974), when assisting his clients engage in what he described as "archeological" expeditions into the unconscious, recommended that they cease censoring their thoughts. They were to lie back on his couch and allow whatever came to mind to bubble to the surface. Something similar must occur for college students endeavoring to "discover" who they are and what they are going to be. They too must be open to unanticipated scenarios. Even if a mother or father adamantly disapproves, they must be willing to entertain what their own minds and guts tell them is appropriate.

One of the mistakes many college administrators and politicians make is to press for accelerated rates of graduation. Mesmerized by the traditional four years and desirous of holding costs down, they keep careful tabs on how long it takes the average student to complete his or her studies. This is a serious problem because many students need time to figure out what to do. Apparently adrift, they are frequently as distressed by their indecision, as are outside observers. Even so, they should not be rushed. The extra terms or years they require are a modest investment, considering the many more years of life they might have to endure the consequences of bad choice. After all, they, not others, have to live with their decisions, thus they must be allowed to sort the sheep from the goats.

Oftentimes, this entails shopping for majors. Most traditional students have the sketchiest understanding of what particular fields entail. Having never been exposed to them, they are unfamiliar with their realities. As a sociologist, I regularly witness this phenomenon. Very few students enter college expecting to major in sociology. They are more likely to think in terms of psychology and then to switch to sociology after having been exposed to it as sophomores. I myself started out as a physics major, then changed to psychology, and then to philosophy, before committing to sociology as a graduate student. At the time, I believed this was evidence of a vacillating character. Since then, I have discovered this is a common pattern. The problem thus lies not in experiencing it but in being precluded from doing so because of artificial constraints.

The normal way students go about narrowing their choices is through trial and error. They sample a variety of subjects to determine which they like and are good at before landing on a favored one. Indeed, the conventional pattern is to reject what one does not like before settling on what one does. Choosing essentially begins with excluding. People eliminate prior to committing. It is apparently easier to determine what is unsatisfying, than what is satisfying. This means that there may be multiple blind alleys which ostensibly waste time. Waste, however, should not be the operative word, because if the extra time results in a good choice, the investment is worthwhile.

Moreover, few people enter the adult world fully aware of their assets or deficits. Charles Horton Cooley (1956) explained that infants learn who they are, in part, by seeing a reflection of themselves in their parent's eyes. Having almost no experience in the world, they have no other standard of comparison. College students, in contrast, have a larger range with which to compare themselves. As result, they can develop more accurate assessments of their relative strengths and weaknesses. By taking different classes, surrounded by varying casts of characters, they get to figure out where they stand. Eventually, if they are wise, they settle on majors where they do well. Furthermore, largely because these subjects come easily, they tend to be more enjoyable. By the same token, specialties chosen because they feel right usually lead to greater success than those selected because they are thought to be moneymakers. Too often, what seems to be practical is not, if it traps a person in a hated line of work.

As discussed earlier, the sorts of knowledge higher education can provide embrace the technical, the self, others, and social structures and cultures. Each of these can be explored in the classroom setting but also outside of it. Universities are learning communities, not just sterile libraries of ideas. Students therefore get to compare themselves with their classmates and professors. They can figure out how smart, well liked, or funny they are in relation to these others. They also get to see how they measure up in the dating market or in athletic prowess. For most, this involves both welcome and unwelcome surprises. One's strengths and weakness often lie in unpredicted places. What matters, however, is discovering the truth, because the adult world can be unforgiving when fantasy overrides accuracy.

The same applies to learning about the strengths and weaknesses of others. The competition is what it is and will not change because one would have it do so. This too is a vital piece of information in deciding where to stake one's future. So too is being able to figure out who might be a reliable ally and who not. Stereotypes imported from childhood can be misleading; hence, experience with diverse others is apt to be enlightening. But this is true only for students who are prepared to interact with people who initially appear different. For many, the biggest surprise is discovering that these others are as human as they.

With respect to diverse social structures and cultures, a student's explorations are only as good as he or she allows them to be. Book learning is important and can introduce persons and events one might never experience directly; nonetheless, some things cannot be known without first-hand exposure. For one thing, bureaucracies are an omnipresent feature of modern societies. Thus, the fact that the young may not previously have encountered their frustrations and possibilities can be a liability. Fortunately (and unfortunately), colleges too are bureaucracies. As such, they can provide practice in dealing with such institutions. They also provide opportunities to engage in political transactions. Either by being politically active on campus or in the larger community, students can ascertain what these entail. Most young people arrive at the doorstep of adulthood burdened by satchels full of impossible ideals. Attempting to put them into action can therefore be a useful corrective. It can begin the process of disillusionment whereby adults discover what is actually possible (Fein, 1999).

With respect to diverse cultures, it turns out that there are many ways to journey through life. People have different beliefs, norms, values, and so forth. But contrary to what relativists tell us, these are not equally rewarding (Moynihan, 1993). Others who come from different backgrounds, as a student's peers and instructors almost surely will, deserve to be treated with respect, but this does not require a suspension of judgment. Not all cultures endorse the sorts of expertise that facilitate social mobility in a techno-commercial society (Murray, 1986). Thus, students should be able to test whether getting routinely inebriated, or festooned in tattoos, or sex addicted, or bereft of book learning brings the rewards they desire. As long as they do not engage in irreversibly destructive behavior, they may learn valuable lessons. This said, in many cases the best way to learn is still by observing rather than doing.

Since self-direction includes more than knowledge, one's motivation can also be explored. College students should be encouraged to figure out what they like and what they dislike; what they find satisfying and/or disconcerting. They ought also be engaged in personal maturation. As a result, they may find that what was once rewarding when they were younger no longer remains a top priority. Moreover, special attention has to be placed on emotional maturity. Individuals who do not learn how to master their fears or frustrations are in for a rough ride. Children are allowed to be capricious, but self-directed adults must be more stable. If they cannot keep their anxieties under control or express their anger in a socially acceptable manner, then whatever decisions they make are likely to be irrelevant.

As people step out into the larger world, they are sure to encounter unfamiliar tests. Yet for many, that which they do not understand can be frightening. Indeed, for some this is a cue to run away and hide. Obviously, this is not the best mode of making decisions in an environment of uncertainty. Successful learners must therefore discover how to maintain their composure as they figure out the appropriate response to an unanticipated challenge. Universities, as it happens, provide many occasions to deal with the unforeseen. Whether a difficult subject or an unsettling fellow student crosses one's path, scrutinizing one's habitual responses can be rewarding. Woody Allen joked that "showing up" was the most important aspect of being successful. Unfortunately, people who do not learn to confront their fears tend not even to do this.

Anger too must be handled with care. Students who have not discovered how to manage their frustrations are often, to their great dismay, provided with opportunities to explore this too in a college setting. There can be no doubt that universities supply their share of frustrations. Things go wrong. Papers thought to be brilliant get low grades. Science experiments blow up in one's face. Dates don't pan out. One's finances go on life support. Complete strangers insult one in the dining hall. What, then, to do? Running home to cry on Mother's shoulder will not suffice. Neither will going on a screaming jag. If, however, a student looks around to determine how others cope, useful models generally present themselves. Even professors can demonstrate mechanisms for self-control unavailable in one's family of origin. These templates may then be tested to determine what works best for oneself.

Colleges are cosmopolitan places. They offer a wide range of options within a confined space. This makes them ideal for engaging in personal explorations. The diverse courses offered, the extra curricula activities available, and the different sorts of students and professors one encounters all provide opportunities for self-discovery. One does not have to travel around the world (although this too is available), in order to encounter unexpected lessons. It is a matter of being prepared to absorb them and to expand upon one's previous horizons.

Independence

Growing to maturity is not a spectator sport. Nor is becoming effectively self-directed an exclusively intellectual exercise. These are only realized in the doing. But because they are, individuals must accomplish them for themselves. Achievements of this sort cannot be delegated to families or friends. Like it or not, college students have to navigate what is necessary on their own. They must, in this sense, become independent adults. Indeed, mature adulthood is a pre-condition for self-direction. Without it, one's dependence continues, while one's ability to make competent choices is arrested.

Nonetheless, it is not necessary to accomplish this transition unassisted. Going to college offers a rite of passage. It can provide a period during which the required metamorphosis occurs. By furnishing the appropriate setting and suitable supports, it can make the requisite changes both less stressful and more complete. A person's emotional quotient can be given a lift and his or her sense of self materially strengthened. Internal controls that were once tenuous can be reinforced, at the same time that one's understanding of where one fits in the larger world is clarified.

Growing up is not easy (Fein, 2011a). It begins with a separation from one's family of origin. As a long as a person remains tethered to his or her parents and siblings, their judgments and desires are apt to trump his or her own. For many, a need to avoid alienating Mom and Dad suppresses objectives with which they might disagree. Breaking this attachment is therefore a *sine qua non*. One's ties to home do not have to be completely severed, but they must be sufficiently weakened to allow for independent thinking. Self-directed people cannot be forever asking, what would Mom or Dad do?

In any event, letting go of what had been axiomatic can be traumatic. This ordeal is, in fact, the major source of teenage angst and rebellion (Erikson, 1968). Individuals teetering in the edge of adulthood, in their ambivalence, can oscillate between raucous oppositionalism and obsequious submissiveness. One moment they are telling their parents they are the worst human beings in the history of the world, while at the next they are begging to be rescued from an ill-considered fiasco. This is the stage where peer groups take precedence and when conforming to a transient style seems laden with lifelong consequences. Nevertheless, the point of this conventionalized unruliness is to use non-family members as temporary life preservers while one tests the waters of independence.

Going to college, especially a residential one, can provide a definitive separation. For most students, this opportunity arises when they are exiting their teenage status. Yet because it can feel absolute, it may be distressing. Not a few students (e.g., ones who have never been away from home for extended periods) experience homesickness. They feel alone and threatened, and desire nothing more than a return to familiar surroundings. Some also traverse a period of wildness. Finally freed from parental supervision, they go on drunken binges and/or engage in imprudent sexual escapades (Bogle, 2008). Despite appearances, they too are consumed by anxieties they are attempting to suppress by denying their existence.

Clearly, a person's fear of aloneness must be addressed. For unless it is, adult self-direction is impossible. But herein lies the possibility of emotional growth. If a student does not go overboard, this fear can be mastered. And if it is, it is possible to undergo an emotional reorientation. Achieving a new status entails more than letting go; there must also a change in how one perceives the world. Nonetheless, letting go is alarming (Fein, 2011a). There can be an interlude during which the past has not been relinquished, but the future is not yet in view. Such moments can bring doubts that reliably safe patterns of life will ever emerge.

Meanwhile, the reorientation process is fraught with confusion. If one's family-based standards are to be modified, what new standards are to take their place? Similarly, if childhood aspirations have become obsolete, which new objectives will provide genuine satisfactions? First and foremost comes the challenge of taking responsibility for one's own choices. Young people are often described as feeling bulletproof. They imagine that nothing they do will harm them. In fact, they are all too aware of their vulnerabilities and hence hasten to repudiate these weaknesses. Being responsible, however, means accepting the consequences of one's decisions. It entails an awareness that one might make serious mistakes, but also the confidence that one can cope with the wreckage.

College can facilitate the development of this orientation, not just via classes that illuminate what must be decided, but also by immersing students in a peer group undergoing similar stresses. Many of one's classmates will similarly be feeling alone and unsure of their destinies. This provides something in common to talk about, as well as sympathetic sustenance. Students will also find themselves within an environment where foolish decisions may be more readily rectified than if they were plunged into fully adult responsibilities. This may not sound like an important advantage, but it is. Our society requires so much learning that a milieu where one does not have to be rushed offers the time to think and to feel things through.

Eric Erikson's (1964, 1968) psychosocial moratorium may not merely furnish a hiatus for individuals in emotional trouble but an interval during which those who will later exercise crucial social responsibilities can become the persons they are expected to be. As leaders in our Gesellschaft society, they will be joining a social stratum that is required to be intellectually and emotionally superior. If they are to be professionalized, they must be transformed into genuinely self-motivated experts. But if they are to be competently self-motivated, they need to acquire a robust sense of self. This takes time. It requires the explorations previously discussed but also emotional experience in dealing with uncertainties. As it happens, the separation entailed in going to college is laden with uncertainty. It entails a long apprenticeship, wherein managing both complexity and discretion are acquired via an extended period of intellectual and emotional learning.

Student Culture

Unlike for-profits and online learning, traditional colleges and universities provide more than technical learning. They offer crucial social experiences. This has been true since the Middle Ages, where the term "college" derived from the shared living quarters students arranged for themselves (Haskins, 1957). But in doing this, something else—something unexpected—emerged. This was a common culture (Horowitz, 1987). We humans are social animals and therefore how we live is not entirely self-determined. Much is derived from learned and shared ways of doing things. The communities in which we find ourselves teach important lessons that may subsequently be enforced by our role partners. We are not only told that *this* is the proper way to use a fork, but that if we do not comply, complete strangers may cast a disapproving eye our way. This might not sound potent, yet because we are social, we are sensitive to this sort of negative attention.

The cultures in which we live teach us the languages we speak, inform us about how to dress, and instill standards of beauty. Our families, colleagues, and strangers mold our norms, values, beliefs, technologies, rituals, symbols, and emotional reactions. We do not invent these. Rather, we are taught to wear shoes; hence, if we appear barefoot for a concert, we are treated as pariahs. Some of these standards are imposed so vigorously that nonconformity can be life-threatening. This is the case with moral standards, where a failure to respect the rule against murder can prompt the death penalty.

So vital are many cultural lessons that they are strongly internalized (Fein, 1997). We do not merely respond to what others desire but are motivated to think, feel, and behave as expected. Thus, the language we have been taught becomes the language in which we dream, while the currently fashionable music becomes the music we enjoy. The same goes for the manners we practice, the sports we play, and religious beliefs we hold. What is more, once these have been firmly established, they are difficult to change. Having become part of who we are, it does not occur to us that they might be altered. This is why many of us become ethnocentric (Boas, 1928). That with which we are familiar seems normal and therefore correct. Merely to question it causes a tightening in our gut.

Cultural conservatism is a universal phenomenon (Fein, 1999; Harrison and Huntington, 2000). Change is possible but in most cases is slow in coming—and wrenching. This includes the student cultures prevalent on college campuses. These have evolved over decades and even millennia and therefore can be deeply entrenched (Horowitz, 1987). Why this matters is because the nature of a student culture can either facilitate or impede the journey toward self direction. It can support the personal growth required to become a responsible decision maker or discourage the necessary lessons. Much of this, however, depends on the missions pursued by the institutions to which they belong. Much also depends on the composition of their student bodies. Boards of trustees, battalions of administrators, phalanxes of professors, and platoons of parents all help shape what schools do and expect. Over the course of many years, individually and in concert, they craft the demands and provide the resources that make a difference. Nevertheless, students—ostensibly the persons upon whom others enforce their will—also contribute to the mix. What they want and are willing to tolerate can be the deciding factor in determining what is done. They are not passive recipients but active participants in cultural formation.

Earlier, it was stressed that a genuine higher education, one that aims at grooming a self-directed elite, cannot be for everyone. Who gets admitted to universities can therefore be decisive in deciding which standards the entrants support. Colleges that do not impose limitations but take all comers are bound to differ from those that are more selective. Clearly, elite students differ from third-raters. The latter generally have few academic aspirations. Many of them enroll in college because they have been pressured to do so. Consequently, they are there not to learn technical skills or develop self-directed attitudes but to graduate as painlessly as possible. They seek credentials, not an education. Such students cannot initially be expected to enforce norms or espouse values that advance professionalization. Nor do they covet demanding courses or extracurricular activities oriented toward personal growth. Many just want to have fun, not to belong to a community of learners. The more scope they have to engage in mindless entertainments, the better they like it. If they are to do their best, these attitudes need to be revised by a college ambiance that propels them in a more academic and personal growth directions.

This is not to say that colleges should be academic monasteries or that all students must be transformed into medical school-type grinds. This is neither necessary nor desirable. The sort of professionalization useful for would-be physicians is not obligatory for most other employments. Indeed, the flexibility that produces a first-rate executive is different in kind. Doctors are renowned for their prodigious memories, whereas effective managers rely more on their people skills. One is not better than the other; rather, the tasks they perform demand different emphases. This applies in spades when it comes to university employments. Many academics believe that college programs should be geared to turning out the next generation of academics. Students whose ambitions lie elsewhere are therefore regarded as second-rate. This is unfortunate, for many of these less scholarly types eventually make the world go around.

In any event, even if it made sense to seek a culture aimed at generating millions of scholars, this will not happen. Students won't allow it. This includes the good students. Many want to do well but not at the cost of ignoring other interests—especially social ones. Self-direction is not exclusively technical or intellectual. Much has to do with emotional maturity and socially oriented aptitudes. Too dedicated a concentration on academics can produce too a narrow focus. Most students realize this, even if those who design their programs do not. Consequently, they arrange their schedules to include more than study hours. What is more, they encourage their peers to do the same. Indeed, fellow students who study too much are regarded as the equivalent of rate-busters.

What then should a student culture that reinforces the value of self-direction look like? To begin with, it cannot buttress the entitlement mentality. It must recognize that some students will do better than others and should be commended for their achievements. Cultures that celebrate dumbing everyone down have a way of succeeding in this ambition. Too often they turn out graduates who have difficulty tying their shoelaces. Good universities, in contrast, feature large numbers of students who are prepared to compete for precedence. These scholars believe in merit and wish to see it rewarded (Guy, 1997). While they do not like to lose, they understand that quality must be sought if it is to be attained. They further understand that even if they do not come out on top, they will be better off than they would have been had they not competed. In the end, because they value competence, they take pride in their own accomplishments.

An entitlement culture, in contrast, is a lazy one. It is a dependence culture, which is the opposite of self-directed. An entitlement culture honors the complaints of the mediocre students, whereas a self-directed one is appalled at their temerity. An entitlement culture winks at students who pursue easy A's, whereas a self-directed one distinguishes the good courses (and professors) from the inferior ones. Last, students who believe in entitlement rarely blame themselves for their failures, while those who believe in self-direction are prepared to acknowledge their limitations and to seek improvements.

It should not need saying, but a self-directed culture applies the same rules to everyone. Race, gender, age, religion, social class, and sexual orientation are all deemed irrelevant; hence, special programs designed to provide advantages for particular categories are frowned upon. It is understood that treating people as members of groups frequently precludes treating them as individuals. Affirmative action may be well intended, but it flies in the face of self-direction and the universalistic values crucial to the operation of a market economy and a democratic polity (Kinder and Sanders, 1996). Student cultures that discriminate, for whatever reason, ipso facto discourage personal competence.

On the other hand, student cultures that promote personal exploration open the possibility of personal growth. Individualism has long been an American trait, yet people cannot be who they are—certainly not their best selves—if they do not take the time to figure out the sort of person they are and what they do best. Button-down cultures that force people into predetermined slots—because these seem to make sense—do not, in fact, make sense. In their presumed rationality, they are the antithesis of practicality. Although they claim to promote pragmatism, in shoehorning people into uncomfortable roles, they actually facilitate failure. Consequently, students should not be made to feel guilty about their uncertainties. Given the chance to figure things out, they will discover that their doubts are not resolved by pretending they do not exist or by forcing premature decisions.

This, of course, implies a culture that values independence (Bellah et al., 1985). One of the most important supports any student can have is a community of peers that understands and does not condemn his or her dilemma. Letting go of one's childhood status is made easier when respected others validate a new status. High-school peers tend to affirm rebellious deeds, whereas college peers, assuming they too are preparing for professionalized roles, are more likely to confirm the legitimacy of steps toward self-awareness and self-sufficiency. Instead of dismissing these as evidence of ingratitude, as family members may be wont to do, these are approved of as markers of personal strength. Learning about one's self, others, and diverse social arrangements can thus be valued as laying the foundation for a revised personal identity. If so, this authenticates the primary purpose of a higher education.

All of this is premised on a student culture that subscribes to emotional maturity. Obviously, party cultures do not. These encourage students to get away with as much juvenile revelry as they can. This philosophy is grounded in the belief that if one only lives once, one should enjoy the trip. Nevertheless, a truly satisfying life is rarely devoted to non-stop hedonism. The genuinely good life is one that can be looked back upon with a sense of accomplishment. It is a responsible life and thus one lived courageously and soberly. Children usually do not realize this. In many instances, theirs is a sheltered existence that does not demand such emotional insights. For many college students, this has not changed. Still, for those who expect to achieve something once they graduate, gaining control of their passions should be a priority. Those who do not cannot know who they are, what they want, or why others behave toward them as they do.

To reiterate, knowledge is important, but not merely traditional academic knowledge. Practical—albeit difficult to attain knowledge—is also critical. A student culture that appreciates this can provide valuable feedback. When student leaders are selected because of their maturity and sound knowledge, they too can provide role models. Furthermore, an acceptance of the importance of sociability and personal growth imparts the conviction that learning can be both pleasurable and pragmatic and hence, unproblematic. A consensus regarding this can therefore make these aspirations feel normal. In this case, becoming a well-educated person will feel less of a burden.

Yet student cultures do not exist in a vacuum. What parents believe, as well as what communities endorse, can be decisive regarding what occurs on campus. Parents who do not favor excellence, exploration, independence, or personal growth are unlikely to have children who subscribe to these standards. Mothers and fathers who pander to a student's sense of entitlement and stress the utility of practical majors undermine the sort of learning that should be taking place. Such imperatives are unfortunately communicable. Furthermore, if students have internalized these, they may demand them of a school. Rather than break loose and pursue self-direction, they may conclude that this would entail familial disloyalty.

More potent still, because it can elicit defensive attitudes up and down the campus spectrum, is the culture of the larger society. If most ordinary citizens do not understand what colleges are for, they may be scandalized by activities that do not fit their preconceptions. Similarly, if they believe that a quick turnaround, centered on practical majors, is necessary, students too may fall into line. As participants in the larger community, they will know what is expected of them. Thus, even if they disagree, most will conform. This may make politicians happy, but it sabotages efforts at self-direction.

To sum up, useful student cultures should be serious, yet compatible with student needs. Merit should not be regarded as fraudulent, nor should adulthood be considered a betrayal of personal fulfillment. Students should be future-oriented, even as they struggle to come to terms with the past. Likewise, they should value being well balanced. Few social leaders are narrowly focused. Last, they should collectively support an introduction to the complexities of a diverse and unexpected world. For most persons, this entails some disillusionment (Fein, 1999); nonetheless, illusions are debilitating. Student cultures that are comfortable with self-direction should therefore endorse an acceptance of reality, even though it may be harsh.

Practice

Years ago, when I was in the military, I trained to be an artillery mechanic. According to the test scores, my mechanical aptitude was off the charts. Soon, my group began by familiarizing ourselves with the manuals on 105 howitzers. As an academically minded person, I did extremely well on the exams regarding what these contained. Nonetheless, I was far from the best mechanic in my cohort. Several of my fellow students were much better at fixing artillery pieces. They didn't mind getting their hands dirty and enjoyed the challenge of figuring out what was wrong. As the years went by, they became quite proficient at their duties, whereas I, a reservist, did not keep up.

The moral of this story is that practice matters. Intellectual knowledge that remains disconnected from the real world has the consistency of smoke. It may look substantial from a distance, but it does not get the job done. Indeed, theory and practice are often considered mortal enemies. Theorists are presumably big-brained intellectuals who are capable of unraveling daunting puzzles. More practical people, in contrast, believe in getting down to business. Their concern is what works; hence, they spurn pie-in-the-sky solutions. Yet so far as the theorists are concerned, these practical folks are hidebound conformists. They presumably do not learn new ways of doing things because they do not seek them. Practical people, in their turn, dismiss the feasibility of theoretical solutions. They make jokes about eggheads who are too smart for their own good.

In fact, theory and practice are inextricably bound. Either without the other is incomplete. Thus, theory that is never tested in the real world may be nothing other than idle speculation, whereas practice that is uninformed by theory is blind to unexpected possibilities. The good news is that universities are a place where theory and practice can achieve a détente. The best schools are not ivory towers where students are locked away, memorizing scholastic arguments. While some academics are prepared to debate the equivalent of how many angels can dance on the head of a pin, many get out their microscopes to count them as they cavort. Although it is true that some scholars are absent-minded, many are not. More important, few students are. Most know that what they are capable of doing will ultimately be evaluated in the real world.

Accordingly, it is essential that university programs provide students the opportunity to practice and apply the information learned in class. College campuses cannot supplant the lessons acquired by doing productive work, but they can provide introductory experiences regarding what to expect. In fact, many do. Nor do most reformers suggest that they desist. Almost no one believes higher education should be all theory and abstruse abstractions. Most know that practical experience is also of value.

The fact is that writing and then writing some more is the best way to learn how to write well. Similarly, learning to read intelligently is best accomplished by doing a great deal of reading. As it happens, one of the beneficial side effects of reading is the acquisition of a large vocabulary, which when later put to use can provide symbolic evidence of one's education. This outcome also makes it more difficult for others to intimidate college graduates. To paraphrase the former British Prime Minister Harold Wilson, going to college makes it easier to spot rubbish when it is later encountered. The mysteries of elite culture, having been stumbled upon in the classroom and textbooks, lose their ability to terrorize.

But to continue, learning to speak before groups is best learned by practicing how to speak before groups. Likewise, engaging in research facilitates doing competent research. The same can be said for creating art, participating in politics, competing in athletics, acting in theatricals, or perusing business balance sheets. In many fields, such as social work and psychology, interpersonal skills can also be mastered by partaking in role-playing. Students do not have to work with actual clients in order to rehearse how to deal with them. In addition, independent thinking is an expertise best honed by thinking independently and by defending one's conclusions before others who are well versed in the issues. Colleges that provide experience in these, as most do, thereby expedite self-direction by allowing students to engage in it.

Still unmentioned is practice in socializing. For many students, college is their first significant opportunity to interact with adults as an adult. Online programs frequently boast that they enable learners to participate in conversations with other learners, yet these are a feeble simulation of the real thing. Electronic intermediaries cannot replace the subtle facial cues, the emotional ambiance, the linguistic delicacy, and the body language of face-to-face encounters. They are not adequate substitutes for the personal relationships that flower only in personal meetings (Putnam, 2012). Without these, students cannot learn who they are, who others are, or how they stand vis-à-vis actual human beings. People deprived of human contact never discover their own strengths and weaknesses. As a result, they never develop the interpersonal tools necessary for leadership or for loving relationships. Oftentimes what a young person imagined would be his or her fate is utterly altered in the give-and-take of campus life. To underrate this aspect of higher education is a mistake. This is why extracurricular activities must never be discounted when contemplating reform.

Nor should the importance of internships or service learning be slighted. These too furnish unexpected challenges. Our techno-commercial society is so complex that children are never exposed to the full panoply of occupational and/or relationship possibilities. Aside from the limitations imposed by their immaturity, they get to glimpse but a few high-profile positions, and even then romanticism distorts their view. Often the only way to find out what a particular job entails is to be exposed to it. I cannot tell you how many times I have heard students say the equivalent of "I always wanted to be a teacher until I did student teaching and discovered that I am not cut out for working with children." By the same token, I have often been told something like "I thought I would hate being a police officer, but riding around with the cops made me realize this is what I want to be; this is a job I can handle."

Many times internships introduce students to careers they never contemplated. Thus, in sociology few majors begin by considering human resource occupations; that is, until they are exposed to them. In psychology, the same goes for industrial psychology. Internships therefore deserve to be integrated into college programs. Aside from the direct practice they provide, they allow for indirect practice in the form of information exchanges with fellow students who are experiencing other occupations.

Diversity

Good colleges are cosmopolitan places. Their faculties and student bodies are drawn from disparate backgrounds. This provides learners with an opportunity to interact with a wider world and therefore to expand their repertoires of ideas and experiences. In making them more knowledgeable, this also makes them more tolerant of differences. They become less ethnocentric and, as a result, are open to solutions never previously entertained.

To this end, many universities have promoted what is usually described as "diversity" (Lynch, 1997; Wood, 2003; Dobbin, 2009).

There is, however, a huge element of hypocrisy in this endeavor (Clegg and Rosenberg, 2012). Recruiting minorities was originally instituted as a tool to end segregation, but it soon came under political fire as "reverse discrimination." Schools at first responded that they were not using quotas to allocate entrance slots; they were merely setting goals. Yet when court decisions began going against them, they switched to the diversity rationale. They were now supposedly favoring minorities, not because they were minorities but because other students benefitted from exposure to unfamiliar cultures. Besides, the assumption that some cultures and peoples were superior to others was balderdash. It was judgmental and betrayed more than a whiff of nativist hegemony.

The problem with the diversity policy, however, is that it is group-oriented (Connerly, 2000). Candidates for admission are selected according to their community membership, as opposed to their personal qualifications. As a result, different standards are applied based upon racial and/or ethnic identity. This often means that minority members, including those who lack the academic preparation for demanding programs, are accepted to schools where they subsequently fail out. These dropouts are not helped by this charade. In fact, many never complete degrees that they could manage elsewhere. Research, such as that of Richard Sander (Sander and Taylor, 2012), as presented in his book *Mismatch*, demonstrates that many would do better if they were matched with schools that suit their qualifications. In this case, they would not suffer the frustration and personal doubts created by falling behind better-prepared peers. The problem is exacerbated by a cascade effect whereby the most elite schools accept the best, albeit still unqualified, students, leaving even less qualified ones for less the elite schools. This means that even non-demanding schools must admit learners who cannot keep up with their less challenging curricula.

A further difficulty with ill-disguised quotas is that they are inherently coercive (Entine, 2000). Instead of allocating admission according to merit, they thrust unqualified students in, to the detriment of more capable ones. This is unfair and violates principles of universality. Nonetheless, their classmates are required to remain silent, lest they suffer unpleasant consequences. This, however, contradicts the premises of the diversity rationale. Students who are expected to learn about the irrelevance of category differences are actually confronted with partiality based on group membership. Instead of the same standards being applied to everyone, they are forced to keep quiet in the face of well-intended discrimination. Although they may believe this wrong, they must, for prudence sake, keep their opinions to themselves.

The fact is that diversity works only where it is voluntary. When it is not, people close their hearts and minds. They resent being manipulated, and as a result, learning about others is stymied. Instead, the lesson is that some people are not good enough to make it on their own. Despite assertions of equality, they are really treated as inferior. Paradoxically, excuses are made on their behalf and biases are portrayed as fairness. Nonetheless, few are fooled; including those provided the "benefits." These minority members feel singled out as different—which they are—while at the same time they are allowed to slide by without facing the same demands as their classmates (Feagin and Sikes, 1994). The implication is that they could not meet these and hence, they must be treated with kid gloves (Thernstrom and Thernstrom, 1997, 2003).

All this flies in the face of self-direction (Skrenteny, 1996). It ignores the fact that only individuals who are able to live up to demanding standards can fulfill professionalized responsibilities (Carter, 1991; McWhorter, 2003). The reality of a socially acknowledged expertise is grounded in universalized criteria. Professionals are regarded as competent at what they do because strangers can be confident that they will measure up to exacting guidelines. Once special allowances are granted based on skin-color, religion, gender, social class, or national origin, this assurance is eroded. Indeed, it is likely that later tests of strength will not be met by the recipients of affirmative action; hence, their weaknesses will be revealed. This is not only inimical to their personal interests but to the reputations of other professionals. What is more, it undermines the role integrity of techno-commercial societies.

Consequently, college administrations and faculties that promote artificial diversity do neither their students nor society a favor (Espenshade and Radford, 2009). Worse still, they weaken the foundations of higher education. Thus, they inadvertently undercut the standing of their schools when they use surreptitious means to circumvent laws requiring color-blind admission (as was done in California and Michigan). Fairness is a worthwhile goal, but introducing new forms of unfairness cannot foster it. If the objective is to strengthen universal standards, then universal standards ought to be applied.

Of course, a half a century ago, it was assumed that giving the victims of racial discrimination a leg up would help them overcome disabilities imposed by centuries of maltreatment. The analogy used was of a "head start" that would enable the handicapped to develop the strengths necessary to compete on an even footing. This was a reasonable theory. Nevertheless, it did not work as imagined. Individuals allowed to get by doing less often became content to do less. Rather than develop self-direction, they became dependent on preferences. This favoritism was subsequently both rationalized and institutionalized. Diversity programs are today maintained, not because of their demonstrated effectiveness, but because they have become a way of life.

Gender issues too have been dealt with more along ideological than pragmatic grounds. Once more good intentions have morphed into an assault on middle class values. False dreams of equality have been allowed to threaten the liberties of both men and women (Hochschild, 1995). This is evidenced by efforts to promote "cooperation," as opposed to "competition" (Gilligan, 1982). The former is presented as a feminine attribute that has been suppressed in favor of the latter (Horowitz, 1998). Accordingly, today many college courses aim to encourage collaborative endeavors. They assume that male efforts to outdo one another are anti-democratic and injurious. It is argued that if students are instead taught to be mutually supportive, together they can achieve more than they could individually. The self, in other words, should not be allowed to become egoistic. As per the neo-Marxists, it must be subordinated to the good of the many.

In fact, men do tend to be more competitive than women (Moir and Jessel, 1989). Yet it is also a fact that self-directed success is frequently dependent on such competitive efforts. People who attempt to outdo others, as many men do, often achieve significant results. To close this channel down on the grounds that some people are hurt by it is to sponsor stability at the expense of progress. It is to favor a warm and fuzzy status quo over the turmoil of a vigorous market system.

These facts matter as the number of women on college campuses approaches twice that of men. Higher education is in the process of becoming a feminine ghetto (DiPrete and Buchmann, 2013). This has altered the ambience of many universities, especially the less elite institutions. It has made them more congenial to feminized values and less to masculine ones. This transformation is celebrated in some circles, but it may not bode well for the future of higher education. If colleges historically trained men to occupy positions of social authority, what does it mean if more women acquire a college education than men do—or that this education discourages competition?

Does anyone imagine that the feminization of college attendance implies that ours will become a female-dominated society

(Whittier, 1995)? Or does it suggest that men who are motivated to achieve social dominance will adopt other avenues toward success? If the latter, then universities may be paving their way toward irrelevance. Thomas DiPrete and Claudia Bachmann suggest that this can be averted if college programs essentially teach men to be more feminized and less aggressively competitive. But wouldn't this undermine efforts to assist them in becoming self-directed leaders? If their biological nature is subverted, how can their strengths be harnessed to serve larger social purposes? Might it not be better to accommodate masculine needs rather than dismiss these as uncivilized? As of today, many academics take it for granted that women have been discriminated against; hence, they advocate additional programs designed to promote female success (Lorber, 1994). But what of the men (Sommers, 2000)? Feminists insist that males are oppressors who need no special assistance. But doesn't this discriminate against them?

There can be no doubt that most universities will continue to be co-educational. Yet what will become of their ambience? At this point, it is difficult to say. For the moment, few regard the campus gender ratio as problematic. Consequently, few offer correctives to what is not regarded as perilous. This is changing, but that collegiate atmospherics discourage the muscular self-direction necessary in a Gesellschaft society is not on many radar screens. This itself is a problem. It is a failure to look ahead that might invite unanticipated crises.

For the present, what must be addressed is the prevalence of political correctness on campus. If biased affirmative action and an unacknowledged feminization have come to characterize contemporary higher education, then an inability to discuss these candidly is also unfortunate (Sowell, 2004). Nowadays students who openly express disapproved opinions are apt to find themselves discriminated against. Where once colleges prided themselves on being marketplaces of ideas, they today confine controversial viewpoints to "speaker's corners." Unpopular attitudes, specifically those about race and gender, are considered offensive. Expressing them aloud is therefore thought to create a "hostile" environment (MacKinnon, 1987). Those who might be offended are believed to have a right not to be made uncomfortable. Meanwhile, that the suppression of free speech might discomfort those denied the right to be heard is considered irrelevant.

Not long ago, free speech was protected by the first amendment of the Constitution. Intellectuals parroted what they believed to be Voltaire's assertion that although he disagreed with his opponents, he would fight to the death for their right to speak their minds. This is a shame in that self-direction is quashed when out-of-favor ideas are quashed. The explorations that stimulate independent thought are hampered when limited to socially acceptable shibboleths. Once upon a time, those currently promoting political correctness understood this. When their ideas were punished (e.g., by Joseph McCarthy), they flew to the barricades to defend civil rights. They would never have condoned the destruction of student newspapers because they printed unpopular leftist ideas. Nor would they have expelled students who advocated detested attitudes. Those days are gone. The homogeneity in campus political attitudes is such that it has been imposed on students as well. This means that self-direction not in accord with approved political attitudes is rarely tolerated.

The extent of this "neo-totalitarianism" has been documented by Greg Lukianoff (2012) in *Unlearning Liberty: Campus Censorship and the End of American Debate.* As the president of the Foundation for Individual Rights in Education, (French, et al., 2005) and as an attorney, he has been deeply involved in resisting efforts to restrict free speech. Those who believe the suppression of unpopular thought is a minor academic blemish may be surprised at how pervasive it has become (Kors and Silverglate, 1998). The number of examples Lukianoff presents is stunning. As discouraging is the degree to which colleges and universities engage in moral indoctrination (Kramer and Kimball, 1999). Not only is this prevalent in classrooms, it has migrated to residence halls where students may be harassed into expressing politically correct sentiments. Worse still, as with affirmative action, administrators and professors alike oppose efforts to excise these transgressions. But this stance too is inimical to self-direction.

Conclusions

Colleges and universities need to maintain high standards. They must consequently curb grade inflation. As long as students continue to be awarded grades they have not earned, they will retain inflated opinions of their abilities. When distinctions about who has learned and who has not become blurred, the incentive to learn is eroded. Only honest evaluations can protect genuinely high standards.

The widespread student sense of entitlement must consequently be challenged. The United States has been the wealthiest and most powerful nation in the world for the better part of a century, but this does not mean that every American is entitled to be a secular aristocrat.

Professors must have the courage to challenge this misconception so that students can make more valid appraisals of their potential. It is especially at lower-level institutions that academic standards must be upheld. This is because the temptation to dilute these is greatest where the emphasis on academics is weakest. Schools with large numbers of poorly prepared students must therefore resist demands to allow easy graduation.

By the same token, student explorations should be encouraged. Accordingly the opportunity to change majors should not be curtailed. Most students come to higher education unaware of the sorts of persons they are or the types of occupations best suited to their abilities and desires. Oftentimes they discover these in the process of testing alternatives. It is frequently by ruling out unacceptable choices that they determine the appropriate ones. This means that "major shopping" should not be discouraged.

A corollary of this is that students should not be rushed into making choices. It often takes time to figure out what is appropriate. Efforts to force students to graduate according in accord with a predetermined schedule may therefore be counterproductive. Individuals mature at different rates and face a range of diverse challenges; hence, the timetable that is best for one may not be for another. Students should also be encouraged to make their own choices. They must live with whatever majors they choose; hence, they should choose something that works for them. Parents and professors may have ideas about what is best; nevertheless, students are better situated to decide what suits them. Furthermore, it is in making these decisions that they hone their skills in self-direction.

Professionalization is also facilitated when colleges and universities strive to create a community of learners. Students who interact with one another learn from one another. Higher education is a social phenomenon. Much of it occurs outside the classroom. Colleges and universities ought therefore provide an ambience where this can occur. Residential schools can achieve this via their dormitories and eating facilities. Commuter schools can do so with student lounges, extracurricular activities, and school spirit.

More particularly, students should be encouraged engage in peer-level discussions. Colleges must not intimate that all knowledge is to be derived from their faculties. Student bull sessions also provide an opportunity to explore ideas and test intellectual skills. The young may be relatively callow, but their immaturity is surmounted in learning to deal with the differences between themselves. The resultant stresses likewise assist in developing emotional maturity. Stress is not inherently bad. As psychologists have learned, eustress can build character and promote emotional toughness.

Neither should social activities be neglected. At first blush, socializing with one's peers may not seem to provide intellectual benefits, but this is untrue. Learning about oneself and others via intimate relationships is an essential aspect of exploring the real world. A steady diet of abstractions not only makes for dull students, but it detaches them from reality. Circumstances must therefore be arranged so that students can be emotionally and intellectually supportive of one another. Providing multilevel venues for this allows learners to be available to one another in ways that authority figures cannot. Sometimes it is only peers (i.e., those experiencing similar challenges) that can provide the supports acceptable to vulnerable individuals. This makes them feel "understood" without feeling judged.

Perhaps the most important circumstance higher education can provide an opportunity for a psychosocial moratorium. The transition to adult responsibilities can be demanding and may therefore need to be cushioned. Ironically, allowing people the time to grow up can make the process go faster. Pressuring unready individuals to make binding decisions is a formula for failure. It causes mistakes that later have to be rectified. Many individuals on the cusp of adulthood therefore benefit from a time off, during which they test themselves and the world they are entering. Allowing a reduced level of responsibilities during this phase is thus in their interest. So may be the foolishness that goes with a reduction in social demands. Often the most indelible lessons are derived from silly mistakes—assuming these are subsequently corrected.

Unfortunately some students have serious issues that must be addressed before they can take advantage of learning opportunities. In a perfect world, everyone would have a perfect childhood during which to develop emotional maturity and social independence. Since this is not the case, institutions for higher education, especially at the mid and lower levels, must make provisions for these learners by offering the space and the support to overcome earlier handicaps. Counseling centers and peer advisors are therefore good ideas.

Next students should be afforded an opportunity to rehearse what they learn. Schools should organize activities in which students practice the skills they acquire in the classroom. Colleges may, for instance, sponsor debating societies, model United Nations, musical events, and the like, during which students gain experience in doing what they are studying. This contributes both to their motivation and budding expertise.

Internships should also be a regular feature of the learning experience. Oftentimes students believe that they will enjoy working in fields that later prove unsatisfying. Requiring them to participate in internships enables them to avoid this pitfall. While some internships lead to jobs, more often they forestall reality shock. For a parallel reason, student clubs should be allowed to organize protests and demonstrations. Undergraduates are notoriously idealistic. Many wish to reform the world, even though their knowledge of it is incomplete. Likewise, they think in broad strokes. Protests and other expressions of this romanticism can, as a result, introduce them to the difficulties in implementing their preferred solutions.

Then, too, students can profitably be encouraged to take trips, attend conferences, and publish articles. The college experience should foster a cosmopolitan orientation. Horizons can be expanded by study abroad, by participation in disciplinary activities, and by making contributions to their fields of endeavor. Much like the apprenticeships of old, these are able to assist in making the transition to an adult mentality. So can engaging in authorship. Thus, student publications should remain largely under the control of students. Undergraduates need to be encouraged to publish, even if only on a local level. Much of what they compose may be imprudent, yet these excesses help them distinguish rubbish from wisdom. It is especially important that neither administrators nor faculty members impose their own convictions.

Next, affirmative action must be phased out. When these programs were introduced, it was with the understanding that they would provide a head start for those left behind. Whether these were minorities, women, or pariah communities, they would be to allowed to catch up. The intention was never to introduce perpetually different standards, which would violate the American dream of equal opportunity for all. An unanticipated side effect was that lowering standards for targeted groups reduced their incentive to perform. We humans respond to the demands made of us. When these are lowered—for whatever reason—we tend to do less. As a result, the very programs designed to help the victims of discrimination placed millstones around their necks. Many never lived up to their potential because they discovered they could get by with reduced efforts. In the end, they were robbed of the respect they might otherwise have earned.

Universal standards, it must be emphasized, are best instilled by being uniformly applied. Minorities formerly treated unfairly deserve equal treatment now. By the same token majorities that indulged in discrimination must learn to refrain from bigotry. Nevertheless, visiting unfairness on the descendants of its perpetrators is not the most effective way of institutionalizing fairness. Fair-mindedness is best taught by being fair. Diversity should thus be achieved organically and voluntarily. It is a worthwhile goal that can, in fact, expand the horizons of students. But if it is to be achieved, it must not be artificially enforced.

In sum, a relevant higher education is a well-rounded package. Far more than providing an appropriate curriculum, it addresses the whole person. Individuals do not become self-directed experts merely by consuming facts and statistics. They must also be immersed in a community that instills the attitudes and cultural capital needed to make good decisions in an environment of uncertainty. They must also be allowed to grow at their own pace. Cookie-cutter reforms that inhibit the development of individual strengths or that undercut historically constructed college supports are therefore ill-conceived. They may seem well crafted, but they leave out the human dimension.

8

Self-Directed Faculties

Administrative Bloat

As universities have grown larger, they have also grown more bureaucratic. With more to coordinate, the machinery designed to do so has increased in size and complexity. This, in turn, has amplified the pressures directed against faculty professionalization. Instead of encouraging professors to be more self-directed, efforts have been made to make them less so. Specifically, rather than increasing their control over the classroom, they have had to contend with attempts to curtail their prerogatives. This unfortunately has adversely affected the ability of faculty members to transmit self-directed attitudes to their students. Ironically, although the need for professionalization has escalated, the autonomy needed to promote it has been suppressed.

More bureaucracy means more administrators, whereas multiplying administrators invites further efforts at top-down control. Managers specialize in exercising power. They perceive their job as directing the activities of others. Indeed, they feel duty-bound to impose external controls. Where work is complicated yet routine and/or where uniformity is essential, this attitude can be useful. Where, however, responsiveness and discretion are needed, it can be detrimental (Grusky and Miller, 1970). The latter is the situation with respect to higher education.

There can be no doubt that university administrations have exploded in size and intrusiveness. The number of administrators has grown at almost twice the pace for professors, while the disparity in salaries has accelerated at least as quickly. Less well recognized are the rigidities instituted as a result of these disparities. Because administrators have different goals than front-line academics, they frequently support organizational policies inimical to superior teaching. Despite the fact that they proclaim an allegiance to educational quality, their programs often have the opposite effect. This is not because they are evil, but because the nature of their positions propels them in these directions.

Management is about control (Whyte, 1956; Perrow, 1970). Historically, it is about making sure that subordinates do what they are supposed to do. In non-professionalized organizations, direction routinely comes from the top down. This being the norm, it can be difficult for managers to cede authority to professionalized underlings. Even when this makes sense, it does not feel comfortable. Quite understandably, people who perceive themselves as in charge do not appreciate pressures emanating from below. This includes demands from college faculties, despite the social prestige that professors enjoy. In the university setting, the drive toward control is manifested in a number of ways. One is empire building, a second is efforts to impose "accountability," and a third is standardization. Each of these has its place; nevertheless, all militate against professionalization and faculty self-direction. As such, they are responsible for many problems that contribute to the college bubble.

If we begin with empire building, we must realize that this tendency characterizes executives as a social category. People who go into management often do so because they crave power. They hope to control others and to garner the stature that goes with such control. This translates into perceiving success as contingent on obtaining ever-greater influence. The more subordinates led, the more important decisions made, the more eminent a manager feels. What is actually accomplished pales in significance compared with perceptions of what seems to have been accomplished.

And so college administrators seek to increase the number of their subordinates (Ginsberg, 2011). One reason why the ranks of educational managers have swelled is that the more underlings presidents and vice presidents directly control, the more important they feel. The same applies to the inflated titles awarded junior administrators. Where once college presidents were content to deal directly with deans and provosts, today they are surrounded by legions of vice presidents. Deans and assistant deans and discipline coordinators have similarly multiplied as the number of colleges into which universities are divided has grown. As if this were not enough, the salaries of these bureaucrats have increased apace. Those at the top feel more important when those below them also have large incomes—in that this confirms their comparative importance. As a consequence, faculty members get left in the dust (Jaschick, 2012e). Subordinate to even junior administrators, they must earn less to corroborate their inferiority. This is especially so at mid- and lower-level schools where the professors cannot bring national reputations to the bargaining table.

Empire building also extends to the level of students. Obviously, the more learners a school enrolls, the more noteworthy it must be. And so enrollments continue to rise. So too do the numbers of majors offered, because the more of these an institution has on its books, the higher its relative standing. This, of course, dictates that there must be buildings to accommodate the overflow. Nor does it hurt if these are fancy. Then, too, successful athletic programs can bring favorable publicity. Even thriving research programs fetch prestige. To be more like Harvard suggests that a school's administrators must be worthy of comparable respect.

And so we get an endless game of follow the leader. Everyone wants to do what the prestigious schools are doing and/or what the prestigious foundations recommend. Moreover, since each school is ratcheting up its enrollments, its offerings, and its administrative ranks, its immediate competitors feel compelled to do the same. They do not develop innovations based on local conditions but copy what seems to have worked elsewhere. Hence, if interdisciplinary departments are being created at other schools, or if university colleges have become a craze, or if women's studies are perceived as a gauge of modernity, these are implemented irrespective of the need or the consequences. Administrators who do not want to be caught with their pants down follow what others do, because this is safer. It is also liable to bring kudos. On one level, therefore, they cannot be faulted. True innovation is dangerous. Idiosyncratic mistakes can topple a rash leader, whereas conforming to the pack is less likely to tempt the public to demand the scalp of a wayward president, provost, or dean.

Empire building extends down to faculty members as well. Administrators know they can count on the support of subordinates upon whom they shower favor. Professors promoted into the executive suite usually make more money for doing less work than they did in the classroom. As a result, they are grateful to their sponsors and eagerly carry their water. This loyalty is rewarded and reproduced downward as junior administrators hasten to appoint assistants loyal to them.

Most schools tell faculty members that advancement in rank depends on success in research and teaching. Service is theoretically relegated to lesser significance. Yet the reality of the college pecking order is somewhat different. Yes, eminence in research can lead to promotion to associate and/or full professor, but the addition to one's salary, at smaller schools, rarely exceeds four thousand dollars. Meanwhile, promotion into a managerial position can add ten, twenty, and even fifty thousand dollars to one's income. Worse still, salary compression has been proceeding at an alarming rate. Because of the current economic conditions, the amount paid senior faculty has remained stagnant; whereas that paid junior faculty has increased so as to attract competent applicants. The result is that the difference between what is disbursed to the most experienced and least experienced faculty members has virtually disappeared and in some cases has been reversed (Flaherty, 2013). Professors know this and thus, those desirous of organizational power and additional dollars put their eggs into the service basket. Sooner or later, if they can make themselves useful to those capable of promoting them, they profitably escape the academic grind. An unanticipated side effect of this bureaucratic escalator is, of course, that experienced teachers often opt out of teaching, thereby leaving less qualified ones to fill the void.

There is also the practice of co-optation. Administrators increase their authority by assigning faculty members to complete tasks ostensibly in accord with their underlings' objectives. As a result, programs are launched that feed faculty egos, while simultaneously making them feel part of the team. Thus, there are committee duties to complete and prestigious reports to write. Accordingly, a professor can sit on the academic senate, a budget committee, or a core curriculum team without making an ounce of difference to learning outcomes. Nonetheless, as a valued part of the governing machinery, he or she feels obliged to refrain from making waves.

Another recent manifestation of the expansion of bureaucratic control has been the call for greater *accountability*. Administrators are presumably responsible for maintaining the quality of the education. Although they are not in the classroom, their alleged academic superiority makes them responsible for ensuring that students receive the promised academic benefits. Indeed, the public demands this. Ordinary citizens and the parents of potential students want to make certain the money spent on college is wisely expended. They don't want dead wood teaching subjects their children do not need.

As the symbolic heads of universities and colleges, administrators are frequently asked to explain—and sometimes demonstrate—how their institutions fulfill their mission. How is it that heads-in-the-clouds professors are allowed to get away with teaching so few hours and producing such lame results? There must be an answer laypersons are prepared to accept. Not surprisingly, administrators seek to provide one. But once more, it is at mid-level institutions that these pressures are most felt. Dependent as many are on public funds and staffed by non-prestigious professors, citizens have doubts they feel a right to express, and thus administrators experience anxieties they wish to allay.

But here is the problem. Administrators are not in the classroom. They do not see what professors are doing. Nor are they experts on all of the subjects the professors teach. They may themselves have been trained as political scientists, accountants, or educators. How then are they to tell what should be taught in mathematics and nursing, or whether this is being taught effectively? In fact, whatever they say, they cannot be certain. Nevertheless, they feel impelled to say something, for to suggest that they have done nothing to improve institutional outcomes might be regarded as gross incompetence.

What then to do? Some gauges of effectiveness must be put in place. And hence they are. The trouble is that these rarely measure what they purport to measure. Because they must be simple to administer and outwardly fair, they tend to leave out subtleties. Among the most popular techniques are student evaluations. At the end of each term, students are asked to fill out forms on which they rank their teachers on a variety of dimensions—did the profs know their materials, did they teach them effectively, were they fair graders, were they available to provide assistance, and so forth. On the face of it, this sounds reasonable, but experience has demonstrated serious flaws. For instance, professors who teach difficult courses are liable to be evaluated more harshly. On the other hand, likeable professors usually rate high. As winners of a popularity contest, they seem, on paper, to be better educators than their more exacting colleagues. Meanwhile, controversial professors are in a bind. Students who agree with them may be effusive in their praise, while those who don't are apt to be scathing critics. Besides, how insightful are students who do not know what they need to know? Some studies suggest that graduates come to different conclusions as the years pass by. In fact, the more experience they have, the more accurate their assessments are liable to be.

Nonetheless, student evaluations may be all administrators have to go on. They too may realize these are deficient, yet what is the alternative? Something similar applies to judgments regarding faculty achievements in research and creative activities. Once more, personal limitations preclude a direct assessment of what has been accomplished.

And so here too, administrators resort to indirect measures. Thus, they count the numbers of papers a professor has published and rank of the journals in which they appeared. Or they tally the number of citations a professor's work receives. How many times have other scholars mentioned his or her writings? This is "publish or perish" at ground level.

On the face of it, this also seems like a sensible procedure, yet it too is fraught with misleading conclusions. For one thing, many highly accomplished scholars are not prolific writers. They know their materials and may even be innovative in the classroom, but they publish few papers. George Herbert Mead immediately comes to mind. Often regarded as the father of symbolic interactionism, his printed output was meager. Indeed, his magnum opus, *Mind, Self, and Society* (Mead, 1934), derived from student notes. In addition, quantity may not be correlated with quality. Nowadays many academics have learned they can collaborate with partners to produce dozens of multi-authored papers. They have also discovered that they can rework the same materials so that they are published in different journals under different titles. This looks good but is poor evidence of scholarly achievement.

Even the number of citations an author receives can be misleading (Bauerlein, 2013; Hollander, 2013; Weisberg, 2013a). If an academic is producing works consistent with mainstream opinions, other colleagues may utilize these to bolster their own claims. But if an author is outside the disciplinary consensus, his or her work may be ignored. Conventionality is a feeble indicator of validity. Moreover, it is an incentive to refrain from innovation. Intellectual breakthroughs rarely emanate from the establishment, yet is it consistency with establishment views that administrators reward.

This last piece of information is in line with administrative desires for predictability (Ritzer, 2011). Bureaucratic leaders are generally not disposed to favor subordinates who cause trouble. That which is unexpected is difficult to control. And so most of the people who run universities rate those who go along to get along the highest. These are the folks they promote; these are the ones they shower with honors and large salaries. Rule breakers, on the other hand, are singled out for punishment. Unlike their more accommodating colleagues who are allowed to get away with small indiscretions, they are not.

Then there is the bureaucratic penchant for *standardization*. Here too the arguments in favor of homogeneity are based in a supposed need to improve educational quality. Administrators contend that if uniformly high standards are imposed, teaching and research will improve.

The notion is that there are empirically recognized "best practices" that, if insisted upon, generate improved outcomes (Christensen and Eyring, 2011). Professors who have hitherto been allowed to improvise their own must therefore be reined in and instructed to conform to techniques with demonstrated effectiveness. This, however, is based on propaganda. Its utility has not been substantiated in practice.

For proof that educators have not discovered a foolproof formula for enhancing pedagogical efficiency all one must do is cast a wary eye on K–12 schools. The amount of money and expertise directed toward these have been prodigious, but standardized tests do not corroborate their efficacy. It is one thing for alleged experts to assert their know-how but quite another to demonstrate it in action. The sad truth is that many professional educators hope to do to universities what they have done to primary and secondary schools. They want to validate their theories, not via consequences but via universality. Presumably, if everyone does what they claim is best, they must be right.

In fact, the central point of standardization is control. Managers really do like predictability. They want to be certain that what they tell others to do is done. Delegating control to subordinates leaves too many uncertainties. What are those professors doing behind closed doors? Are they insisting students learn what they should? The best way to be certain is to demand that faculty members implement predetermined patterns. College administrators do not, however, know what works best. Nor can they demonstrate that identical techniques work well under all conditions. What is, in reality, coveted is *consistency* because this makes it easier to monitor what is done. Since discretion is the enemy of uniformity, it is feared.

This is why many administrators love technology. Machines facilitate standardization. Computers and online learning have risen to prominence, in part, because they reduce the human element in education. They can be programmed to do the same thing the same way every time, which permits further centralization. A smaller number of persons, under the direct supervision of higher-ups, can thereby be controlled so as to produce practices capable of being scrutinized by non-experts. Flexibility and responsiveness are lost, but uniformity and predictability are gained. Spontaneity and innovation are sacrificed, but the power of those who crave power is enhanced.

Cookie-cutter programs introduce a comparable reliability. It is not so much that these have established their efficacy as they can be initiated from above. Standardized syllabi, identical teaching rubrics, flashy graphics, universal evaluation measures, prepackaged classroom exercises, and preapproved learning outcomes can all be justified as "best practices." That they may not mesh with the personalities and/or skill sets of particular professors is deemed irrelevant. Likewise, that they may not have the predicted consequences, especially for self-direction, is ignored.

Once, when I was working as a vocational counselor, I sought to develop new therapeutic techniques (Fein, 2011). After my supervisor got wind of this, he told me to stop. When I asked if he had doubts about the effectiveness of what I was doing, he admitted that this was not the issue. The problem, he said, was that he did not understand what I was doing and therefore, I must stop. This same mentality infects college administrators. Because they can neither see, nor control, nor even understand what is occurring in diverse disciplines, they often enforce a limited array of policies that they believe they do understand.

This attitude produces a shallowness and inflexibility inimical to pedagogical or scholarly advancements. Mao Tse-tung encouraged a hundred flowers to grow and then beheaded those with whom he disagreed. The sad truth is that many heads have been rolling on American campuses. Professors who do not wish to be homogenized have been put on notice. They must conform or be judged incompetent.

Yet variety is productive of invention. Diverse ideas are the seedbed of progress. No doubt they are untidy. They do not make for orderliness or predictability. This is one reason some politicians despise the free market. Nonetheless, it is from free markets that democracy and prosperity arose (Spencer, 1969). The same applies to universities. Allowing professors to remain unstandardized allows them to be creative. When freed from arbitrary constraints, they can come up with new ideas. They can also be inspirational in ways that uniformly disciplined pedagogues are not. Although it is true that some willful professors go off half-cocked, this is a small price to pay for unforeseen—and unforeseeable—improvements.

Meanwhile, administrators in quest of standardization wallow in a follow-the-leader mentality. They boast of the new programs brought to campus, the overwhelming majority of which were cribbed from elsewhere. Whether these are interdisciplinary departments, university colleges, orientation courses, equal-opportunity directors, or special facilities for the developmentally handicapped, the odds are they were pioneered at other schools and/or advocated by prestigious think tanks. Most college administrators are risk-averse. They do not want to be the flower picked before its time. And so they conform. Talk about critical thinking may be all well and good, but if standing out invites criticism, this could be career-threatening. As a result, they too go along to get along, which ironically includes posturing about being innovative.

The sociologist Michel Crozier (1964) made an interesting observation that throws light on the managerial mentality. In researching a French cigarette factory, he discovered that its manager was happiest when doing something. During those periods that the plant was operating almost automatically, he was bored. It was when engaged in reorganizing its operations that he flourished. He might be the number-one authority on site, but this did him little good unless he was exercising this power. As a consequence, he invented things to do.

College administrators also need things to do. Were they to delegate significant responsibilities downward, they might feel superfluous. The result is that they feel impelled to make changes. These are rationalized as improvements, but this enhancement is rarely vindicated. A prime example is core curricula. These are forever being tinkered with, albeit without evidence of greater learning. Largely missing from these efforts is a clear-sighted understanding of what is necessary. The mission of higher education is understood in banal of terms. Indeed, the goal of promoting professionalized self-direction is almost never consciously entertained. And so, there is a lot of bravado and claims about distinctive successes, without much forward movement.

A Professionalized Faculty

If college administrators and faculty members are at odds about what the faculty role should be, professors are themselves vague about the objectives they should pursue. Most think of themselves as professionals, but they do not purposefully apply the criteria of professionalism to what they do. They certainly are aware, however, that they are often at odds with their superiors. Furthermore, they know their bosses frequently disrespect them. Nevertheless, they rarely contemplate what distinguishes them from these managers.

As might be expected, most professors are oriented toward their own disciplines and their own teaching assignments. Thus, if their emphasis is on research or creativity, they are focused on breakthroughs that might garner recognition from their peers (Glendon, 2011). Or if they are focused on the classroom, their chief concern is liable to be what happens between them and their students (Lang, 2008). The nuts-and-bolts of coordinating a bureaucratic institution are far from their thoughts. While they must make adjustments to meet administrative demands, these are generally unwelcome intrusions. The upshot is that they are unlikely to plan how to preserve professional perquisites against encroachments from their superiors. While they may value academic freedom, most remain naïve when it comes to the political maneuvers needed to keep administrators at bay.

As discussed above, for many administrators maintaining or enhancing their control is the central issue of their careers. For professors, this is a side issue. That they have not been completely overwhelmed by their organizational betters owes more to the complexity of their tasks than their political acumen. For the most part, their bosses do not tell them what to teach because they do not know what needs to be taught. Still, if the discretion required to pass along a self-directed expertise is to be preserved, academics must have a better grasp of what is at stake. If they are to uphold professionalization, they must understand what this entails.

Let us therefore examine the basics of professionalization (Greenwood, 1957). This begins with a specialized knowledge. College professors have to be authentic experts in their specialties. They cannot be dilettantes who pretend to know what they do not. If they attempt this, they will be found out and disrespected. They must also participate in expanding and refining the boundaries of their disciplines. As the stewards of discrete branches of knowledge, they need to be dedicated to keeping these vibrant. But this endeavor must be sincere. Pretenses to developing new insights will also be found out. Consequently, not all adherents to a discipline need be equally involved in research or creativity. Because not all are equally talented, a relatively few require the resources to pursue additions to our collective knowledge.

From these specialized understandings, assuming they are real and relevant, should flow social authority and self-policing. That which professors understand better than others deserves to be respected by their organizational superiors, by their students, and by the public. Indeed, if their greater knowledge does not command admiration, collective ignorance is liable to be placed in the driver's seat. Nevertheless, reflexive deference is not necessary in that even knowledgeable people make mistakes. Still, though professors can, and should, be questioned about their claims, suppressing their autonomy is seldom a good idea. This includes demands that they teach their courses in the particular way that pedagogical experts or ideological activists believe best.

Professors who know their business ought be modest enough to learn from others but not so compliant that they automatically conform to bureaucratic mandates.

Professors must also have control over the professional discipline exercised within their fields. Thus, they deserve the primary say regarding who is qualified to teach their subjects. The right to hire and fire, as well as to set ethical standards, should largely be vested in them. As the experts in what needs to be taught, they must be delegated the freedom to make these decisions. Were their careers at the mercy of individuals who cannot recognize academic competence, incompetence would be rife. This, however, also requires restraint on the part of professors. Were they, too, to be arbitrary, the results would be as dangerous as those derived from administrative arrogance.

Academic professionals must also maintain high ethical standards. They cannot be dishonest or coercive. If they are to be delegated control, others must be certain they will not abuse it. Professors cannot be gods in their classrooms. They must possess the modesty to recognize their frailties; hence, they must enforce limits on themselves. Research that violates elementary principles of human decency, as well as classroom behaviors that infringe upon student rights, ought to be barred. This too is a minimum that should be expected of professionals.

All of this is dependent upon an adequate professional socialization. Self-motivated experts are not born; they are made. Their expertise is inculcated during an extended period of apprenticeship and maintained within a community of like-minded professionals. In short, college professors cannot be competent professionals unless they participate in a professional culture. The special knowledge they defend, and the authority to exercise it wisely, must be internalized and reinforced. They have to be the kinds of persons who are capably self-directed and who remain so without pressure from organizational superiors.

If this sounds simple, it is anything but. Many of the above pages have been expended on detailing the structural foibles of administrators. Much of what they do is, in fact, contrary to the interests of higher education. This is not, however, because they are contemptible people but because the nature of their positions pushes them in unconstructive directions. The same, however, can be said about professors. They too are imperfect human beings who can be driven astray by the attributes of their positions. What can go wrong and how this can be corrected must therefore be our next focus attention.

Professional Expertise

College professors are supposed to know more about their subjects than others humans—much more. As a result, they are assumed to make superior independent decisions regarding these than laypersons could. This presumably is why students choose to be inducted into their specialties. It is why they too wish to become expert in them. But what if professors are not as knowledgeable as they claim (Solway, 2012)? What if they are like the soothsayers of old who pretended to predict the future by reading the cracks in chicken bones? Should we, as a society, invest billions of dollars in charlatans who only simulate a special competence? Are we paying for the appearance of understandings that do not exist?

Life is fraught with uncertainties; ergo, we humans sometimes fool ourselves into believing we have more control than we do. Ironically, if universities merely specialize in a simulation of control, as paradoxical as it sounds, this too is a useful service. Simply allaying our shared anxieties helps us get on with business. Nonetheless, actual understandings are far more valuable in that they better assist in performing necessary work. Academics should therefore strive to expand what they—and hence, we—know. Thus, they do need to engage in productive research. They should also participate in authentically creative activities. The question, however, is, ought all professors do this? Does it instead make sense to limit the ranks of those required to increase our intellectual patrimony?

In recent years, as hundreds of universities have sought to emulate Harvard, the answer has been that all professors should engage in research and creative activities. Thus, they are told that they need to be "triple threats." Tenure-track academics, as a category, are asked to be productive in teaching, scholarship, and service. If they are, all three prongs will presumably benefit. Thus, with more researchers, schools will accelerate the acquisition of knowledge. And with more dedicated teachers who are active scholars, these pedagogues will have more to offer students. Likewise, with more colleges developing expansive repositories of applied knowledge, society will gain from its application. This is clearly a win-win situation that should elicit universal approbation. Who indeed would question the validity of judiciously harnessed knowledge? Or who would doubt that professors should be encouraged to be all that they can be?

Scholarship. Although it is true that effective scholarship can be synergistic with effective teaching, this interaction presupposes uniformly sound scholarship (Hutchings et al., 2011; Phelps, 2012). This premise, however, is not being met—and never will be (Hamilton, 1996). The unwelcome truth is that not all academics are competent researchers or creative artists. As in any profession, most are run-of-the-mill. They may know their subject matter but do not possess the genius to add significantly to it. Hence, to demand that they do will divert their attention from things that they do well, while simultaneously flooding the marketplace with mediocre ramblings. It is not that average professors cannot contribute useful additions but that they often clog the system with debris that gets in the way of more valuable contributions.

Some observers have complained about what they decry as the new "scholasticism" (Mead, 2011). During the Middle Ages, many scholars devoted their careers to churning out theological trivia that was forgotten soon after their dominance ended. Nowadays, we see an analogous explosion in inconsequential journal articles. Every discipline and sub-discipline has generated new periodicals, frequently online, to concentrate on ever more arcane issues. Academics themselves complain that these materials are often so technical that only a few dozen scholars are interested in reading them. These articles are also so larded with jargon as to be undecipherable by any but a few cognoscenti (Best, 2003).

In reality, the problem is more serious. Much of what is published is of extraordinarily low quality. Once these articles have been decoded, they turn out to add little, if anything, to our knowledge. Often they merely repeat what has been said better elsewhere. In this sense, they offer up old wine in new bottles in the hopes of sounding innovative. Because genuine creativity enhances professional reputations, the objective is to appear to have made a breakthrough. Thus, too often what others have achieved is not cited and in many cases is not known. In part, this is because there is so much extraneous noise in the system that, to mix metaphors, it is difficult to separate the wheat from the chaff. The banal and the insightful sit side by side, making it difficult to distinguish which is which. The result is that most academic articles go unread. Given that the great majority are not worth reading, this does not constitute a serious loss. What does, however, is the incentive to do good work. If all that counts is the number of articles an academic publishes, their quality or influence are of little relevance.

Genius has always been in short supply and remains so today. The difference is that we have many more people pretending to be geniuses because their jobs depend on it. So many pseudo-scholars demand attention that quality gets short shrift, especially in the humanities and social sciences. What tends to take the place of scientific or creative merit is ideological purity. Sadly, much of what professes to be scholarship is moralism in disguise. With neo-Marxism having gained currency on college campuses, its adherents have swamped the intellectual marketplace (Horowitz, 1961). Where once religious divines promulgated theological viewpoints from the pulpit or in avowedly religious tracts, today's left-wing reformers clandestinely peddle their wares in the classroom or in journals that portray them as scientific, scholarly, and/or artistic (Hutchings, et al., 2011).

So ideologically lopsided have these publications become that it is difficult for authors who are not politically correct to acquire a hearing. A recent issue of *Social Forces* (March 2012) provides an instructive example. As the flagship journal of the Southern Sociological Society, it might be expected to reflect the political sympathies of the area of the country in which most of its members reside. This would be wrong. More than half of the articles dealt with inequality as understood from a conflict-theory perspective. Thus, they concerned income inequality in retirement; the impact of slavery on racial inequality; the consequences of right-wing extremism; environmental pollution by large US corporations; the segregation of gay, lesbian, and bisexual youths; and the impact of race, ethnicity, and immigration on structural constraints. In fact, one would be hard-pressed to discover overtly conservative positions expressed in most mainstream academic journals. They are simply judged as not up to the standards of these publications by reviewers who harbor antagonistic ideological preferences.

The reason for this tilt is that on-campus biases have themselves become extreme (Adams, 2004; Yancey, 2012). Attitudes are so uniformly leftist that those who hold them perceive these as moderate. John Ellis and Charles Geshekter (2012) have illustrated the trend to liberal dominance with respect to California state universities. Whereas in 1969, the ratio of Democrats to Republicans on these campuses was five to three, the ratios are now 18:1 in the humanities, 21:1 in the social sciences, and even 10:1 in the natural sciences. Most alarming, the ratio of left to right for new hires is 64:1. In other words, left-leaning professors are reproducing themselves to a degree that is making campus conservatives an endangered species.

Nonetheless, this bias is not thought to be prejudicial by those who enforce it (Gross, 2013). Utterly sincere in their convictions, they are certain they are defending academic quality. They may even blame those excluded from the university for their own dilemma. Thus Neil Gross, a professor of sociology at the University of British Columbia, suggests that conservatives themselves may be discouraging students who agree with them from going to graduate school. By bad-mouthing institutions of higher education, they make academic careers less attractive—with predictable results.

The depressing truth is that many liberal professors are protecting what they regard as moral purity. What matters to them is an author's or a colleague's conclusions, not his or her intellectual rigor. This attitude, however, converts the pursuit of truth into a farce. That which is not considered desirable cannot be discovered to have merit if the gatekeepers will not let it in. Journals refereed thusly claim to uphold scholarly standards. Yet once moralism becomes the criteria for admittance, ideas are no longer allowed to contend in a test comparative of mettle.

The humanities and social sciences have suffered the most from these trends (Attard, 2013). Having jettisoned the neutral quest for specialized knowledge, they have become bastions of radical exhortation masquerading as wisdom (Kimball, 1990). Naturally, those perpetrating this deceit do not comprehend it as such. They argue that even if they have a point of view, it is a valid one. Those who disagree, however, are not apt to be impressed. Regrettably, although professors who endorse the status quo thereby dismiss this leftward drift, they are in the process of undercutting their authority. The intellectual even-handedness they pretend to exhibit may be difficult, yet rejecting it is shortsighted. It robs these would-be professionals of the respect needed to make them socially influential by broadcasting their partisanship.

One smaller impediment is likewise hampering the generation of original ideas. This is the proliferation of IRBs (Institutional Review Boards). These were created to prevent ethical abuses by researchers. No one wanted to see a repetition of the callous disregard for life evidenced by the Tuskegee studies of syphilis patients (Reverby, 2009). These refused treatment to infected subjects, even after a cure had been discovered. The well-being of innocent victims meant less to the researchers than the data obtained by keeping them ill. Once this insensitivity was made public, it reminded people of the brutal "studies" the Nazis perpetrated on concentration camp inmates.

IRBs were to eliminate such ill treatment by requiring academic researchers to receive prior approval from a committee of colleagues before beginning their inquiries. On the face of it, this seems a modest demand. Yet in practice, it too has become a bureaucratic nightmare. As is the case with most bureaucratic agencies, these boards are risk-averse. They would rather say no than allow investigations that might prove harmful. As a result, they tend to throw cold water on any study whose outcome is unpredictable. But this is just what scientific studies are supposed to be. They need to be allowed to tread where others have not gone if they are to uncover the unexpected. Add to this the cumbersome paperwork appended to the research process, and many projects never get off the drawing board. Breakthroughs, especially in the social realm, are never made because they are never attempted.

Teaching

An excess of moralism has also harmed the professionalization of teaching. Many professors believe it is their mission to inculcate the values to which they subscribe (Wood and Toscano, 2013). Just as religious colleges once perceived their task as perpetuating the tenets of their denominations, so today's secular professors hope to instill the standards they believe vital to our collective well-being. This commitment, however, does not stress self-direction. Despite the lip service to "critical thinking," the critiques generated are remarkably one-sided (Weisberg, 2013b). Given the social-democratic allegiances of contemporary academics, this means that collectivist principles tend to be praised, whereas conservative ones are spurned. Those who engage in these distortions may not be fully socialist, but a large number come perilously close.

More than a few professors seek disciples in their classrooms (Horowitz, 2006). They hope to indoctrinate a cadre of students to carry their perspectives forward (Glenn, 1997; Shapiro, 2004). In so doing, these academics fail to distinguish descriptive from prescriptive exercises (Loewen, 1995). Because they believe strongly in particular reforms, they assume that their values are tangible facts. Much as natural rights philosophers imagined that the "rights" they championed were objective, contemporary moralists assume the same about the ones to which they adhere. As a result, they treat students who disagree as having failed to grasp elementary truths. By the same token, those who approve are perceived as intellectually gifted.

Many contemporary academics insist that it is as impossible to keep values out of their lessons as it is to keep them out of their research or creative productions. Furthermore, they defend their biases on the grounds that everyone is biased (Derrida, 1997). Yet what they leave out of this defense is the assumption their own prejudices are beneficial, whereas those of their opponents are not. This conclusion, however, is wholly unwarranted. That which left-wing ideologues desire may be advantageous; nevertheless, they need to prove it. In any event, they are not completely mistaken in asserting that we all incorporate unexamined premises into our work. Where they go wrong is supposing that these should remain unexamined. The fact is that they are not self-evident and ought not be treated as such.

When intellectual positions are derived from value commitments, their advocates have an obligation to acknowledge that they are. This, however, does not mean that college professors must be moral eunuchs. They can retain strong ethical leanings. They can also promote these in their role as private citizens. Yet in the classroom, they have a duty to confess their biases. Students have a right to know what is fact and what is personal preference. If learners are to be self-directed—that is, if they are to make up their own minds about what to believe—they deserve not to be manipulated. When scholars take advantage of their authority, it is they who are being unethical.

Nonetheless, value judgments are inextricably linked to the social sciences and humanities. This makes it imperative that their practitioners be open and aboveboard. If these disciplines are to retain a reputation for expanding student horizons, those who teach them must present both sides of controversial questions. They do not need to avoid controversy or maintain silence about their personal judgments. These must, however, be put in perspective. All that is necessary is to make students aware of competing points of view. Converts acquired under false colors are done no service. Nor do disciplines that specialize in proselytizing do themselves a favor. In the long run, they lose their persuasiveness.

Despite the danger of classroom bias, however, bureaucratic correctives are not called for. Instructional quality is not improved by standardized teaching practices. Forcing professors to teach the same things in the same ways obviates the advantages of a professionalized faculty. Self-directed professors, who are experts in what they know and are personally motivated to do their jobs well, introduce pedagogical benefits that no prepackaged bureaucratic programs can match. By permitting well-qualified professors to exercise discretion, colleges gain the rewards available via their knowledge and passions. Primary and secondary schools, where what is taught is less complex, can be routinized, whereas higher education, even below the elite level, ceases to be "higher" when deprived of the spontaneity of genuine experts sharing hard-won insights.

Teaching is a human endeavor (Taylor, 2010). It depends on the interactions of actual human beings. Information is transferred from educator to learner, albeit not in the manner of inserting a flash drive into a computer. If human students are to integrate what they are taught into their long-term memories, their emotions, not just their memory cells, need to be aroused. Neuroscience is making it clear that competent decision making depends upon using our affects as gatekeepers (Damasio, 1994). How facts are brought together in our unconscious minds and how they are retrieved when deciding what actions to take turns out to be mediated by our emotions. Anyone who believes that human brains are neutral computers does not understand how thinking occurs. This is why education can never be reduced to mechanically transferring data into receptive minds.

Schooling has always been an interpersonal experience. Its achievements have never been replicated in a society of autodidacts. Human-to-human contacts make a difference. They did when Aristotle was lecturing at the Lyceum. They do when Miss Ann is teaching Johnny how to read. To assume that somehow computers can supplant this is absurd. Professors, even bad professors, bring their humanity into the classroom. And when they do, things happen over and above what can be derived from reading a book or viewing a tape. Good professors are inspirational. They can turn lives around by helping students to understand materials they might not otherwise assimilate. They can also motivate students to follow career paths they might never have considered or to participate in relationships that might have seemed impossible.

All this signifies that professors should be allowed to be themselves (Lang, 2008; Ambrose, et al., 2012). Instead of being constrained by normative rubrics, they must be allowed to design courses as they see fit and teach them according to their own lights. As it happens, there is no single best teaching style. What works for an individual academic may not serve well for another. Some are born storytellers; others feature a dry sense of humor; still others are restrained and introverted. Indeed, some may be so shy that they have difficulty interacting at a personal level. These differences dictate that how instructors present their lessons must also differ. Although this may seem like an obstacle to effective communication, it is not. Students react positively to professors who are themselves, even when these selves are vastly dissimilar. When teachers reveal their personal enthusiasms and display unexpected quirks, they become engaging personalities. Students pay attention and subsequently care enough to learn. Not all listeners, of course, become equally engaged, but enough do to make good things happen. In fact, this ability to stimulate personal identification is one of the most important sources of student motivation.

That professors differ in their expertise and ideological stances is also advantageous. If students are to become self-directed—that is, if they are to develop skills in making good choices—it helps to obtain practice in choosing between different options. When professors disagree, this makes some students uncomfortable, but this very discomfort provides the impetus to think things through. By the same token, when professors disclose their ideological interests, not only does this allow them to impart information that may not be available elsewhere, but their disparate concerns may spark an awareness that there are multiple directions learners can pursue. These also give students permission to be their unique selves. They do not have to be standardized when those charged with inaugurating them into adulthood are not. In the end, this diversity provides knowledge, as well as well-rounded leadership.

Nowadays, as earlier discussed, there has also been a craze for PowerPoint (Conway, 2013). Virtually every classroom comes equipped with projectors that permit instructors to display illustrative materials. In many cases, this allows instructors to present the entirety of their class notes on-screen. As they teach, students are invited to read along. This might seem an excellent method for introducing clarity, yet it almost never is. The customary result is boredom. Instead of reading with depth, minds wander off into daydreams as professors drone on. In-class teaching of this sort is little better than distance learning. When it is mechanical, it loses its emotional impact. Graphic illustrations should not be forbidden, but they ought to be used sparingly. As long as they do not substitute for the professor's humanity, they are useful.

Nor should professors be afraid to tell stories—including those drawn from their personal experience (Gottschall, 2012). Many novice academics fear that this might be unprofessional. Accordingly, they concentrate on abstract concepts drawn from textbooks. These unfortunately can be too dry to comprehend or too disengaged to be remembered. We humans are storytelling and story-consuming animals. Narratives are often how we make information hang together. They are also tools used to store ideas in memory. Often emotionally laden, this brings concepts to life and makes them worthy of being retained. That a particular professor's examples may be idiosyncratic is not a disadvantage but part of what makes them memorable.

Last, we come to adjuncts. In an effort to economize, most universities have taken to filling classrooms with adjuncts. This is a mixed blessing. In some cases, these temporary instructors bring unique qualifications to their task. Frequently having worked out in the real world, they furnish practical experience many traditional academics lack. Unhappily, a large number of professors have a well–deserved reputation for naiveté. In moving directly from graduate studies to a teaching role, they never pause to test their expertise in practice. As a result, many never discover the hands-on difficulties of implementing their theories. Practitioners, however, are usually aware of the limitations imposed by reality. Making some of these persons available to students, therefore, opens minds to unsuspected obstacles. To illustrate, my department at KSU includes a criminal justice component. As might be expected, many of our students are preparing for careers in law enforcement. To have actual police chiefs, lawyers, and detectives teach policing methods and/or legal procedures is therefore a great boon. These teachers have the authority of experience and command attention mere book learning—or even research—might not.

On the other hand, a majority of adjuncts have yet to complete their advanced degrees. In this case, teaching is used to supplement their income and educational experience. Consequently, my department finds many adjuncts uneven in their performances. Some are natural pedagogues who can take a class in hand and run with it. Others are halting and disengaged. In general, especially when new, novices are academically limited. As a result, we make it a practice to assign them introductory courses. This way, they are not in over their heads.

As to the college bubble, commentators have suggested contradictory approaches to utilizing adjuncts. Those who favor routinization and/or technological solutions generally believe adjuncts lower costs, while maintaining quality (Wildavsky et al., 2011). If what they are asked to do is standardized via expert rubrics, they can presumably deliver the same product as more experienced instructors. If, however, professionalization is valued, then this strategy is shortsighted. Those who believe—as I do—that qualified professors can provide unique insights also believe that eliminating them undermines "higher" education. We are of the opinion that self-motivated experts, as a consequence of years of study, research, and teaching, can, by way of their humanity, open the eyes of learners in a manner that less expert pedagogues usually cannot.

There is, as it happens, an even graver problem to over-dependence on adjuncts. If amateurs thoroughly replace qualified professors, what is the incentive to become a self-motivated expert in an academic discipline? If there are no university jobs waiting at the end of years of rigorous study, why devote the time to what will have no payoff? Already we are seeing cynicism developing among graduate students as they witness those who went before them struggle to obtain full-time jobs. This difficulty is most extreme in the humanities, where enrollments are declining. Moreover, do we really want a society from which professional intellectuals are absent? How would we make advances in the knowledge these people create and defend?

Let me conclude this section by providing an illustration of what I believe is necessary if college teaching is to flourish. For many years I worked side by side with a colleague who was the epitome of self-directed professorship. His name was Vassili Economopoulus. Trained as a demographer, he taught sociology at KSU for many years, specializing in gender and family studies. Not only was he a popular professor, but students and colleagues alike respected him. Vassili did not do research, but he was careful to keep up with the research done by others. His chief concern was that he teach his students what they needed; what both he and they perceived as relevant. He made this palatable by telling scores of jokes—very bad jokes, whose punch lines he invariably mangled. But this was part of his charm, for he too laughed as his gaffes. He was also extraordinarily caring, a trait that was transparent to his students. I, for instance, did not discover that he kept a drawer full of toys for his students' children until after he was deceased. For these reasons (i.e., his combination of academic competence and personal kindness), his peers awarded him teacher-of-the-year honors.

To this, I must add a word about intellectual integrity. Vassili was a liberal. I am not. We disagreed about many subjects. This, however, never prevented us from discussing our positions with passion and candor, nor from being friends. Often we aired our viewpoints while driving together to professional conferences. Then, after we exhausted our arguments, we would sing songs at the top of our lungs. Vassili never held a grudge and never forced his opinions on others. He was always willing to hear others out and then share his own views lucidly and honestly. This remains my ideal of what a teaching-oriented professor should be and what universities too often lack.

Professional Autonomy

College professors who do not control their work are not and cannot be professional (Delbanco, 2012). If most of their decisions are imposed from above, they are neither self-directed nor able to apply their accumulated expertise effectively. Professionalized academics must be able to create their own syllabi. They must also be permitted to choose their reading lists and organize their classroom schedules. Likewise, the exercises they employ should be of their selection, while the grades they give have to be based on their judgment. Different professors will choose to stress different topics and handle them in different ways. This is as it should be. Were it not, discretion would be absent. Uniformity is possible only when it is prescribed from a central source and rammed down the throats of those liable to resent it.

Intellectual Discretion

Food manufacturers have found that individual palates prefer different blends of tomato sauce (Gladwell, 2008). Why should intellectual subjects be different? Among other things, homogenized rubrics preclude responsive teaching. They interfere with pedagogues exercising personal discernment when answering student questions. They also discourage unique responses based on a professor's skill set. When only one way is assumed best, however good it may be, it becomes an albatross that prevents improvements.

Professors must similarly be allowed discretion in developing research agendas. When they are told what to study by bureaucratic superiors, we may be sure that what they find is consistent with what their bosses desire. The truth is that outliers have made many of the most significant human discoveries. Some important thinkers were downright strange—including Isaac Newton (Gleick, 2003) and Albert Einstein. To have shut them down because they did not conform to the preconceptions of individuals who were not familiar with their research would not only have been foolish; it would have been perilous. Many improbable strategies lead to dead ends, but some do not; hence, these must not be strangled in the crib. When research projects are vetted according to bureaucratic priorities, they are converted into a charade. Investigators merely go through the motions. The outcomes, unfortunately, are almost always hackneyed nonsense.

This is another reason for allowing professors to have the chief say in hiring and firing. Although they too can be conformists, they are apt to be more flexible than administrators. They are also likely to be more in tune with the demands of actual teaching and research, because they almost certainly possess a more relevant expertise than their organizational superiors. Thus, while they too are constrained by personal and group biases, they are also influenced by empirical considerations. This might seem to contradict my earlier assertion that liberal professors hire liberal colleagues, yet this trend is not written in stone. Once faculty members realize that uniformity is not in their or their students' interest, it can be modified.

Tenure. In recent years, professorial discretion has been under assault. Thus, a variety of commentators have argued that academic tenure is outmoded (Riley, 2011). They tell us that academic freedom is not in danger and therefore faculty members do not need protection from administrative interference. The problem, as these critics see it, is that professors have too much freedom. They are, as a result, unaccountable. Ensconced in an artificial bubble of security, they go off in half-baked directions, utterly unconcerned whether what they are doing makes sense. Moreover, many become lazy. They do not have to be productive to retain their jobs, and so they are not. In the end, they become arbitrary, egocentric, and ridiculous. Why, then, should society subsidize this retreat from reality? Doesn't it make more sense to expose professors to the same sort of competition that others must endure?

The gravamen of this argument is essentially that college professors are not true professionals. They are not genuinely self-motivated experts and hence cannot be trusted to make independent decisions. Sadly, it must be admitted that this is sometimes true. Some professors do become caricatures of themselves. Yet this is not the norm. It is not even the norm for academics who have become intellectually stagnant. Most work harder than is realized. Nonetheless, the point of providing academics with special protections is to arrange space for novelty. Creativity and genius are, as earlier noted, scarce commodities. They also make for prickly personalities. People who are different from average can be difficult to understand or tolerate. Indeed, it may be when they are at their most inspired that they are their most insufferable. Only later—when and if their innovations find wider currency—are they hailed for their contributions. In the meantime, they benefit from being allowed to pursue their visions in peace (Ginsberg, 2011).

The counterargument to this proposition is that tenure ends up defending conformity. Because the consensus of academic opinion tends to be inflexible, a reigning establishment can exclude mavericks while rewarding drones. Some contend that this is, in fact, the current state of affairs. Liberal, and left of liberal, opinion is so dominate on college campuses that upwards of 90 percent of faculty members routinely vote Democratic. Furthermore, these ideologues admit to excluding colleagues who differ in political outlook (Jaschik, 2012c). They will not hire or promote avowed conservatives on the grounds that they are not smart enough to be professors. So prevalent has this practice become that on my campus, a number of my peers have confessed in private that they are conservative but immediately swore me to secrecy in the belief that if their opinions were known, it would ruin their careers.

But if this is the case, then wouldn't tenure serve only to preserve the perquisites of those currently in power? Wouldn't it continue to exclude nonconformists? This is a good question in that it frequently does. Yet happily, frequently is not always. I am, in point of fact, evidence of this. When I went up for tenure at KSU, my liberal department chair and the liberal vice president of academic affairs sought to deny it. Three bitter years went into fighting their resolve, but in the end, I prevailed. I did, because many of my colleagues, including several administrators, came down on my side. Although they disagreed with my political attitudes, they would not consent to what they perceived as an injustice. Not to put too fine a point on the matter, their integrity trumped their politics. Such professional honor, it is safe to say, is more widespread than on a single campus. In any event, having been awarded tenure, I was freed to be a dissident. My enemies may snipe at me, but I continue to do the sort of work I desire.

It is also safe to say that the contemporary academic consensus will not last forever. The current politically active establishment that rose to prominence in the wake of the Vietnam War is in the process of disintegrating. My age peers are slowly retiring and being replaced by another generation. Although it is true that their understudies were trained to follow in their footsteps, the young have a tendency to march off in new directions. They do not always want to be subservient to the old and therefore seek groundbreaking ventures. Intent on being their own persons, they too hope to innovate. If so, tenure should be available to them as they trod unfamiliar shores.

Compensation

Also as alluded to above, most professors are paid less than administrators. With the exception of academic stars at the elite institutions, they receive much lower compensation than is generally understood. We frequently hear about how poorly paid K–12 teachers are; nevertheless, high school teachers in major metropolitan areas receive tens of thousands more than most college-based academics, especially those in the humanities and social sciences. Indeed, I discovered, much to my chagrin, that when I was an associate professor I was earning considerably less than local elementary school guidance counselors. College professors may stand high in social prestige, but they rank low in pecuniary rewards. The fact is that so many intellectual types aspire to a university career that the competition keeps salaries down. Except in disciplines such as business—and nowadays, nursing—where off-campus employment is better compensated, would-be professors must take what they can get.

Given that we live in a market economy, this is understandable. The supply of potential academics outstrips the demand. What it does not outstrip, however, is the supply of high-quality aspirants. As long as it is understood that professors are not well paid, a large proportion of the best minds will seek their fortunes elsewhere. They will perhaps bypass teaching and research in favor of Wall Street or government service. This is a shame, in that it means that those left behind are deprived of the prestige needed to compete with their bureaucratic bosses. As long as they earn less, they are apt to be treated as inferior.

The respect and independence of the professoriate are further eroded by the crush of adjuncts. With so many aspirants to academic positions willing to take so little they essentially constitute what Marx (1967) referred to as a "reserve army" of the unemployed. As a result, fiscally sane administrations will continue to hire them in large numbers. This makes economic sense, but it does not make sense in terms of quality. For as long as professors continue to be underpaid compared with what PhDs can command in the marketplace, the incentive remains for the best minds to migrate elsewhere. In the end, their professionalism will decline, with students and society being the biggest losers.

Good teachers are hard to identify, but when they are, they should be rewarded. Colleges can get away with doing less, at least in the short run, but in the long term they lose what makes them socially valued. Fine-dining facilities may attract students, but once the word gets out that a school's professors are second-rate, its reputation for excellence is liable to be a thing of the past.

Maturity

Professional authority can also be damaged by the foibles of the professoriate. When professors act more like children than mature adults, they undercut their reputations. Henry Kissinger once observed that college politics can be so cut-throat because so little is at stake. He might also have noted that professors can be ridiculously naïve because so many of their decisions have little consequence. Anyone who has paid attention to activities of academic senates will have noticed how out of touch these can be. By the same token, anyone who has sat in on a large number of college courses will have heard some preposterous claims. In not having to make decisions with immediate impacts, many academics develop a habit of not thinking through their recommendations. What comes to mind is a conference I attended where a prominent scholar told his listeners that Democrats were unlikely to elect a president until they nominated someone like Oprah Winfrey or Tom Hanks. This was said in dead earnest, but what was most surprising was how well this proposal was received by his audience.

Too many academics are eternal students. All they know is the classroom. They lack a sense of responsibility because they have never dealt with non-academic responsibilities. It is remarkable how many faculty members admit to not wanting to grow up. It is equally remarkable how many concede that they never wanted to immerse themselves in the competitive atmosphere of the marketplace. For them, the college campus was to be a safe cocoon in which to think exalted thoughts. Since they would never be in charge of making anything work, they could dabble in esoteric daydreams without taking the blame if things went wrong. Besides, many were not sure they had the toughness to weather the ravages of a non-sheltered lifestyle.

This attitude has made for a detached attitude toward reality. I once had a discussion with a humanities colleague who insisted that some academic programs should move forward irrespective of the cost. As far as she was concerned, this was the right thing to do, even if it bankrupted the university. This unwillingness to consider the consequences of one's schemes is relatively harmless if it stays within the confines of the classroom, but it can be catastrophic if these are intended for implementation. Those whose professional status depends on being specialized experts should find this prospect chilling. If all they do is spin fantasies to entertain immature students, they may not deserve the authority to which they aspire. Therefore, as prestigious adults, they should comport themselves like adults. In short, they need to be concerned with testing their ideas against reality.

Maturity, especially emotional maturity, is not a sentence to stagnation or misery. Consequently, it should not be anathema for self-directed students or self-directed professors. As importantly, if universities are to be seedbeds for new ideas, those who produce them ought to be grown-ups. Creativity does not have to be confined to childish mentalities (Fein, 2011a). Indeed, the sorts of social restructurings that produce genuine improvements are most apt to come from individuals who understand the problems of adulthood. It is adults who are—or should be—sensitive to the complexities and contradictions of a Gesellschaft society.

Mentoring

It may sound self-evident to some ears, but educators should be dedicated to educating. This is worth saying because so many professors despise the classroom. They perceive themselves as scholars and researchers whose efforts are diverted by having to attend student needs. Far from valuing the synergies of interacting with learners, they find contact with the young distressing. It is also understood that research and creative activities, not teaching, are the road to professional prestige. They know that the fewer hours spent teaching, the higher their status will be among their peers.

This is not to imply that research and scholarship are unworthy. They are, after all, the heart and soul of professional expertise. But they are not the heart and soul of what universities should be. Higher education is about passing along knowledge, not merely developing it. Universities ought to embrace a collegiality that includes students. These schools are at their best when they are a community of scholars that incorporates neophytes, most of whom are transitioning to something else. Universities that are totally separate from the larger society are on the way to becoming useless appendages. Correspondingly, professors who hope to be entirely separate from students sentence themselves to irrelevance.

Professors should also be role models (Delbanco, 2012). If the objective of a college education is preparation for self-directed leadership, then those who advertise themselves as stewards of the required expertise should exhibit this in action. If they cannot be effective guides to mature responsibility, they do not deserve to be allocated the resources expended in the belief that they are. Students who are in the process of developing independent senses of self benefit from contact with respected, non-familial adults. This can furnish examples of how to be successfully adult without limiting oneself to the patterns with which one grew up.

But mentors need not—and cannot—be surrogate parents. They may pay attention to students who are both worthy and desirous of it, but the vast majority must accept something less. Still, that less does not have to be insignificant. Mature and successful adults (i.e., persons who care about the futures of those under their tutelage) should be willing to share of themselves. The best professors are engaged in the classroom. They put themselves on the line with sufficient transparency that they can epitomize how self-direction works. Academics need not be perfect human beings. None of us is. But in their uniqueness, hobbled by shortcomings as we all are, they can still demonstrate that self-direction is possible. In being themselves, and making decisions they are prepared to revise, they can show others that learning is possible. As living exemplars of being flawed, yet esteemed, they can encourage learners, who are aware of their own deficits, that they too can grow into estimable human beings.

Too often life is a fraud. People pretend to be more than they are in an effort to extract deference from others. College should not be like that. It should be real, supportive, and helpful. While it is true that as a human institution it displays—and will always display—the limitations associated with being human, the professionals who are at its core should strive to be their best, most competently self-directed selves. They will, of course, fall short, but in making the effort to be professionalized, they can encourage the next generation to do the same. This, even more than their technical expertise, is the legacy academics should endeavor to leave behind.

Conclusions

The single most important step that can be taken to prevent an academic bubble is to slash the bloated administrative edifice. Thus, the number of college administrators should be cut in half. As long as this distention is allowed to increase, the bureaucratic model will continue to infringe on faculty professionalism. Since administrators are not motivated to curb these excesses, trustees, regents, and legislatures must impose firm targets. Given that many administrative positions are redundant, this goal needs to be draconian. Although politicians have their own hobbyhorses, they will find that universities can do much better once their bureaucratic excesses are reduced.

And one of the first places to begin cutting costs is by slashing administrative salaries. As long as administrators continue to make far more than professors, the incentives to leave the professoriate will remain significant. This has deleterious consequences for the professionalism of the faculty and is therefore inimical to student needs. It also creates a sense of superiority among administrators that encourages egotism.

Administrative meddling in academic affairs should also be restrained. Continued efforts by academic managers to control what is taught results in rigidities that discourage faculty members for deploying their expertise. Rationalizations about a need for accountability are exactly that: rationalizations. They do not improve the quality of education. This also implies that make-work routines need to be reduced. As long as administrators feel that they must justify their existence, they will continue to make demands that serve no sensible purpose. Meaningless reports will be written, foolish projects inaugurated, and time-consuming committee assignments proliferate. These costly ventures must therefore be identified and ruthlessly eliminated.

In contrast, the professionalism of college faculties needs to be respected and enhanced. If professors are to encourage self-direction, they must first themselves be self-directed. They need to be authentically self-motivated experts who are delegated authority accordingly. Yet they must be worthy of this trust. This requires that their own biases be held at bay. Although professors are entitled to express political opinions, they are not entitled to impose these on students. Colleges and universities are supposed to be repositories of knowledge, not a locus of indoctrination. Professors ought to share information, not seek disciples. It is consequently essential that they allow students to reach their own conclusions, and not grade according to whether or not they agree with faculty predilections.

Indeed, colleges and universities should present both sides of controversial subjects. While individual preferences are inevitable, this can be converted into an asset. Faculty members can use their passions to present information in a memorable fashion. But they should also make students aware that other viewpoints are equally respectable. Furthermore, schools should employ professors who advocate a spectrum of positions. This will enable students to hear multiple sides of important questions, which, in turn, will facilitate making up their own minds.

The humanities and social sciences, in particular, must accommodate greater intellectual balance. The current ratio of liberals to conservatives is grossly distorted. This imbalance is, in part, maintained by the inclination of liberal professors to hire and promote other liberals (Goldberg, 2012). Not only is this unfair, but it undermines the legitimacy of the humanities and social sciences. One reason these subjects have declined in popularity is that parents and students regard them as repositories of liberal clichés. In other words, too much political correctness is tantamount to professional suicide.

This said, good teaching must be nurtured. Therefore, all college and university professors should be required to teach. Research or service responsibilities should not excuse professors from sharing their expertise with students. The central concern of higher education is, after all, education. Other objectives may be worthwhile, but they must not be allowed to eclipse this fundamental mission. Requiring all professors to teach reaffirms this commitment.

Nor should faculty members be forced to be triple threats. Demands that all be equally productive in teaching, research, and service are unwise. Instead of recognizing and taking advantage of their different strengths, it forces many to be mediocre in one or more areas. While teaching and research can be synergistic, they are not always; hence, efforts to impose this can backfire. This means also that if promotion and tenure are denied to superior teachers merely because they are dedicated teachers, classroom excellence is thereby discouraged. When only outstanding researchers are rewarded, the message that instruction is an afterthought is unmistakable. To correct this, schools may, for instance, need to provide separate research and teaching trajectories.

Nor should administrators impose standardized teaching rubrics. If faculty members are to share their unique specialties, they must be allowed to develop their own syllabi. Furthermore, because there is not one best teaching style, professors must be permitted to utilize their own strengths in the classroom. Only in this way can they take advantage of their expertise and/or encourage self-direction by way of example. Classroom experience, especially in the humanities and social sciences, is to a large degree emotionally laden. Yet professors who are not allowed to be themselves cannot share their passions. As a result, they rarely inspire a desire to learn or to make the intellectual connections that link abstract concepts with real-world experiences. What teachers bring to the classroom differs, but this too is crucial to allowing students to deal with human differences.

Good teaching, especially in the humanities and social sciences, is responsive teaching. Professors who are allowed to be themselves respond to students in the here and now. They notice small cues and make adjustments in how they frame their lessons. As a result, their students are more engaged. Aware that the instructor is concerned with their needs, they are apt to reciprocate.

In the end, of course, professors should be remunerated according to their skills. Colleges that pay faculty members less than high school teachers get what they deserve. While the marketplace must, to some extent, determine salaries, if excellence is not rewarded, it disappears. Moreover, money and respect go hand in hand; hence, inappropriately low compensation decreases professional esteem. So does the excessive use of adjuncts. The complex subjects taught at the university level require disciplinary expertise. While some adjuncts provide unique capabilities and others are competent at teaching introductory level courses, too great a reliance on them reduces quality. In addition, to the degree that adjuncts substitute for tenure-track professors, the incentive to pursue PhDs is reduced. If this occurs, the pool of potential adjuncts will eventually dry up.

Next, scholarship should not become a modern version of scholasticism. If not all faculty members are competent scholars, then insisting that all engage in scholarly activities diminishes the quality of research and creative activities. Contributions diluted by reams of mediocrity do not advance our knowledge. To the contrary, they make it more difficult to distinguish that which has merit from that which does not. With hundreds of thousands of professors seeking to make their mark and therefore motivated to inflate their achievements, judgments of quality are distorted and advances in knowledge fail to accumulate.

Indeed, faculty members who are coerced into producing second-rate scholarship become cynical. They realize that they are merely playing an academic game and lose their incentive to be proficient. The fact is that because professionalism entails a self-motivated expertise, once this expertise becomes artificial, professionalism is converted into a travesty. This lessens the quality of both scholarship and teaching.

Professors might also be encouraged to participate in "faculty internships." Too great an immersion in an "ivory tower" culture contributes to inferior scholarship and teaching. Lifelong scholars (i.e., those who never experience the demands of actual practice) often produce work that is detached from the real world. One way to avoid this is to urge professors to take paid leaves of absence, during which they gain practical experience in their specialties.

We, as a society, might also consider the possibility of expanding the role of dedicated research institutions. If colleges and universities are to remain in the education business, it makes sense to distinguish them from institutions whose primary emphasis is research. Full-time researchers in the hard sciences and engineering might be concentrated in places like the Rockefeller Institute, while technical specialists in the social sciences could migrate to think tanks.

Last, tenure must be preserved. Academic freedom is always in danger. The temptation to punish dissent is a constant. Universities may celebrate academic freedom, yet administrators, professors, and laypersons who are offended by unpopular viewpoints do not always hesitate to censor them. Excuses are found, and rationalizations are honored, but the end result is that nonconformists are punished.

Fortunately, today's majorities may one day be tomorrow's minorities. Although tenure tends to entrench the current intellectual majority, it also preserves turf for struggling minorities. The latter might now seem to constitute a token presence, but change does occur. And when it does, tenure should be there to protect the new outliers. A freshly minted minority may take comfort that their forebears had the good sense to keep these protections in place when they were in charge.

9

An Evolutionary Perspective

Evolutionary Change

Change can be difficult. Major changes can be especially so. We humans tend to grow comfortable with the social arrangements that we know; hence, even when we desire improvements, even when these are necessary, we are apt to resist them. And because significant alterations are habitually regarded as both jarring and uncertain—and thus, dangerous—they are honored more in our imaginations than in practice. This applies as much to overhauling higher education as to any other human endeavor. However well educated the reformers may be and however dedicated to fixing what is broken, it is easier to conceive of dramatic correctives than it is to implement them.

Moreover, when change does occur, it tends to be slower and more halting than we might like. In our mind's eyes, we build visions of an ideal future that we yearn to inaugurate immediately, but then the real world intervenes. Those indistinct blueprints that seductively beckon from what appears to be the road just ahead have a way of receding from view as we attempt to bring them to fruition. Somehow what we envisaged does not turn out as expected. Then we are left to pick up the pieces. Nor are other people always cooperative. Too often they refuse to do our bidding. In fact, they may have conflicting aspirations. Thus, in the end we are forced to make accommodations that strike us as half measures.

Sometimes, of course, we do not desire change but have it thrust upon us. Things go wrong in unforeseen ways, and we are forced to adjust irrespective of our desires. We may even be required to accede to modifications we detest. For example, the college bubble was not something most educators expected, nor is it something they welcome. Yet it is here and therefore, it has commanded the attention of academics and laypersons alike. Something must be done; nevertheless, there is no agreement as to what this should be.

Whatever the answers turn out to be, however, they are apt to be wrenching. Higher education is not a simple institution It has many moving parts and millions of interested players. The reforms that eventually emerge are therefore bound to include both cultural and structural factors. Long-established ways of life, as well as long-established patterns of interpersonal interaction, will be thrown askew. Much as an earthquake can tear structures asunder for thousands of square miles around, thereby interrupting the plans of millions of inhabitants, tinkering with how colleges and universities are put together normally causes greater disruptions than activists envisage.

The result is that changes tend to be evolutionary rather than revolutionary (Lopreato and Crippen, 1999). Cosmic transformations that totally redo long-standing traditions are generally figments of sanguine imaginations. Just as political revolutions—be they the French, Russian, or Chinese—did not produce the societies their architects promised, so educational upheavals never turn out precisely as planned. There are simply too many variables for all to be appreciated ahead of time. Nor do the most competent social engineers have as much control over events as they assume. Like Soviet central planners, they may attempt to be rational, but this is within a context that resists complete rationality.

In the real world, improvements do occur and problems are solved, but mostly piecemeal and by means that no one totally foresaw. Ultimately, many individuals contribute to a process that is not fully coordinated or even fully understood. In the end, multiple small innovations and countless insignificant adjustments add up to a whole that is appreciated only in retrospect. This was the case with the Industrial Revolution; it was the case with the advent of the American nation. And it will be the case with how we solve the challenge of the academic bubble—assuming, of course, that we do.

Because what happens is likely to evolve, it is important to appreciate how social evolution occurs. Not unlike biological evolution, this process is partly Lamarckian and partly Darwinian. Also like its biological counterpart, it is a messy progression over which no one has all-embracing control. Perhaps Daniel Chirot (1986, 1994) provided the simplest conception of how this transpires. Building upon the work of Talcott Parsons (1951), he has offered a straightforward set of stages that are easy to grasp, albeit devilishly difficult to traverse. To begin with, these steps are similar to those navigated in Darwin's natural selection in that they facilitate the gradual emergence of features that advance the survival of an organization or society. Nonetheless, they are different in that they operate on acquired characteristics rather than genetically transmitted ones.

As Chirot sees it, social evolution begins with a long-established set of cultural and structural elements. These, having developed together, are integrated into a conservative whole (Tylor, 1881). They are, in Chirot's words, "institutionalized." But then something happens. Formerly functional ways of life are disrupted. A "stressor" impinges upon the system. Whether this derives from internal or external sources, it upsets the previous balance. Suddenly the needs of the system or of the individuals comprising it are not met, and there are pressures to adapt to this new circumstance. In some cases, if nothing is done, there is a danger of collapse (Diamond, 2005). In others, there is merely a great deal of discomfort that motivates efforts toward relief.

The next question is, where is this relief to be found? There may be a solution close at hand, but then again, there may not be. If there isn't, an innovative response will have to be found. Chirot describes this phase as "adaptive radiation." Many of those disrupted by the stressor will seek an answer to the challenge. These persons may be social leaders; they may be anonymous underlings. It is impossible to tell in advance from whence the best ideas will arise. Nor is it easy to distinguish good ideas from bad ones. Indeed, people may promote solutions that have even more disastrous consequences than the problem that initiated their search. Much as brainstorming can veer off on tangents, there is no way to be certain which improvisations will work.

And so evolution moves to the next phase, which is to separate the wheat from the chaff. Just as with natural selection, proposals must be tested and sorted according to whether they achieve what is needed. Ultimately, this is an empirical process. Impassioned advocates may champion one solution over another, and they may for a time be persuasive, yet in the end, it is reality that usually triumphs. The object, it must be remembered, is the survival of the system. Since not all proposals are equally effective in achieving this, some will be shouldered aside by others. Herbert Spencer (1969) described this process as "the survival of the fittest." He also spoke of "nature red in tooth and claw." The point is that the competition to determine what works best is neither tidy nor always fair. Individuals, and/or groups fight vigorously for their favorite solutions. They may even seek to undermine rival solutions. But in the end, success is generally awarded to answers that satisfactorily address what went wrong.

It should also be noted that this sorting-out process is frequently saturated with moralism. Competing parties often seek to develop bandwagon effects on the grounds that what they are seeking is morally superior. Portraying themselves as "good guys" who are holding the gate against bad ones (Fein, 1997), they demand orthodoxy with their own positions, while simultaneously dismissing those of their rivals as not worthy of consideration (Tilly, 2004). The last thing these moral combatants desire is an objective appraisal of their relative merits. This impulse, however, tends to obscure what is going on and makes it difficult to arrive at an optimum solution.

In any event, answers that "satisfice" in Herbert Simon's (1947) sense of the term, i.e., that are "good enough," are usually found because the alternative can be extinction. The problem is that these solutions are rarely as clear-cut as those proposed by the most vocal advocates. The moral propositions in which they specialize must generally be simple in order to attract significant numbers of adherents. Hence, they normally entail appealing narratives that provide an easily grasped account of the problem and an equally undemanding response. The real world, however, almost always turns out to be more complicated. Indeed, it is so complex that in most cases, the participants never fully understand all that is happening—or why.

Still, those whose lives have been disrupted must act—and so they do. This brings us to Chirot's final phase of the evolutionary process. It is the period of re-institutionalization. Here the many smaller sub-answers generated from disconnected sources are integrated into a new whole. Both cultural and structural factors are aligned with one another so that they mesh. Social revolutionaries are rarely aware of all of these pieces or even how they interact; hence, they almost never seek to combine them in a cohesive package. This merger generally occurs unconsciously as uncounted participants attempt to reduce the dissonance produced by contradictory elements (Festinger, 1957).

Personal understandings, social norms, symbolic representations, public rituals, innovative technologies, aesthetic preferences, interpersonal relationships, social roles, exchange processes, hierarchical rankings, and reconciliation communities must all fall into place before a stable equilibrium is reached. This is not a matter of theory and hence only occurs in the doing. Nor is it liable to happen smoothly. Differences in interest and perspective are likely to be worked through in grating conflicts that are both uncomfortable and uncertain. No one knows—or can know—the final resolution beforehand. Actually, there may be no "final" resolution because new and unanticipated stressors tend to pop up. These then demand fresh innovations and additional efforts at sorting them out.

All of this, of course, applies to higher education. Like any other complex human endeavor, it cannot escape the vagaries of social evolution. Just because its stewards are more intelligent and more knowledgeable than most others does not mean they can short-circuit the process. They too are limited human beings (including this author) and, as a result, may expect surprises. Nonetheless, this should not prevent us from innovating or from winnowing out proposed answers. Mistakes will surely be made along the way, but one of the virtues of evolution is that there are numerous opportunities to correct these.

The Evolution of Higher Education—the Problem

Let us therefore look at how higher education has evolved, how it currently seems to be evolving, and where this course is likely to wind up. No one can be sure about any of these things. The past, the present, and the future are all, to some degree, opaque. Because each of us sees only a small portion of vast panoply of events to which we also bring the distortions of our own biases, errors are made and fantasies are entertained. But this does not mean that we cannot improve our focus of what we observe. The truth, as the post-modernists insist, is not fully knowable (Derrida, 1997). Even so, we can develop better approximations of it. So let us review where we are.

It has been alleged that we are at the brink of an academic bubble and therefore must act, lest it bursts. Our task is presumably to modify colleges and universities so that they survive this threat. We are not, however, starting from the beginning; hence, we are not required to invent higher education from scratch. The institution has a long history and retains many vibrant traditions. Things have gone wrong and may even go more radically wrong before they get better; nonetheless, we have a robust foundation upon which to build. Thus, reform does not have to be revolutionary in the sense of imposing total change. As a result, we need not throw out all that has preceded us.

Nor could we. With the roots of higher education as deep as they are and with so many people committed to its present configuration, efforts to tear it all down and replace it with something profoundly different are doomed. Academics are accused of being conservative when it comes to their own careers (Wildavsky et al., 2011), but this is not altogether a bad thing. It prevents ill-conceived correctives from destroying what has been achieved. Letting go of what one has in hand in favor of what has only been promised is rarely a good idea.

Be that as it may, there is a problem—or rather, a basketful of problems—that demand our attention. Higher education is under stress; few doubt that. But what is the source of this stress? Several of the proximate causes have already been enumerated. To wit: costs have escalated. Enrollments have stagnated. The time students take to get their degrees has become excessive. The humanities and social sciences are under siege. A gender gap exists and is widening. Worst of all, the quality of higher education seems to be slipping.

Most observers agree to all of these, yet liberals and conservatives are sharply divided regarding several other issues. Thus, liberals fear that our schools continue to discriminate against minorities and whereas they should be aggressively pursuing social justice and equality, they are dawdling. Meanwhile conservatives counter that this emphasis on social concerns detracts from quality, while simultaneously ignoring valuable traditions. Each side of this moral divide is certain that its principles must prevail and that if those of its opponents do, the consequences will be tragic.

There is, however, a more fundamental source of stress. It is not merely that higher education has been changing; our society as a whole has been transformed. Colleges and universities are merely struggling to keep pace with these developments (Ogburn, 1922). Ours has become a middle-class society—the first in history (Fein, 2005). It is the first in which the upper middle classes, as opposed to the upper classes, have set the social agenda. This has occurred because ours has become a more professionalized society. As a mass techno-commercial society, it requires the services of legions of self-motivated experts. Many millions of ordinary people need to exercise competent discretion in abstruse specialties if they are to keep the wheels of a post-industrial economy spinning or democratic institutions democratic.

The challenge submitted to higher education has been to produce this self-directed elite. It must accommodate millions of ordinary young people, many of whose family backgrounds have not prepared them to exercise discretion, and help them develop into mature adults capable of making high-quality decisions independently, even in an environment of uncertainty. This is a difficult assignment. So complex is it that there have been many slips along the way. Indeed, the proximate problems with which most commentators are concerned derive from this underlying difficulty. It is the central stressor that is upending the academic apple cart. Consequently, it is what needs to be addressed if we are to return to equilibrium.

Unfortunately, this underlying cause is not usually perceived for what it is. As a result, those who would fix the problems plaguing higher education generally concentrate on the overt difficulties. They look to costs, enrollments, etc., as requiring immediate attention. Accordingly, when they propose solutions, it is correcting these they have in mind. The upshot is that the process of adaptive radiation gets sidetracked. Many innovations are suggested, but most are tangential to the principal difficulty. Some, to be sure, make good sense. The trouble is that they do little to meet the most crucial challenges.

Among the solutions that have been proposed are making schools more business-like, and, in particular, employing technology so as to make them more productive and therefore less costly (Belfield and Jenkins, 2013). Schools are also asked to be more "relevant" by being more multicultural, more interdisciplinary and, in general, more politically correct (Glazer, 1997). This, it must be admitted, is not thought to make them cheaper to operate but to make them more attractive to enrollees whose needs will be better met. Then there is the matter of fairness. Higher education is said to be unfair to less well-prepared students and especially to minorities. This is to be corrected by making schools more affordable, making the subjects they teach less abstruse, and obliging all who apply for admission. In many cases, affirmative action is also demanded in order to reverse past injustices. These reforms are thought to open the doors to those previously excluded and, in the process, to enable the rest of us to take advantage of historically ignored talents. But most important, this is demanded because it is regarded as a moral imperative.

Last, there are the structural improvements urged by those convinced that higher education is handicapped by how it is currently organized. These commentators ask, for instance, that tenure be eliminated. They claim that this amounts to excessive job security that robs faculty members of the incentive to do their best. Or they recommend increased dependence on adjuncts. This they tell us would lower costs, while not reducing quality. Or they insist on more emphasis on research. This would presumably make universities more productive by increasing the contributions they make to the larger society.

Each of these proposals deserves a fair hearing, yet they have not been derived from the foremost challenge confronting our colleges and universities. Thus, they tell us little about how we are to produce the self-directed elite required by a professionalizing civilization. Innovations decoupled from what most needs to be fixed can be useful, but they are patently insufficient. Whatever good they achieve pales in comparison with the problems they leave untouched. There is another issue here as well. To the degree that innovations are morally inspired, they can confuse matters. Morality has a way of clouding our judgment. It is so emotionally insistent that it often prevents us from seeing facts considered contrary to ethical objectives. Regrettably, moralists can be so self-righteous that they deny potentially fatal dangers inconsistent with their agendas.

The Evolution of Higher Education—Solutions

If we are to deal with the fundamental stressor bedeviling higher education, we must therefore step back to get a clearer view of what is required. If we are to develop innovations that solve our most pressing difficulties, we must understand our basic mission. As has been argued, the most vital task confronting higher education is to produce an elite commensurate with our social needs. It is not about being business-like or multicultural. It is not even about being fair—although fairness, if possible, is worthy of being pursued. As to relevance, the fundamental relevance required pertains to keeping our society afloat. Any social entity that decides it is more important to uphold idealistic standards than to survive will neither survive nor sustain those standards.

So first we need to prepare self-directed leaders who can keep food on our tables, clothes on our backs, roofs over our heads, and enemies from breaching our boundaries. This may sound less elevated than pursuing moral heights—that is, until one recognizes that maintaining moral standards is also necessary to pursuing economic or political objectives. Indeed, how we define these standards flows as much from practical considerations as the other way around (Fein, 1997, 1999). Being a self-directed leader does not imply being a selfish tyrant. If anything, being rudimentarily fair is essential to working effectively with others. Today's professionalized leaders must, if anything, be able to work effectively with a very diverse cast of other human beings.

And so if colleges and universities are going to prepare a self-directed professionalized elite, they must put in place programs that inculcate the knowledge and the motivation needed to make high-quality decisions autonomously. The courses they teach, as well as the ambiance they foster, should be designed with this in mind. The goal is to deal with the stresses created by the demands of a techno-commercial marketplace, not merely to teach what has already been taught or to replace these with offerings with others in line with what romantics believe essential. Traditional courses may remain appropriate, but they should be evaluated in terms of our current needs, as opposed to historic conditions.

As to what needs to be learned, this involves knowledge of technology, of oneself, of others, and of society. Contemporary higher education has to cast a wide net. There is so much that deserves to be understood that a cosmopolitan approach is crucial. Narrow technical skills should be part of this mix, yet in a complex division of labor, not everyone has to be expert in every specialty. Social and personal knowledge are more fundamental because their application is more broadly relevant, especially in navigating our incredibly variegated communities. Professionals and those who are becoming professionalized work more with people and data than they do with things (Hughes, 1958). They must therefore be comfortable with people and how we humans organize our societies. But first, leaders must be comfortable with themselves, or they will be unable to penetrate the mysteries of either individuals or groups.

But knowledge is not enough. People must be motivated to employ what they know and proficient enough to employ this well. Unfortunately, motivation is difficult to instill. If it and the ability to apply it are not, to some degree, already present, they may be impossible to implant. Consequently, colleges and universities need to be selective. People of all classes and ethnic or racial backgrounds must have an opportunity to prove themselves; nevertheless, they should be matched with the institutions best suited to assist them.

Next, the ambiance of these schools must be such that they encourage students to grow into their best, most dedicated selves. Becoming internally motivated is something learners do on their own, but if they are furnished the time and the appropriate resources, large numbers can manage it. This begins with schools that are appropriately professionalized, as opposed to bureaucratized. It continues with student bodies that are encouraged to interact and to be mutually supportive. Simply sitting at an electronic device or even reading a book is no substitute for human relationships. This is because positive human relationships are imperative for creating personal goals.

Nor should the complexity of contemporary societies be overlooked. Finding an appropriate niche within a welter of obscure possibilities is one of the chief difficulties that today's learners face. Not surprisingly, self-direction begins with finding a direction that fits who one is. It is therefore essential that students be allowed to explore their options. Education has too often been about molding the learner to meet the needs of others. Self-directed universities must avoid this trap by permitting students the time to make personal discoveries and the room to make mistakes. The worse blunder of all is forcing young people to enter occupations they despise; occupations at which they are likely to be inept and that will make them unhappy for a lifetime.

If we turn now to the practices that enable faculty members to promote student self-direction, the starting point must be professorial self-direction. Unless professors are themselves allowed discretion, they can hardly model this for their students. Too often proposed reforms leave out what professors should be if they are to provide learners with what they need. Frequently, the goal is instead to discipline them into doing what others desire. The bureaucratic model of social organization is so pervasive that to many, making it operate more effectively within higher education seems no more than common sense. Find the most efficient ways to deliver what students require and then make sure teachers deliver this in the most effective manner. This is no more than Taylorism updated to apply to colleges and universities (Taylor, 1911). The problem is that it is the antithesis of self-direction. Paradoxically, this model, having failed to establish its validity in the commercial sphere (Grusky and Miller, 1970), has been exhumed so as to rearrange organizations where it is even less applicable.

So many of the reforms recommended for higher education either come from administrators or require additional administrators, that Ginsburg (2011) was absolutely on target to write about "the rise of the all-administrative university." Instead of encouraging professors to be more professional, ever-greater resources are dedicated to getting them under control. Rather than allow these academics to make independent decisions, they are, in the name of "accountability," forced into a straight-jacket of "best practices." In other words, their expertise is spurned and their motivation questioned. Outsiders, often their organizational bosses, are presumed to know best. Although to judge from the results, this is absurd. Quality education cannot be had when those who are its natural stewards are treated like lackeys who must remain subservient to administrators, who are unfamiliar with what needs to be taught.

Of course, this implies that professors have a responsibility to live up to the requirements of professionalism. Sadly, this is not always the case, and so it too must be addressed. Just as there has been a moralistic tilt among some of those who wish to reform higher education, so there has been an ideological tilt on campus. Too often faculty members are more concerned with promoting a moral program than with assisting students in becoming self-directed. Nowadays, this attitude is concentrated in left-wing quarters, but it would be just as ominous were it on the right. Universities have historically been thought of as marketplaces of ideas. They were supposed to be neutral ground on which new concepts were tested and perfected. This, however, is only possible where no particular orthodoxies prevail. Once official tenets are prescribed, this trial by fire ceases to exist. Only socially sanctioned beliefs can be safely expressed, and they may never be challenged.

Since universities are supposed seedbeds of knowledge, a socially enforced uniformity in inimical to one of their central functions. Research may continue to be produced, but it will be research in name only. The object will no longer be to discover the truth, because the truth is believed already to be known. This converts the university into a church and not an educational institution. As important, it interferes with implanting self-direction. To be self-directed, students must learn to think independently. But if only a circumscribed set of views is allowed, how can they think on their own? In this case, if they came to unapproved conclusions, their freedom would be quashed.

It is therefore in the interests of professors, both in terms of their scholastic freedom and their ability, to transmit genuinely critical thinking that they support intellectual diversity (Arum and Roska, 2011). Moreover, this is not only in the interests of a society that requires professionalization, but it is in the interests of their occupational survival. The special expertise of faculty members that makes them valued mentors of the young ceases to be an expertise if it is only repeats a stereotyped catechism. As of now, many professors are in a state of denial. They refuse to believe that they defending "officially" sanctioned truths. Caught in an academic echo chamber, they do not realize that they are sabotaging freedoms that they themselves hold dear.

In any event, the sorts of changes that promote self-direction frequently differ from those that speak to less fundamental problems. Indeed, they suggest that some of the most popular ideas circulating among potential reformers would be counterproductive. Instead of strengthening higher education, they would make it less viable. Instead of graduating the professionalized leaders our society requires, they would make themselves irrelevant by producing a generation of intellectual clones.

Which brings us to Chirot's selection stage of the evolutionary process. Adaptive radiation generates a wealth of contradictory proposals. These are difficult to sort through, in part because they have different aims. Having analyzed the underlying problems differently, their suggested solutions often differ. How, then, are we, as a society, to determine which paths to follow? In the Darwinian model, some creatures survive, while others do not. Some possess characteristics that enable them to feed, protect, and reproduce themselves, whereas their competitors are less successful and therefore decline in numbers. The same—or nearly the same—applies to cultural and structural innovations. Thus, some ways of life, in time, prove superior to others. They too enable people to feed, clothe, and protect better than do rival lifestyles. Likewise, some social organizations enable those who subscribe to them to outdo the competition. This may not be nice, but survival is not about being nice—it is about surviving.

At any rate, like it or not, proposals for social reform will be tested in action. However persuasive their proponents, the time comes to demonstrate whether they can deliver what they promise. Academics specialize in verbal skills. They are generally intelligent and articulate enough to make a compelling case for even bad ideas (Sowell, 2009). Being applied under fire, in contrast, exposes these concepts to revealing their weaknesses. Errors, to be sure, can be rationalized, yet in the long run those innovations that work outperform those that do not. It may take a while to get there, but some individuals and communities prosper, whereas others wither on the vine. In other words, only some endure, irrespective of how enticing they sounded at the beginning.

We are now at the selection stage with respect to educational reform. Actually, we are in the midst of both adaptive radiation and the sorting out of what works from what does not. Even though conditions remain in flux and new ideas continue to surface, some proposals have been sufficiently tested for us to get an inkling of whether they will pan out. Analysts differ on how things are proceeding, but there are straws in the wind. The results may change as further adjustments are made, but some preliminary findings are worth stating. Preliminary outcomes indicate that particular schemes will probably disappoint, even on their own terms; that notwithstanding the benefits they promise, they have not been able to achieve the predicted end points.

And so the enormous expansion of for-profit schools billing themselves as universities has been a disaster. These may boast of how efficient they are, but there is a reason a disproportionate share of their resources is dedicated to advertising and recruitment. Given that they teach so little, and that their graduates have such a difficult time obtaining quality employment (Jaschik, 2012b), and that they induce enrollees to take out student loans they may never be able to repay, it is no wonder that their enrollments have stagnated and may be declining. They may be "efficient," but they are certainly not skilled at instilling self-direction—especially given the caliber of students they draw. If this is supposed to be what a business-like stance produces, it should be shunned as a model for higher education.

Nor has computer-based instruction proved significantly more successful. This mode of education continues to attract ardent support and is continuing to expand as more colleges and universities multiply their offerings. Yet this is no indicator of quality. Despite studies that laud how well and cost-effectively this method teaches, a growing body of data suggests otherwise (Lederman, 2013). Neither cheaper nor more inspirational than traditional courses, despite the convenience, online programs are not geared toward encouraging self-direction. Their impersonality and tediousness, irrespective of recent technical advances, does not lend itself to instilling the knowledge or motivation to be effectively self-directed. The fact is that in eschewing the benefits of human contact, they ignore the sorts of learning that only take place face-to-face.

Nor, given their physical remoteness from the traditional campus, do they provide the benefits of extracurricular programs. This is unfortunate, in that they provide neither the practice entailed in interacting with others nor the emotional spur of direct human feedback. That this interferes with quality education is demonstrated by the reluctance employers have to treat online degrees as if they were equivalent to traditional degrees. Even universities are reluctant to hire online graduates for their tenure-track positions. They may claim these courses are as good as any others when selling them to their students, but when it comes to trusting those who specialized in them to teach others, they demur.

Nor has the all-administrative university been a roaring success. The bureaucratic model, in suppressing professionalism, has not demonstrated improved student outcomes (Ginsberg, 2011). Its so-called "best practices" have not unequivocally proven to be best. These may be easy to administer, but like online classes, they subtract the humanity from the educational endeavor. Worse than this, they subtract the expertise and personal dedication of a professionalized professoriate. Colleges and universities that convert their faculties into poorly paid drones, in the process, undermine the rationale for higher education. Once professors are forced into one-size-fits-all molds, the special expertise that attracted learners in the first place is obliterated. This, then, is not a formula for transmitting competent discretion by modeling competent discretion. Nor is it a recipe for reducing costs. The proof, once again, is that costs have been escalating while quality has, at best, stagnated.

As to faculty members themselves, rampant ideological purity has jeopardized their reputations for wisdom and impartiality. Far from promoting the desired moral outcomes, a uniformity of thought undercuts the traditional marketplace of ideas. Conformity has taken the place of intellectual adventurism with the consequence that critical thinking is discouraged (Arum and Roska, 2011; Lukianoff, 2012; Wood and Toscano, 2013). But independent thinking is the life-blood of self-direction. It is also the font of social progress. This is true in the classroom, where open discussion can stimulate original thoughts; it is true in research, where truly "thinking out of the box" brings unexpected discoveries. Sadly, in fields like English and sociology, there has been a mind-numbing repetition of politically correct incantations.

As for opening a college education to all, this has been idealism taken to unreasonable limits. A democracy should provide opportunity for everyone; whereas it cannot provide success for all. In human societies, where hierarchy is omnipresent, and in a complex techno-commercial society, where self-motivated expertise is at a premium, not everyone can arrive at the top. There will be an elite; it is just a question of what sort of elite. To pretend otherwise is to offer some people false hope. Like it or not, talent and motivation are not equally distributed (Davis and Moore, 1945); hence, some people will out-compete others. Nor would an artificial equality benefit society at large. If everyone, irrespective of competence, were allowed access to every job, perhaps by lottery, then mistakes would not only be made, but they would proliferate. The same is true of higher education itself. If ability is not a factor in attaining success, then the only way to provide equal instruction for all is to eliminate quality as a consideration. This tactic is especially threatening at mid- and lower-level institutions where the pressures to graduate all comers are great.

Nevertheless equal opportunity is of value. Democracy cannot thrive where only some people are allowed access to education. Still, access is not tantamount to success. Schools do—and should—differ in their standards and methods, while they simultaneously ensure that their respective criteria for achievement are met. Only this can actually produce the desired social mobility. Similar considerations apply to diversity. Learners can benefit from being exposed to individuals unlike themselves. Yet this only occurs when standards are uniformly applied. Universalism (i.e., the same rules for all) is promoted only when the rules are, in fact, impartially enforced. To do otherwise, whether with respect to ability, or gender, or race, or social class, or sexual orientation produces cynicism. Moreover, when people are cynical, they cease being self-directed in the sense of honestly utilizing their special expertise. They instead become game-players who attempt to subvert the system to their own advantage (Sander and Taylor, 2012).

This may be a harsh judgment, but we in the United States seem to have lost faith in many of our historic values (Sowell, 1999, 2007, 2009). Our old platitudes about freedom, honesty, competition, family solidarity, personal responsibility, universalism, and merit strike many ears as mean-spirited. Nevertheless, it is at our colleges and universities where these have traditionally been instilled in up-and-coming leaders. If we now choose to do otherwise, we had best be careful. If the qualities that make for self-directed professionalism are eschewed, what do we propose to put in their place?

Finally, as to Chirot's last stage in the evolutionary process—namely, reinstitutionalization—we have clearly not arrived there yet. No consensus on how we wish to reform higher education has been widely adopted. Thus, we cannot integrate what remains contradictory nor consolidate what has not been decided upon. In other words, we are liable to experience a great deal more conflict before these issues are resolved.

Conclusions

We have all seen the movie and most of us were enchanted by it. *The Wizard of Oz* is a classic for very good reasons. It stirs our imaginations, in large part because it deals with issues with which many of us have struggled—such as the meaning of home and family. Happily, at its conclusion, all of the major players have their wishes granted by the wizard. The Tin Man gets a heart, the Lion gets courage, and Dorothy gets to return to Kansas.

As for the Scarecrow, he has been singing all picture long about how if he only had a brain, he would be able to think wondrous thoughts. Oz ostensibly solves this problem by providing him with a college degree. The wizard explains that back where he comes from there are men who are no smarter than the Scarecrow, but what sets them apart intellectually is that they have this piece of paper. The Scarecrow is so enthused that he immediately begins spouting mathematical formulae and historic facts.

This, of course, is fiction. College graduates do not automatically become world-class thinkers. Paradoxically, Frank Baum, in including this vignette into his tale, expressed his own doubts about the value of university training. Nevertheless, we as a society seem intent on providing everyone with a sheepskin. We have apparently taken it into our collective heads that if all are so equipped, they will all be brilliant successes. Little thought has gone into what about higher education is supposed to provide these benefits. It is just assumed that something good will emerge. The credential itself is regarded as magic; hence, just going to college will produce the desired results.

It has been my contention in the preceding chapters that this is largely untrue; that unless colleges and universities instill the self-direction needed by a professionalizing society, they will be a waste of time and resources for many people. On the other hand, if they inculcate the appropriate forms of knowledge and motivation, they can furnish us with the sort of leadership needed by a mass techno-commercial society. I have further suggested that many of the tools required to achieve this are at hand; that our schools do not have to be transformed into something completely different from what they have been. As long as we understand the appropriate mission of higher education, we can make the modifications to do the job.

In fact, the traditional college education did seek to impart the knowledge and the wisdom needed to exercise social leadership (Bok, 2013). Thus, many of the traits that support self-direction are part of what universities have long attempted to teach. What is different today is that we are trying to transmit these qualities to larger numbers of persons, many of whom come from diverse social backgrounds. To paraphrase Abraham Lincoln, in a democracy, this is altogether fitting and proper. Furthermore, given the growth of our middle class and therefore the need for more upward mobility, it is to colleges and universities that we have turned to provide the requisite socialization.

Furthermore, because many individuals aspiring to leadership roles do not come from backgrounds that instill the fundamentals of self-direction, our institutions of higher learning have inherited this task. Fortunately, they can fulfill it, but only if they tailor their offerings to this mission. What they have to do differs according to the sorts of students they admit, but certain basics apply. All of these schools must be more professionalized and therefore less bureaucratized. All must address themselves to the human dimension of inspiring motivation, as well as to transmitting knowledge. And all must be honest and uniform in the standards they apply and the abilities they certify. Technical gimmicks will not work. Nor will moralistic conformity. We must get back to the old notions of a marketplace of ideas and a community of learners. Ultimately, they must lead by example. They must embody what they preach.

Of one thing we can be certain: the future will not replicate the past. Nor can we discern exactly what tomorrow will hold. Consequently, there will be differences of opinion. What is needed is thus an open dialogue and equally open minds. Conflict is inevitable, whereas orthodoxy is not.

Bibliography

Abrams, R. M. 2006. *America Transformed: Sixty Years of Revolutionary Change, 1941-2001*. New York: Cambridge University Press.

Acton, Lord. 1887. *Letter to Bishop Mandell Creighton*.

Adams, M. S. 2004. *Welcome to the Ivory Tower of Babel: Confessions of a Conservative College Professor*. Augusta, GA: Harbor House.

Adler, M. (Ed.) 1952. *The Great Books of the Western World*. New York: Encyclopedia Britannica,

Agresto, J. 2011. " The Liberal Arts Bubble." *Academic Questions*, Vol. 24, No. 4.

Alba, R. D. 1990. *Ethnic Identity: The Transformation of White America*. New Haven: Yale University Press.

Ambrose, S. A., Bridges, M. W., DiPietro, M., Lovett, M. C. and Norman, M. K. 2010. *How Learning Works: Seven Research-Based Principles for Smart Teaching*. San Francisco: Jossey-Bass.

Ambrose, S. E. 1987. *Nixon: The Education of a Politician 1913–1962*. New York: Simon and Schuster.

Anderson, J. Q., Boyles, J. L. and Rainie, L. 2012. *The Future of the Internet*. Washington, DC: Pew Research Center.

Anderson, M. 1992. *Imposters in the Temple: American Intellectuals are Destroying Our Universities and Cheating Our Students of Their Future*. New York: Simon & Schuster.

Aristotle. 1941. *The Basic Works of Aristotle*. Edited by R. McKeon. New York: Random House.

Armstrong, E. A. and Hamilton, L. T. 2013. *Paying for the Party: How College Maintains Inequality*. Cambridge, MA: Harvard University Press.

Arum, R. and Roska, J. 2011. *Academically Adrift: Limited Learning on College Campuses*. Chicago: The University of Chicago Press.

Arum, R. Et al. 2012. "One Hundred Great Ideas for Higher Education." *Academic Questions*, Vol. 25, No. 3.

Ashton, T. S. 1965. *The Industrial Revolution 1760-1830*. New York: Oxford University Press.

Association of American Colleges and Universities. 2013. "It Takes More than a Major: Employer Priorities for College Learning and Student Success." Washington, DC: AAC&U.

Attard, J. 2013. "In Defense of Liberal Education: Criticizing the Critical." *Academic Questions*, Vol. 26, No.3, Fall.
Auchincloss, L. 1989. *The Vanderbilt Era: Portraits of a Gilded Age*. New York: Scribner.
Axelrod, A. 2006. *Patton: A Biography*. London: Palgrave MacMillan.
Bailyn, B. 1992. *The Ideological Origins of the American Revolution*. Cambridge, MA: The Belknap Press.
Bailyn, B. 2003. *To Begin the World Anew: The Genius and Ambiguities of the American Founders*. New York: Vintage Books.
Bales, R. F. 1950. *Interaction Process Analysis*. Cambridge, MA: Addison-Wesley.
Ball, T. and Dagger, R. 1999. *Political Ideologies and the Democratic Ideal*. New York: Longman.
Bannister, R. C. 1979. *Social Darwinism: Science and Myth in Anglo-American Social Thought*. Philadelphia: Temple University Press.
Barlett, D. L. and Steele, J. B. 1996. *America: Who Stole the Dream?* Kansas City: Andrews and McMeel.
Barnard, C. 1938. *The Function of the Executive*. Cambridge, Mass.: Harvard University Press.
Baron-Cohen, S. 2003. *The Essential Difference: The Truth about the Male and Female Brain*. New York: Basic Books.
Barone, M. 2004. *Hard America Soft America*. New York: Crown Forum.
Barone, M. 2011. "Will College Bubble Burst From Public Subsides?" TownHall. http//townhall.com/columnists/michaelbarone.2011/07/21
Barone, M. 2012. "Colleges Skimp on Science, Spend Big on Diversity." TownHall. http//townhall.com/columnists/michaelbarone.2012/04/05
Barone, M. 2013. "College Bubble Bursts after Decades of Extravagance." TownHall. http//townhall.com/columnists/michaelbarone.2013/05/09
Barzun, J. 2000. *From Dawn to Decadence: 500 Years of Western Cultural Life*. New York: HarperCollins Publishers.
Bauerlein, M. 2009. *The Dumbest Generation: How the Digital Age Stupefies Young Americans and Jeopardizes Our Future (Or Don't Trust Anyone Under Thirty)*. New York: Tarcher.
Bauerlein, M. 2013. "Peer Review and the Productivity Era." *Academic Questions*, Vol. 26, No.2., Spring.
Bauman, Z. 1992. *Intimations of Postmodernity*. New York: Routledge.
Belfield, C. and Jenkins, D. 2013. "Measures of college efficiency too often ignore full chain of production." *Inside Higher Education*, April 19.
Bell, D. 1978. *The Cultural Contradictions of Capitalism*. New York: Basic Books.
Bellah, R. N., Madsen, R., Sullivan, W. M., Swindler, A., and Tipton, S. M. 1985. *Habits of the Heart: Individualism and Commitment in American Life*. Berkeley, CA: University of California Press.
Bennett, W. and Wilezel, D. 2013. *Is College Worth It?: A Former United States Secretary of Education and a Liberal Arts Graduate Expose the Broken Promises of Higher Education*. Nashville, TN: Thomas Nelson Publishers.

Berger, P. and Luckmann, T. 1966. *The Social Construction of Reality: A Treatise in the Sociology of Knowledge.* Garden City, NY; Doubleday.
Bergmann, B. R. 1996. *In Defense of Affirmative Action.* New York: Basic Books.
Bernstein, R. 1994. *Dictatorship of Virtue: Multiculturalism and the Battle for America's Future.* New York: Alfred A. Knopf.
Best, J. 2001. *Damned Lies and Statistics: Untangling Numbers from the Media, Politicians, and Activists.* Berkeley: University of California Press.
Best, J. 2003. "Killing the Messenger: The Social Problems of Sociology," *Social Problems,* 50: 1–13.
Best, J. 2004. *More Damned Lies and Statistics: How Numbers Confuse Public Issues.* Berkeley: University of California Press.
Best J. 2006. *Flavor of the Month: Why Smart People Fall for Fads.* Berkeley: University of California Press.
Blass, T. 2004. *The Man Who Shocked the World: The Life and Legacy of Stanley Milgram.* New York: Basic Books.
Blau, P. 1963. *The Dynamics of Bureaucracy.* Chicago: University of Chicago Press.
Bloom. A. 1987. *The Closing of the American Mind.* New York: Simon & Schuster.
Blumin, S. M. 1989. *The Emergence of the Middle Class: Social Experience in the American City 1760–1900.* New York: Cambridge University Press.
Boas, F. 1928. *Anthropology and Modern Life.* New York: Dover Publishers.
Bogle, K. A. 2008. *Hooking Up: Sex, Dating and Relationships on Campus.* New York: New York University Press.
Bok, D. 2013. *Higher Education in America.* Princeton: Princeton University Press.
Bonevac, D. 2012. "Is Sustainability Sustainable? *Academic Questions,* Vol. 23. No. 1.
Bork, R. 1996. *Slouching Toward Gomorrah: Modern Liberalism and American Decline.* New York: Regan Books.
Bosquet, M. and Nelson, C. 2008. *How the University Works: Higher Education and Low-Wage Nation.* New York: New York University Press.
Bourdieu, P. 1977. *Outline of the Theory of Practice.* Cambridge: Cambridge University Press.
Bowen, W. G. and Bok, D. 1998. *The Shape of the River: Long-Term Consequences of Considering Race in College and University Admissions.* Princeton: Princeton University Press.
Bowlby, J. 1969. *Attachment.* New York: Basic Books.
Bowles, S. and Gintis, H. 1976. *Schooling in Capitalist America: Educational Reform and the Contradictions of Capitalist Life.* New York: Basic Books.
Bozell, L. B. 2004. *Weapons of Mass Distortion: The Coming Meltdown of the Liberal Media.* New York: Crown Forum.
Bradley, M. J., Seidman, R. H. and Painchaud, S. R. 2012. *Saving Higher Education: The Integrated, Competency-Based Three-Year Bachelor's Degree Program.* San Francisco: Jossey-Bass.
Brann, E. 2012. "The Great Tradition." *Academic Questions,* Vol. 25, No. 1.

Brimelow, P. 2003. *The Worm in the Apple: How the Teacher Unions Are Destroying American Education.* New York: HarperCollins Publishers.
Brookhiser, R. 1999. *Alexander Hamilton: American.* New York: Simon & Schuster.
Brooks, D. 2000. *Bobos in Paradise: The New Upper Class and How They Got There.* New York: Simon & Schuster.
Brooks, D. 2004. *On Paradise Drive.* New York: Simon & Schuster.
Brownmiller, S. 1975. *Against Our Will: Men, Women and Rape.* New York: Bantam.
Bruce, T. 2001. *The New Thought Police: Inside the Left's Assault on Free Speech and Free Minds.* Roseville, CA: Prima Publishing.
Bruhn, J. 2001. *Trust and the Health of Organizations.* New York: Kluwer/Plenum.
Buckley, K. W. 1989. *Mechanical Man: John Broadus Watson and the Beginnings of Behaviorism.* New York: The Guilford Press.
Burke, J. 2007. *Connections.* New York: Simon & Schuster.
Caesar, J. [1980] *The Battle for Gaul.* Boston: David R. Godine Publisher.
Cannon, L. 1999. *Official Negligence: How Rodney King and the Riots Changed Los Angles and the LAPD.* Boulder, CO: Westview Press.
Caplow, T., Hicks, L. and Wattenberg, B. J. 2001. *The First Measured Century: An Illustrated Guide to Trends in America, 1900-2000.* Washington, DC: AEI Press.
Carr, N. 2010. *The Shallows: What the Internet is Doing to Our Brains.* New York: W. W. Norton and Company.
Carter, S. L. 1991. *Reflections of an Affirmative Action Baby.* New York: Basic Books.
Carter, S. L. 1998. *Civility: Manners, Morals and the Etiquette of Democracy.* New York: Basic Books.
Chatfield, C. 1992. *The American Peace Movement: Ideals and Activism.* New York: Twayne Publishers.
Chernow, R. 1998. *Titan: The Life of John D. Rockefeller.* New York: Vintage Books.
Chirot, D. 1986. *Social Change in the Modern Era.* New York: Harcourt, Brace, Jovanovich.
Chirot, D. 1994. *How Societies Change.* Thousand Oaks: Pine Forge Press.
Christensen, C. M. and Eyring, H. J. 2011. *The Innovative University: Changing the DNA of Higher Education from the Inside Out.* San Francisco: Jossey-Bass.
Christy, R. D. and Williamson, L. (Eds.) 1991. *A Century of Service; Land Grant Colleges and Universities, 1890-1990.* New Brunswick, NJ: Transaction Publishers.
Chua, A. 2011. *Battle Hymn of the Tiger Mother.* New York: The Penguin Press.
Clegg, R. 2011. "Affirmative Discrimination and the Bubble." *Academic Questions,* Vol. 24, No. 4.
Clegg, R. and Rosenberg, J. S. 2012. "Against 'Diversity.'" *Academic Questions,* Vol. 25, No. 3.
Cole, S. (Ed.) 2001. *What's Wrong with Sociology?* New Brunswick, NJ: Transaction Publishers.

Coleman, J. S. 1990. *Foundations of Social Theory*. Cambridge, MA: Harvard University Press.

Coleman, J. S., Campbell, E. Q, Hobson, C. J., McPartland, J., Mood, A. M., Weinfeld, F. D. and York, R. L. 1966. *Equality of Educational Opportunity*. Washington: US Government Printing Office.

Collier, P. and Horowitz, D. 1976. *The Rockefellers: An American Dynasty*. New York: Holt, Rinehart & Winston.

Collier, P. and Horowitz, D. 1984. *The Kennedys: An American Drama*. New York: Summit Books.

Collier, P. and Horowitz, D. 1987. *The Fords: An American Epic*. New York: Summit Books.

Connerly, W. 2000. *Creating Equal: My Fight Against Race Prejudices*. San Francisco: Encounter Books.

Conway, C. 2013. "Essay on the Teaching Value of Chalkboard." *Inside Higher Education*. April 1.

Cooley, C. H. 1956. *Human Nature and the Social Order*. Glencoe, Ill.: The Free Press.

Coser, L. 1964. *The Functions of Social Conflict*. New York: The Free Press.

Courtois, S., Werth, N., Panne, J. L., Paczkowski, A., Bartosek, and Margolin, J. L. 1999. *The Black Book of Communism: Crimes, Terror, Repression*. Cambridge, MA. Harvard University Press.

Cowelll, F. R. 1961. *Life in Ancient Rome*. New York: G. P. Putnam's Sons.

Cranston, M. 1982. *Jean-Jacques*. New York: W. W. Norton & Co.

Cronk, L. 1999. *That Complex Whole: Culture and the Evolution of Human Behavior*. Boulder, CO: Westview Press.

Crozier, M. 1964. *The Bureaucratic Phenomenon*. Chicago: University of Chicago Press.

Dahl, R. 1967. *Pluralist Democracy in the United States*. Chicago: Rand McNally.

Dahrendorf, R. 1959. *Class and Class Conflict in Industrial Society*. Stanford, CA: Stanford University Press.

Dahrendorf, R. 1968. *Essays in the Theory of Society*. Stanford, Ca.: Stanford University Press.

Dalrymple, T. 2001. *Life at the Bottom: The Worldview that Makes the Underclass*. Chicago: Ivan R. Dee.

Damasio, A. 1994. *Descartes' Error: Emotion, Reason, and the Human Brain*. New York: Penguin Books.

Darwin, C. 1979. *The Origin of Species*. New York: Avnel Books.

Davies, T. 1997. *Humanism*. New York: Routledge.

Davis, K. and Moore, W. E. 1945. "Some Principles of Stratification." *American Sociological Review* 10 (April 242-249.)

Delbanco, A. 2012. *College: What It Was, Is, and Should Be*. Princeton: Princeton University Press.

Demott, B. 1990. *The Imperial Middle: Why American Can't Think Straight about Class*. New Haven: Yale University Press.

Derrida, J. 1997. *Deconstruction in a Nutshell* (Edited by D. Caputo) New York: Fordham University Press.

Deutsch, M. and Collins, M. E. 1951. *Interracial Housing: A Psychological Evaluation of a Social Study*. Minneapolis: University of Minnesota Press.

Deveaux, M. 2000. *Cultural Pluralism and Dilemmas of Justice*. Ithaca, NY: Cornell University Press.

Dewey, J. 1943. *The School and Society*. Chicago: University of Chicago Press.

Diamond, J. 2005. *Collapse: How Societies Choose to Fail or Succeed*. New York: Penguin Books.

Diamond, J. 2013. *The World Until Yesterday: What Can We Learn from Traditional Societies*? New York: Viking.

DiPrete, T. and Buchmann, C. 2013. *The Rise of Women: The Growing Gender Gap in Education and What It Means for American Schools*. New York: The Russell Sage Foundation.

Dobbin, F. 2009. *Inventing Equal Opportunity*. Princeton: Princeton University Press.

Doty, C. S. (Ed.) 1969. *The Industrial Revolution*. New York: Holt, Rinehart and Winston.

Douthat, R. 2005. *Privilege: Harvard and the Education of the Ruling Class*. New York: Hyperion.

D'Souza, D. 1991. *Illiberal Education: The Politics of Race and Sex on Campus*. New York: The Free Press.

Duchesne, R. 2011. *The Uniqueness of Western Civilization*. Boston: Brill.

Dulles, F. R. 1966. *Labor in America: A History*. Arlington Heights, Ill.: Harlan Davidson.

Dunbar, R, Knight, C. and Power, C. 1999. (Eds.) *The Evolution of Culture*. New Brunswick, NJ: Rutgers University Press.

Duncan, O. D. 1965. "The Trend of Occupational Mobility in the United States." *American Sociological Review*, 30: 491–498.

Durant, A. and Durant. W. 1967. *Rousseau and the Revolution*. New York: MJF Books.

Durden, W. G. 2012. "Essay on the Idea of a Useful Liberal Arts." *Inside Higher Ed*. November 26.

Durkheim, E. 1915. *The Elementary Forms of Religious Life*. New York: The Free Press.

Durkheim, E. 1933. *The Division of Labor in Society*. New York: The Free Press.

Durkheim, E. 1961. *Moral Education*. New York: The Free Press.

Ebenstein, A. 2001. *Friedrich Hayek: A Biography*. New York: Palgrave.

Eberstadt, M. 2004. *Home-Alone America: The Hidden Toll of Day Care, Behavioral Drugs, and Other Parent Substitutes*. New York: Sentinel,

Edin, K. and Kefalas, M. 2005. *Promises I Can Keep: Why Poor Women Put Motherhood before Marriage*. Berkeley: University of California Press.

Edman, I. (Ed.) 1928. *The Works of Plato*. New York: The Modern Library.

Edmonds, D. and Eidinow, J. 2006. *Rousseau's Dog: Two Great Thinkers at War in the Age of Enlightenment*. New York: HarperCollins.

Edmundsen, M. 2013. *Why Teach?: In Defense of a Real Education*. New York: Bloomsbury Publishing

Elias, N. 1983. *The Court Society*. New York: Pantheon Books.

Elias, N. 1998. *On Civilization, Power, and Knowledge*. (Edited by Stephen Mennell and Johan Goudsblom) Chicago: University of Chicago Press.

Ellis, J. J. 1979. *After the Revolution: Profiles of Early American Culture*. New York: W. W. Norton & Co.

Ellis, J. J. 1993. *Passionate Sage: The Character and Legacy of John Madison*. New York: W. W. Norton & Co.

Ellis, J. J. 1996. *American Sphinx: The Character of Thomas Jefferson*. New York: Alfred A. Knopf.

Ellis, J. M. 1997. *Literature Lost: Social Agendas and the Corruption of the Humanities*. New Haven: Yale University Press.

Ellis, J. M and Geshekter, C. L. 2012. "Democrats Dominate UC CSU Faculties." San Jose Mercury News, July 4, 2012.

Ellis, R. J. 1998. *The Dark Side of the Left: Illiberal Egalitarianism in America*. Lawrence: University of Kansas Press.

Elshtain, J. B. 1995. *Democracy on Trial*. New York: Basic Books.

Engels, F. 1972. *The Origin of the Family, Private Property, and the State*. New York: International Publishers.

Entine, J. 2000. *Taboo: Why Black Athletes Dominate Sports and Why We're Afraid to Talk About It*. New York: Public Affairs.

Entwisle, D. R., Alexander, K. L. and Olson, L. S. 1997. *Children, Schools & Inequality*. Boulder, CO: Westview Press.

Epstein, C. F. 1970. *Woman's Place: Options and Limits in Professional Careers*. Berkeley: University of California Press.

Erlich, P. 2000. *Human Natures*. New York: Penguin Books

Erikson, E. 1950. *Childhood and Society*. New York: W. W. Norton.

Erikson, E. 1964. *Insight and Responsibility*. New York: W. W. Norton.

Erikson, E. 1968. *Identity: Youth and Crisis*. New York: W. W. Norton.

Espenshade, T. J. and Radford, W. A. 2009. *No Longer Separate, Not Yet Equal: Race and Class in Elite Admission and Campus Life*. Princeton: University of Princeton Press.

Etzioni, A. 1961. *A Comparative Analysis of Complex Organizations*. New York: Free Press.

Etzioni, A. 1993. *The Spirit of Community: Reinvention of American Society*. New York: Simon & Schuster.

Everitt, A. 2001. *Cicero: The Life and Times of Rome's Greatest Politician*. New York: Random House.

Fain, P. 2011. "For-Profits Lag Behind Other Colleges in Student Outcomes." *Inside Higher Ed*. December 7.

Fain, P. 2012a. "CUNY Faculty Sue to Block New Core Curriculum." *Inside Higher Ed*. March 22.

Fain, P. 2012b. "Harkin Releases Critical Report on For-Profits." *Inside Higher Ed*. July 30.

Fain, P. 2013a. "Gates Foundation Helps Colleges Keep Tabs on Adaptive Learning Technology." *Inside Higher Ed*. April 4.

Fain, P. 2013b. "On-line Courses Are Second Choices for Community College Students in Some Subject Areas." *Inside Higher Education*, April, 26.

Farley, R. 1996. *The New American Reality: Who We Are, How We Got Here, Where We Are Going.* New York: Russell Sage Foundation.
Feagin, J. R. and Sikes, M. P. 1994. *Living with Racism: The Black Middle-Class Experience.* Boston: Beacon Press.
Fein, M. 1997. *Hardball Without an Umpire: The Sociology of Morality.* Westport, CT: Praeger.
Fein, M. 1999. *The Limits of Idealism: When Good Intentions Go Bad.* New York: Kluwer/Plenum.
Fein, M. 2005. *The Great Middle Class Revolution: Our Long March Toward a Professionalized Society.* Kennesaw, GA: Kennesaw University Press.
Fein, M. 2011a. *On Loss and Losing: Beyond the Medical Model of Personal Distress.* New Brunswick: Transaction Publishers.
Fein, M. 2011b. *A Professionalized Society: Our Real Future.* Kindle.
Fein, M. 2012a. *Human Hierarchies: A General Theory.* New Brunswick: Transaction Publishers.
Fein, M. 2012b. *Post-Liberalism: The Death of a Dream.* New Brunswick: Transaction Publishers.
Ferguson, N. 2001. *The Cash Nexus: Money and Power in the Modern World, 1700–2000.* New York: Basic Books.
Festinger, L. 1957. *A Theory of Cognitive Dissonance.* Evanston, Ill.: Row, Peterson.
Festinger, L. Rieken, H. W. and Schacter, S. 1964. *When Prophesy Fails.* New York: Harper & Row.
Fiamengo, J. 2013. "The Fail Proof Student." *Academic Questions,* Vol. 26, No. 3., Fall.
Fischer, D. H. 1989. *Albion's Seed: Four British Folkways in America.* New York: Oxford University Press.
Fishman, R. 1987. *Bourgeois Utopias: The Rise and Fall of Suburbia.* New York: Basic Books.
Fitzhugh, W. 2011. "High School Flight from Reading and Writing." *Academic Questions,* Vol. 24, No. 4.
Flaherty, C. 2013. "A university tries to deal with salary compression among faculty members." *Inside Higher Education,* February 11.
Fonte, R. 2011. "The Community College Alternative." *Academic Questions,* Vol. 24, No. 4.
Fornara, C. 1991. *Athens from Cleisthenes to Pericles.* Berkeley: University of California Press.
Foucault, M. 1979. *Discipline and Punish: The Birth of the Prison.* New York: Random House.
Fox, R. 2012. "The Razor's Edge." *Academic Questions,* Vol. 25, No. 1.
Frank, S. A. 1998. *Foundations of Social Evolution.* Princeton: University of Princeton Press.
Franklin, D. L. 1997. *Ensuring Inequality: The Structural Transformation of the African-American Family.* New York: Oxford University Press.
Frazier, F. 1965. *Black Bourgeoisie: The Rise of a New Middle Class.* New York: MacMillan.

Freeman, D. 1983. *Margaret Mead and Samoa: The Making and Unmaking of an Anthropological Myth*. Cambridge, MA: Harvard University Press.

French, D. A, Lukianoff, G. and Silverglate, H. A. 2005. *FIRE's Guide to Free Speech on Campus*. Philadelphia: Foundation for Individual Rights in Education.

Freud, A. 1966. *The Ego and the Mechanisms of Defense*. New York: International Universities Press.

Freud, S. 1953–1974. *The Standard Edition of the Complete Psychological Works of Sigmund Freud*. (Edited by J. Strachey. London: Hogarth Press and Institute for Psychoanalysis.

Freud, S. 1961. *Civilization and Its Discontents*. New York: W. W. Norton Co.

Friedman, M. 1962. *Capitalism and Freedom*. Chicago: University of Chicago Press.

Fukuyama, F. 1995. *Trust: The Social Virtues and the Creation of Prosperity*. New York: Free Press.

Fukuyama, F. 1999. *The Great Disruption: Human Nature and the reconstitution of Social Order*. New York: Free Press.

Fussell, P. 1983. *Class: A Guide Through the American Status System*. New York: Simon & Schuster.

Galbraith, J. K. 1958. *The Affluent Society*. Boston: Houghton Mifflin.

Gans, H. J. 1988. *Middle American Individualism: Political Participation and Liberal Democracy*. New York: Oxford University Press.

Garder, R. D. 1978. *Horatio Alger: or the American Hero Era*. New York: Arco Publishers.

Gardner, M. 1957. *Fads and Fallacies in the Name of Science*. New York: Dover.

Gerth, H. and Mills, C. W. (Eds.) 1946. *From Max Weber: Essays in Sociology*. New York: Oxford University Press.

Gibbon, E. [1963] *The Decline and Fall of the Roman Empire*. New York: Dell Publishing.

Gibbs, J. 1989. *Control: Sociology's Central Notion*. Chicago: University of Illinois Press.

Giddens, A. 1973. *The Class Structure of the Advanced Societies*. New York: Harper & Row.

Gilligan, C. 1982. *In a Different Voice*. Cambridge, MA: Harvard University Press.

Ginsberg, B. 2011. *The Fall of the Faculty: The Rise of the All-Administrative University and Why It Matters*. New York: Oxford University Press.

Gladwell, M. 2000. *The Tipping Point: How Little Things Can Make a Big Difference*. Boston: Little, Brown and Co.

Gladwell, M. 2008. *Outliers: The Story of Success*. New York: Little, Brown and Company.

Glazer, N. 1997. *We are All Multiculturalists Now*. Cambridge: Harvard University Press.

Gleick, J. 2003. *Isaac Newton*. New York: Pantheon Books.

Glendon, M. A. 1991. *Rights Talk: The Impoverishment of Political Discourse*. New York: Free Press.

Glendon, M. A. 2011. *The Forum and the Tower: How Scholars and Politicians Have Imagined the World, from Plato to Eleanor Roosevelt.* New York: Oxford University Press.
Glendon, M. A. and Blankenhorn, D. (Eds.) 1995. *Seedbeds of Virtue: Sources of Competence, Character, and Citizenship in American Society.* Lanham, MD: Madison Books.
Glenn, N. 1997. *Closed Hearts, Closed Minds: The Textbook Story of Marriage.* New York: Institute for American Values.
Goffman, E. 1959. *The Presentation of Self in Everyday Life.* Garden City: Doubleday and Co.
Goffman, E. 1961. *Asylums.* New York: Achor Books.
Goffman, E. 1963. *Stigma.* Englewood Cliffs: Prentice-Hall.
Goffman, E. 1969. *Strategic Interaction.* New York: Ballantine Books.
Goffman, E. 1974. *Frame Analysis.* New York: Harper and Row.
Goldberg, J. 2012. *The Tyranny of Clichés: How Liberals Cheat in the War of Ideas.* New York: Sentinel.
Goleman, D. 1995. *Emotional Intelligence: Why It Can Matter More Than IQ.* New York: Bantam Books.
Goleman, D. 2006. *Social Intelligence: The New Science of Human Relationships.* New York: Bantam Books.
Good, T. L. and Braden, J. S. 2000. *The Great School Debate: Choice, Vouchers, and Charters.* Mahwah, NJ. Lawrence Erlbaum Associates.
Gordon, M. M. 1964. *Assimilation in American Life: The Role of Race, Religion, and National Origins.* New York: Oxford University Press.
Gottschall, J. 2012. *The Storytelling Animal: How Stories Make Us Human.* New York: Houghton Mifflin Harcourt.
Gould, S. J. 1977. *Ever Since Darwin: Reflections in Natural History.* New York: W. W. Norton & Co.
Gould, S. J. 1981. *The Mismeasure of Man.* New York: W. W. Norton Co.
Gould, S. J. 1996. *Full House: The Spread of Excellence from Plato to Darwin.* New York: Three Rivers Press.
Gouldner, A. J. 1954. *Patterns of Industrial Bureaucracy.* New York: The Free Press.
Gouldner, A. W. 1960. "The Norm of Reciprocity." *American Sociological Review.* 25: 161–78.
Gouldner, A. W. 1970. *The Coming Crisis of Western Sociology.* New York: Basic Books.
Grabar, M. 2013. *Exiled: Stories from Conservative and Moderate Professors Who Have Been Ridiculed, Ostracized, Marginalized, Demonized, and Frozen Out.* Atlanta, GA: Dissident Prof.
Graham, L. 1993. *Science in Russia and the Soviet Union.* New York: Cambridge University Press.
Gramsci, A. 1977. *Antonio Gramsci: Selections from Political Writings.* New York: International Publications.
Granovetter, M. 1973. "The Strength of Weak Ties." *American Journal of Sociology*; 78, 1360–80.

Greenspan, A. 2013. "White Men Alienated in Higher Ed, Survey Suggests." *Inside Higher Ed.* March 22.
Greenwood, E. 1957. "Attributes of a Profession." *Social Work,* II, 3, July.
Greer, C. and Kohl, H. 1995. *A Call to Character.* New York: Harper-Collins.
Gregorovius, F. 1971. *Rome and Medieval Culture.* Chicago: University of Chicago Press.
Griswold, W. 1994. *Cultures and Societies in a Changing World.* Thousand Oaks: Pine Forge Press.
Gross, N. 2013. *Why Are Professors Liberal and Why Do Conservatives Care?* Cambridge, MA: Harvard University Press.
Grusky, O. and Miller, G. A. (Eds.) 1970. *The Sociology of Organizations: Basic Studies* (Second Edition). New York: The Free Press.
Guy, M. E. 1997. "Counterpoint: By Thine Own Voice, Shall Thou Be Known." *Public Productivity and Management Review,* Vol. 20, No. 3, March, pp. 237–242.
Hacker, A. and Dreifus, C. 2010. *Higher Education?: How Colleges Are Wasting Our Money and Failing Our Kids—And What We Can Do about It.* New York: Times Books.
Hall, R. H. 1999. *Organizations: Structures, Processes, and Outcomes.* Upper Saddle River, NJ: Prentice-Hall.
Hamilton, R. F. 1996. *The Social Misconstruction of Reality: Validity and Verification in the Scholarly Community.* New Haven: Yale University Press.
Hardy, G. M. and Everett, D. L. 2013. *Shaping the Future of Business Education: Rigor and Life Preparation.* New York: Palgrave Macmillan.
Harris, M. 1977. *Cannibals and Kings: The Origins of Cultures.* New York: Random House.
Harris, M. 1989. *Our Kind: Who We Are, Where We Came From and Where We Are Going.* New York: HarperCollins.
Harrison, L. E. and Huntington, S. P. (Eds.) 2000. *Culture Matters: How Values Shape Human Progress.* New York: Basic Books.
Haskins, C. H. 1957. *The Rise of the Universities.* Ithaca: Cornell University Press.
Hatab, L. J. 1990. *Myth and Philosophy: A Contest of Truths.* La Salle, IL: Open Court.
Hayek, F. A. 1944. *The Road to Serfdom.* London: Routledge.
Hayek, F. A. 1988. *The Fatal Conceit: The Errors of Socialism.* Chicago: The University of Chicago Press.
Hayes, C. 2012. *Twilight of the Elites: America after Meritocracy."* New York: Crown.
Haynes, J. E. and Klehr, H. 2003. *In Denial: Historians, Communism and Espionage.* San Francisco: Encounter Books.
Hearn, F. 1997. *Moral Order and Social Disorder: The American Search for Civil Society.* New York: Aldine de Gruyter.
Hedstrom, P. and Swedberg, R. (Eds.) 1998. *Social Mechanisms: An Analytic Approach to Social Theory.* New York: Cambridge University Press.
Heilbroner, R. L. 1980. *The Worldly Philosophers.* New York: Simon and Schuster.
Hendershott, A. 2011. "Catholic in Name Only." *Academic Questions,* Vol.24, No. 3.

Herrnstein, R. J. and Murray, C. 1994. *The Bell Curve: The Reshaping of American Life by Differences in Intelligence.* New York: Basic Books.
Hewitt, J. P. 1998. *The Myth of Self-Esteem: Finding Happiness and Solving Problems in America.* New York: St. Martins.
Himmelfarb, G. 1995. *The De-Moralization of Society: From Victorian Virtues to Modern Values.* New York: Alfred A. Knopf.
Himmelfarb, G. 1999. *One Nation, Two Cultures.* New York: Alfred A. Knopf.
Hobbes, T. 1956. *Leviathan; Part I.* Chicago: Henry Regnery Co.
Hochschild, A. R. 1983. *The Managed Heart: Commercialization of Human Feeling.* Berkeley: University of California Press.
Hochschild, J. 1995. *Facing Up to the American Dream.* Princeton, NJ: Princeton University Press.
Hoffer, E. 1951. *The True Believer: Thoughts on the Nature of Mass Movements.* New York: Harper & Row.
Hoffer, P. C. 2004. *Past Imperfect: Facts, Fictions, Fraud—American History from Bancroft and Parkman to Ambrose, Bellesiles, Ellis and Goodwin.* New York: Public Affairs.
Hollander, P. 2013. "Peer Review, Political Correctness and Human Nature." *Academic Questions,* Vol. 26., No.2, Summer.
Horowitz, D. 1998. *Betty Friedan and the Making of the Feminine Mystique.* Amherst: University of Massachusetts Press.
Horowitz, D. 2006. *The Professors: The 101 Most Dangerous Academics in America.* Washington, DC: Regnery Publishing.
Horowitz, H. L. 1987. *Campus Life: Undergraduate Cultures from the End of the Eighteenth Century to the Present.* Chicago: University of Chicago Press.
Horowitz, I. L. 1961. *Radicalism and the Revolt against Reason: The Social Theories of Georges Sorel.* London: Southern Illinois University Press.
Horowitz, I. L. 1994. *The Decomposition of Sociology.* New York: The Oxford University Press.
Howard, P. K. 2001. *The Lost Art of Drawing the Line: How Fairness Went Too Far.* New York: Random House.
Howell, J. T. 1973. *Hard Living on Clay Street: Portraits of Blue Collar Families.* Prospect Heights, IL.: Waveland Press.
Hughes, E. C. 1958. *Men and Their Work.* New York: Free Press of Glencoe.
Hughes, R. 1993. *Culture of Complaint: The Fraying of America.* New York: Oxford University Press.
Hume, D. (1739). *A Treatise on Human Nature.* London.
Humphrey, H. H. 1964. *War on Poverty.* New York: McGraw-Hill.
Hunt, A. 1999. *Governing Morals: A Social History of Moral Regulation.* New York: Cambridge University Press.
Hunter, J. D. 1991. *Culture Wars: The Struggle to Define America.* New York: Basic Books.
Hunter, J. D. 2000. *The Death of Character: Moral Education in an Age Without Good and Evil.* New York: Basic Books.
Huntington, S. P. 1996. *The Clash of Civilizations and the Remaking of World Order.* New York: Simon & Schuster.

Huntington, S. P. 2004. *Who are We?: The Challenges to America's National Identity*. New York: Simon & Schuster.

Hutchings, P., Huber, M. T. and Ciccone, A. 2011. *The Scholarship of Teaching and Learning Reconsidered: Institutional Integration and Impact*. San Francisco: Jossey-Bass.

Isaacson, W. 2003. *Benjamin Franklin: An American Life*. New York: Simon & Schuster.

Jackson. J. L. 2008. *Racial Paranoia: The Unintended Consequences of Political Correctness*. New York: Basic Civitas Books.

Jardine, L. 1999. *Ingenious Pursuits: Building the Scientific Revolution*. New York: Doubleday.

Jaschik, S. 2012a. "Senior Professor's Mass E-Mail Leads to Introspection." *Inside Higher Ed*. June 18.

Jaschik, S. 2012b. "Study Finds Wage Disadvantage for Those Starting as For-Profits." *Inside Higher Ed*. July 3.

Jaschik, S. 2012c. "Survey Finds that Social Psychologists Admit to Anti-Conservative Bias." *Inside Higher Ed*. August 8.

Jaschik, S. 2012d. "Survey Finds that Professors, Already Liberal, Have Moved Further Left." *Inside Higher Ed*. October 24.

Jaschik, S. 2012e. "New Study Analyzes How Faculty Pay Compares Worldwide." *Inside Higher Ed*. March 22.

Jaschik, S. 2013a. "New Study Links Student Motivations for Going to College to Their Success." *Inside Higher Ed*.. April 25.

Jaschik, S. 2013b. "Study Finds Choice of Major Influenced by Quality of Intro Professor." *Inside Higher Ed*, August 12.

Jencks, C. 1972. *Inequality: A Reassessment of the Effect of Family and Schooling in America*. New York: Basic Books.

Jencks, C. 1992. *Rethinking Social Policy: Race, Poverty and the Underclass*. Cambridge, MA: Harvard University Press.

Johnson, A. G. 2001. *Privilege, Power, and Difference*. Mountain View, CA: Mayfield Publishing.

Johnson, V. E. 2002. *Grade Inflation: A Crisis in College Education*. New York: Springer.

Keller, L. (Ed.) 1999. *Levels of Selection in Evolution*. Princeton, NJ: Princeton University Press.

Ketcham, R. 1990. *James Madison: A Biography*. Charlottesville: University of Virginia Press.

Kimball, R. 1990. *Tenured Radicals: How Politics Has Corrupted Our Higher Education*. Chicago: Ivan R. Dee.

Kinder, R. R. and Sanders L. M. 1996. *Divided by Color: Racial Politics and Democratic Ideals*. Chicago: University of Chicago Press.

Kissel, A. 2011. "Will Universities Discover Their Core Mission as They Shrink?" *Academic Questions*, Vol. 24, No. 4.

Klein, M. 2003. *The Change Makers; From Carnegie to Gates*. New York: Times Books.

Kloppenberg, J. T. 2011. *Reading Obama: Dreams, Hope, and the American Tradition*. Princeton: Princeton University Press.

Knight, R. H. 1998. *The Age of Consent: The Rise of Relativism and the Corruption of Popular Culture.* Dallas TX: Spence Publishing.
Kohlberg, L. 1981. *The Philosophy of Moral Development: Moral Stages and the Idea of Justice.* New York: Harper & Row.
Kohn, M. L. 1969. *Class and Conformity: A Study in Values.* Homewood, Ill.: The Dorsey Press.
Kohn, M. L. and Schooler, C. 1983. *Work and Personality: An Inquiry Into the Impact of Social Stratification.* Norwood, NJ: Ablex Publishing.
Kohn, M. L. and Slomczynski, K. M. 1990. *Social Structure and Self-Direction: A Comparative Analysis of the United States and Poland.* Cambridge, MA: Basil Blackwell.
Kolowich, S. 2011. "Survey Shows that as Online Enrollments Have Boomed, Doubts about Online Quality Persist." *Inside Higher Ed.* November 9.
Kolowich, S. 2013. "The Minds Behind the MOOC's." *The Chronicle of Higher Education,* March 18.
Kornblum, W. 2011. *Sociology in a Changing World* (9th Edition). Belmont, CA: Wadsworth Publishing.
Kors, A. C. and Silverglate, H. A. 1998. *The Shadow University: The Betrayal of Liberty on America's Campuses.* New York: The Free Press.
Kramer, H. and Kimball, R. 1999. *The Betrayal of Liberalism: How the Disciples of Freedom and Equality Helped Foster the Illiberal Politics of Coercion and Control.* Chicago: Ivan R. Dee.
Kramer, R. 1991. *Ed School Follies: The Miseducation of America's Teachers.* New York: The Free Press.
Kuhn, T. S. 1970. *The Structure of Scientific Revolutions; Second Edition.* Chicago: University of Chicago Press.
Kurtines, W. M. and Gewirtz, J. L. (Eds.) 1987. *Moral Development Through Social Interaction.* New York: John Wiley & Sons.
Lacey, R. 1986. *Ford: The Men and the Machine.* Boston: Little, Brown and Co.
Ladd, E. C. 1999. *The Ladd Report.* New York: The Free Press.
Lang, J. 2008. *On Course: A Week-by-Week Guide to Your First Semester of College Teaching.* Cambridge: Harvard University Press.
Lareau, A. 2003. *Unequal Childhoods: Class, Race, and Family Life.* Berkeley: University of California Press.
Lareau, A. and Conley, D. (Eds.) 2008. *Social Class: How It Works.* New York: Russell Sage.
Larson, E. J. 2004. *Evolution: The Remarkable History of a Scientific Theory.* New York: The Modern Library.
Larson, M. S. 1977. *The Rise of Professionalism: A Sociological Analysis.* Berkeley: University of California Press.
Lasch, C. 1979. *The Culture of Narcissism: American Life in an Age of Diminishing Expectations.* New York: Warner Books.
Lavin, D. E, and Hyllegard, D. 1996. *Changing the Odds: Open Admissions and the Life Chances of the Disadvantaged.* New Haven: Yale University Press.
Lederman, D. 2013. "Study Finds Some Groups Fare Worse than Others in Online Courses." *Inside Higher Education,* February 25.

Lederman, D. and Jaschik, S. 2013. "Survey of Faculty Attitudes on Technology." *Inside Higher Ed*, August 27.
Lenski, G. 1966. *Power and Privilege: A Theory of Social Stratification.* New York: McGraw-Hill.
Lenzer, G. (Ed.) 1975. *Auguste Comte and Positivism: The Essential Writings.* New York: Harper Torchbooks.
Lemert, E. M. 1967. *Human Deviance: Social Problems and Social Control.* Englewood Cliffs, NJ: Prentice-Hall.
Lewis, M. and Saarni, C. (Eds.) 1985. *The Socialization of Emotions.* New York: Plenum Press.
Lewis, O. 1966. *La Vida: A Puerto Rican Family in the Culture of Poverty.* New York: Random House.
Lipset, S. M. 1996. *American Exceptionalism: A Double-Edged Sword.* New York: W. W. Norton.
Lipset, S. M. and Bendix, R. 1959. *Social Mobility in Industrial Society.* Berkeley: University of California Press.
Loewen, J. W. 1995. *Lies My Teacher Told Me: Everything Your American History Textbook Got Wrong.* New York: The New Press.
Lofland, L. H. 1973. *A World of Strangers.* New York: Basic Books.
Lopreato, J. and Crippen, T. 1999. *Crisis in Sociology: The Need For Darwin.* New Brunswick, NJ: Transaction Publishers.
Lorber, J. 1994. *Paradoxes of Gender.* New Haven: Yale University Press.
Lortie, D. 1975. *Schoolteacher: A Sociological Study.* Chicago: University of Chicago Press.
Ludwig, A. M. 2002. *King of the Mountain: The Nature of Political Leadership.* Lexington: University of Kentucky Press.
Lukianoff, G. 2012. *Unlearning Liberty: Campus Censorship and the End of American Debate.* New York: Encounter Books.
Lynch, F. R. 1997. *The Diversity Machine.* New York: The Free Press.
MacKinnon, C. A. 1987. *Feminism Unmodified: Discourses on Life and Law.* Cambridge, MS: Harvard University Press.
Madsen, A. 2001. *John Jacob Astor: America's First Multimillionaire.* New York: John Wiley & Sons.
Magnet, M. 1993. *The Dream and the Nightmare: The Sixties Legacy to the Underclass.* New York: William Morrow & Co.
Mannheim, K. 1936. *Ideology and Utopia.* New York: Harcourt, Brace, and World, Inc.
Mannheim, K. 1940. *Man and Society.* London: Routledge and Kegan Paul.
Mansfield, H. 2013. "The Higher Education Scandal." *Claremont Review of Books*, Vol. XIII, No.2, Spring.
Mapp, A. J. 1987. *Thomas Jefferson: A Strange Case of Mistaken Identity.* Lanham, MD: Madison Books.
Marks, J. 2012. "Conservative Focus on the Higher Ed Bubble Undermines Liberal Education." November 15.
Marshall, P.D. 1977. *Celebrity and Power: Fame in Contemporary Culture.* Minneapolis, Minn.: The University of Minnesota Press.

Marx, K. 1967. *Das Capital.* Edited by F. Engels. Translated by Samuel Moore and Edward Aveling. New York: International Publishing.
Marx, K. and Engels, F. [1848] 1935. *The Communist Manifesto.* (In: *Selected Works*) London: Lawrence and Wishart.
Maslow, A. 1954. *Motivation and Personality.* New York: Harper and Row.
Massey, D. S. 2007. *Categorically Unequal: The American Stratification System.* New York: Russell Sage Foundation.
Matthews, K. D. 1964. *The Early Romans: Farmers to Empire Builders.* New York: McGraw-Hill.
McCullough, D. 2001. *John Adams.* New York: Simon & Schuster.
McFeely, W. S. 1981. *Grant: A Biography.* New York: W.W. Norton and Co.
McNeill, W.H. 1963. *The Rise of the West: A History of the Human Community. Chicago*: University of Chicago Press.
McWhorter, J. 2003. *Authentically Black: Essays for the Black Silent Majority.* New York: Gotham Books.
Mead, G. H. 1934. *Mind, Self and Society.* Chicago: University of Chicago Press.
Mead, L. M. 2011. "Scholasticism: Causes and Cures." *Academic Questions,* Vol. 24, No. 3.
Mead, L. M. 2012. "The Poverty of Poverty Research." *Academic Questions,* Vol. 25, No. 4.
Mead, M. 1928. *Coming of Age in Samoa.* New York: American Museum of Natural History.
Mead, M. 1930. *Growing Up in New Guinea: A Comparative Study of Primitive Education.* New York: Dell Publishing.
Menchu, R. with Burgos-Debray, E. 1984. *I, Rigoberta Menchu: An Indian Woman in Guatemala.* (Trans. Ann Wright.) London: Verso.
Merton, R. 1949. *Social Theory and Social Structure.* New York: Free Press.
Mill, J. S. 1857. *Utilitarianism.* Indianapolis: Bobbs-Merrill.
Mill, J. S. 1863. *On Liberty.* London.
Millard, C. 2011. *Destiny of the Republic: A Tale of Madness, Medicine, and the Murder of a President.* New York: Doubleday.
Mills, C. W. 1951. *White Collar; The American Middle Classes.* New York: Oxford University Press.
Mills, C. W. 1956. *The Power Elite.* London: Oxford University Press.
Mills, C. W. 1959. *The Sociological Imagination.* New York: Oxford University Press.
Moir, A. and Jessel, D. 1989. *Brain Sex: The Real Difference Between Men and Women.* New York: Delta.
Money, J. and Ehrhardt, A. 1972. *Man and Woman; Boy and Girl.* Baltimore: Johns Hopkins Press.
Montefiore, S. S. 2004. *Stalin: The Court of the Red Tsar.* New York: Alfred A. Knopf.
Moore, M. 2001. *Stupid White Men . . . and Other Sorry Excuses for the State of the Nation.* New York: ReganBooks.
Moore, S. and Simon, J. L. 2000. *It's Getting Better All the Time: 100 Greatest Trends of the Last 100 Years.* Washington, DC: Cato Institute.
Morris, E. 2001. *Theodore Rex.* New York: Random House.

Morris, H. (Ed.) 1961. *Freedom and Responsibility*. Stanford, CA: Sanford University Press.
Morris, R. B. 1985. *Witnesses at the Creation: Hamilton, Madison, Jay, and the Constitution*. New York: New American Library.
Moynihan, D. P. 1965. *The Negro Family: The Case for National Action*. Washington, DC: US Govt.
Moynihan, D. P. 1993. "Defining Deviancy Down." *American Scholar*. Winter.
Moynihan, D. P. 2012. www.goodreads.com/author/quotes
Murray, C. 1986. *Losing Ground: American Social Policy*. New York: Basic Books.
Murray, C. 2012. *Coming Apart: The State of White America, 1960–2010*. New York: Crown Forum.
Murray, D., Schwartz, J. and Lichter, S. R. 2001. *It Ain't Necessarily So: How Media Make and Unmake the Scientific Picture of Reality*. Lanham, MD: Rowman & Littlefield Publishers.
Nasaw, D. 2000. *The Chief: The Life of William Randolph Hearst*. Boston: Houghton, Mifflin.
National Center for Educational Statistics. 2001. *Digest of Educational Statistics, 2001*. Washington, DC. Government Printing Office
Nauert, C. G. 1995. *Humanism and the Culture of Renaissance Europe*. New York: Cambridge University Press.
Neill, A. S. 1960. *Summerhill: A Radical Approach to Child Rearing*. New York: Hart Publishing Co.
Nelson, L. A. 2013. "Education Department Releases Annual Tuition Pricing Lists." *Inside Higher Ed*, June 28.
New York Times Correspondents. 2005. *Class Matters*. New York: Henry Holt and Company.
Norris, C. 1997. *Against Relativism: Philosophy of Science, Deconstruction and Critical Theory*. Oxford, UK: Blackwell Publishers.
Nussbaum, M. 1997. *Cultivating Humanity: A Classical Defense of Reform in Liberal Education*. Cambridge MA: Harvard University Press.
Obama, B. H. 1995. *Dreams from My Father*. New York: Three Rivers Press.
Obama, B. H. 2006. *The Audacity of Hope*. New York: Crown
Oberschell, A. 1995. *Social Movements: Ideologies, Interests, and Identities*. New Brunswick, NJ: Transaction Press.
O'Brien, M. 1987. *Vince: A Personal Biography of Vince Lombardi*. New York: William Morrow and Co.
Ogbu, J. U. 1974. *The Next Generation: An Ethnography of Education in an Urban School*. New York: Academic Press.
Ogburn, W. 1922. (1966) *Social Change with Respect to Culture and Original Nature*. New York: Heubsch.
Olasky, M. 1992. *The Tragedy of American Compassion*. Washington, DC: Regnery Publishing.
Oliver, M. L. and Shapiro, T. M. 1997. *Black Wealth/White Wealth: A New Perspective on Racial Inequality*. New York: Routledge.
Olson, W. K. 1997. *The Excuse Factory: How Employment Law is Paralyzing the American Workplace*. New York: The Free Press.

Orwin, C. and Tarcov, N. (Eds.) 1997. *The Legacy of Rousseau.* Chicago: University of Chicago Press.

Packard, V. 1959. *The Status Seekers.* New York: D. McKay Co.

Palmer, P. J. and Zajonc, A. with Scriber, M. 2010. *The Heart of Higher Education: A Call to Renewal.* San Francisco: Jossey-Bass.

Pantsov, A. V. and Levine, S. 2012. *Mao: The Real Story.* New York: Simon & Schuster.

Papp, P. 1983. *The Process of Change.* New York: Guilford Press.

Pareto, V. 1991. *The Rise and Fall of Elites: An Application of Theoretical Sociology.* New Brunswick, NJ: Transaction Publishers.

Park, R. 1950. *Race and Culture.* Glencoe, Ill: Free Press.

Parsons, T. 1951. *The Social System.* New York: The Free Press.

Parsons, T. and Bales, R. F. 1955. *Family Socialization and Interaction Processes.* New York: Free Press.

Parsons, T. and Shils, E. (Eds.) 1951. *Toward a General Theory of Action.* New York: Harper and Row.

Partridge, W. L. 1973. *The Hippie Ghetto: The Natural History of a Subculture.* New York: Holt, Rinehart and Winston.

Patai, D. 2012. "We, Rigoberta's Excuse-Makers." *Academic Questions,* Vol. 25, No. 2.

Payne, R. 1978. *Leonardo.* Garden City, NY: Doubleday.

Pedersen, O. 1997. *The First Universities: Stadium Generale and the Origins of University Education in Europe.* New York: Cambridge University Press.

Perrow, C. 1970. *Organizational Analysis: A Sociological View.* Belmont, Ca.: Cole/Brooks.

Phelps, R.P. 2012. "Dismissive Reviews: Academe's Memory Hole." *Academic Questions,* Vol. 25, No. 2.

Pines, A. M. 2005. *Falling in Love: Why We Choose the Lovers We Choose.* (2nd Ed.) New York: Routledge.

Pinker, S. 1994. *The Language Instinct: How the Mind Creates Language.* New York: William Morrow & Co.

Pirenne, H. 1936. *Economic and Social History of Medieval Europe.* New York: Harcourt, Brace & World.

Piven, F. F. and Cloward, R. A. 1977. *Poor People's Movement's: Why They Succeed, How They Fail.* New York: Vintage.

Plato, 1928. *The Works of Plato.* (Jowett translation) New York: The Modern Library.

Plumb, J. H. 1961. *The Italian Renaissance.* New York: American Heritage.

Popper, K. R. 1959. *The Logic of Scientific Discovery.* London: Hutchinson & Co.

Popper, K. R. 1971. [1945.] *The Open Society and Its Enemies.* (5th Edition) Princeton: Princeton University Press.

Porter, R. 1982. *English Society in the Eighteenth Century.* New York: Penguin Books.

Potter, J. M. 2000. "Ritual, Power, and Social Differentiation in Small-Scale Societies." In: Diehl, M.W., *Hierarchies in Action: Cui Bono?* Carbondale, IL: Center For Archaeological Investigations.

Price, J. L. 1994. *Holland and the Dutch Republic in the Seventeenth Century: The Politics of Particularism*. New York: Oxford University Press.
Pruitt, D. G. 1981. *Negotiation Behavior*. New York: Academic.
Putnam, M. 2012. "Liberal Arts Colleges Should Ignore Reformers and Reinforce Relationships." *Inside Higher Ed*. April 19.
Putnam, R. D. 1993. *Making Democracy Work: Civic Traditions in Modern Italy*. Princeton: Princeton University Press.
Putnam, R. D. 2000. *Bowling Alone: The Collapse and Revival of American Community*. New York: Simon & Schuster.
Rand, A. 1966. *Capitalism: The Unknown Ideal*. New York: New American Library.
Rauch, J. 1995. *Kindly Inquisitors: The New Attacks on Free Thought*. Chicago: University of Chicago Press.
Raven, B. and French, J. 1959. "The Bases of Social Power." In, D. Cartwright and A. Zander (Eds.) *Group Dynamics*. New York: Harper & Row.
Ravitch D. 2000. *Left Back: A Century of Failed School Reforms*. New York: Simon & Schuster.
Ravtich, D. 2003. *The Language Police: How Pressure Groups Restrict What Students Learn*. New York: Alfred A. Knoff.
Rawls, J. 1971. *A Theory of Justice*. Cambridge, Mass.: The Belknap Press.
Regnery, A. S. 2008. *Upstream: The Ascendance of American Conservatism*. New York: Simon & Schuster, Inc.
Reisman, D. 1950. *The Lonely Crowd*. New Haven: Yale University Press.
Reverby, S. M. 2009. *Examining Tuskegee: The Infamous Syphilis Study and Its Legacy*. Chapel Hill: University of North Carolina Press.
Reynolds, A. 2006. *Income and Wealth*. Westport, Conn: Greenwood Press.
Reynolds, G. H. 2012. *The Higher Education Bubble*. New York: Encounter Books.
Rice, L. and Greenberg, L. (Eds.) 1984. *Patterns of Change*. New York: Guilford Press.
Riech, C. A. 1971. *The Greening of America*. New York: Bantam.
Riley, N. S. 2011. *The Faculty Lounges: and Other Reasons Why You Won't Get the College Education You Paid For*. Chicago: Ivan R. Dee.
Ritzer, G. 2007. *Contemporary Sociological Theory and Its Classical Roots*. (Second Edition) New York: McGraw Hill.
Ritzer, G. 2011. *The McDonaldization of Society: An Investigation into the Changing Character of Contemporary Social Life*. (Sixth Edition) Thousand Oaks: Pine Forge Press.
Rivard, R. 2013. "Despite courtship Amherst decides to shy away fro star MOOC provider." *Inside Higher Education*, April 19.
Rochester, J. M. 2002. *Class Warfare: Besieged Schools, Bewildered Parents, Betrayed Kids and the Attack on Excellence*. San Francisco: Encounter Books.
Rochon, T. R. 1998. *Culture Moves: Idea, Activism, and Changing Values*. Princeton: Princeton University Press.
Rogers, C. 1951. *Client Centered Therapy*. Boston: Houghton Mifflin.

Rogers, C. 1961. *On Becoming a Person*. Boston: Houghton Mifflin.
Rogers, R. 2013. "The Price of Philanthropy." *Chronicle of Higher Education*, July 14.
Rosen, A. S. 2011. *Change.edu: Rebooting for the New Talent Economy*. New York: Kaplan Publishing.
Rousseau, J. J. 1968. (1762) *The Social Contract* (Translated by Maurice Cranston) New York: Penguin Books.
Rousseau, J. J. 1992. *The Discourse on the Origins of Inequality*. (Edited by Roger D. Masters and Christopher Kelly) Hanover, NH: University Press of New England.
Rousseau, Jean-Jacques [1762] 1979. *Emile*. Trans. A. Bloom. New York: Basic Books.
Rove, K. 2010. *Courage and Consequence: My Life as a Conservative in the Fight*. New York: Simon & Schuster.
Rubin, L. B. 1972. *Busing & Backlash: White Against White in an Urban School District*. Berkeley: University of California Press.
Rudolph, F. 1990. *The American College and University: A History*. Athens: University of Georgia Press.
Russell, B. 1929. *Marriage and Morals*. New York: H. Liveright.
Sale, K. 1973. *SDS*. New York: Random House.
Salerno, R. 2013. *Contemporary Social Theory*. New York: Pearson.
Samuelson, R. 1996. *The Good Life and Its Discontents: The American Dream in the Age of Entitlement 1945-1995*. New York: Times Books.
Samuelson, R. 2008. *The Great Inflation and Its Aftermath: The Past and Future of American Affluence*. New York: Random House.
Sander, R. H. and Taylor, S. 2012. *Mismatch: How Affirmative Action Hurts Students It's Intended to Help, and Why Universities Won't Admit It*. New York: Basic Books.
Sanderson, S. K. 1995. *Social Transformations: A General Theory of Historical Development*. Oxford, UK: Blackwell.
Sanderson, S. K. 2010. *Revolutions: A Worldwide Introduction to Social and Political Contention* (Second Edition) Boulder: Paradigm Publishers.
Sarton, G. 1962. *The History of Science and the New Humanism*. Bloomington: Indiana University Press.
Satel, S. 2000. *PC, M.D.: How Political Correctness is Corrupting Medicine*. New York: Basic Books.
Schama, S. 1989. *Citizens: A Chronicle of the French Revolution*. New York: A. Knopf.
Scheff, T. 1990. *Microsociology: Discourse, Emotion, and Social Structure*. Chicago: University of Chicago Press.
Schumpeter, J. A. 1942. *Capitalism, Socialism and Democracy*. New York: Harper & Brothers.
Schwartz, H. 2009. "Antioch Self-Destructs." *Academic Questions*, Vol. 22. No.3.
Seligman, A. B. 1992. *The Idea of Civil Society*. Princeton, NJ: Princeton University Press.

Selingo, J. J. 2013. *College (Un)bound: The Future of Higher Education and What It Means for Students*. New York: Houghton Mifflin Harcourt.

Sennett, R. and Cobb, J. 1966. *The Hidden Injuries of Class*. New York: The Free Press.

Sewall, G. T. 2012. "The Howard Zinn Show." *Academic Questions*, Vol. 25, No. 2.

Shapiro, B. 2004. *Brainwashed: How Universities Indoctrinate American Youth*. Nashville, TN: WND Books.

Shapiro, P. 2011. *Incoming Freshman Attitudes about the Internet*. http://www.gsw.edu/-univrel/news/2009_Incoming_Freshman_Survey

Shaw, J. S. 2011. "What Will Colleges Do When the Bubble Bursts?" *Academic Questions*, Vol. 24, No. 4.

Sherif, M. 1936. *The Psychology of Social Norms*. New York: Harper & Brothers.

Shermer, M. 2011. *The Believing Brain: From Ghosts and Gods to Politics and Conspiracies—How We Construct Beliefs and Reinforce Them as Truths*. New York: Times Books.

Sidanius, J. and Pratto, F. 1999. *Social Dominance: An Intergroup Theory of Social Hierarchy and Oppression*. Cambridge: Cambridge University Press.

Silberman, C. E. (Ed.) 1973. *The Open Classroom Reader*. New York: Random House.

Simon, H. A. 1947. *Administrative Behavior*. New York: MacMillan.

Skocpol, T. 2000. *The Missing Middle: Working Families and the Future of American Social Policy*. New York: W.W. Norton & Co.

Skrentny, J. L. 1996. *The Ironies of Affirmative Action: Politics, Culture, and Justice in America*. Chicago: University of Chicago Press.

Sleeper, J. 1997. *Liberal Racism*. New York: Viking.

Smigel, E. O. (Ed.) 1963. *Work and Leisure*. New Haven: College & University Press.

Smith, A. 1776. *An Inquiry into the Nature and Causes of the Wealth of Nations*. London: W. Strahan & T. Cadell.

Sobel, D. 1999. *Galileo's Daughter: A Historical Memoir of Science, Faith, and Love*. New York: Walker & Co.

Solway, D. 2011. "On Hypertext, or Back to the Landau." *Academic Questions*, Vol. 24, No. 3.

Solway, D. 2012. "Pedagogical Portraits." *Academic Questions*, Vol. 25, No. 2.

Sommers, C. H. 2000. *The War Against Boys: How Misguided Feminism is Harming Our Young Men*. New York: Simon & Schuster.

Sowell, T. 1981. *Ethnic America*. New York: Basic Books.

Sowell, T. 1999. *The Quest for Cosmic Justice*. New York: The Free Press.

Sowell, T. 2004. *Affirmative Action Around the World: An Empirical Study*. New Haven: Yale University Press.

Sowell, T. 2007. *A Conflict of Visions: Ideological Origins of Political Struggles*. New York: Basic Books.

Sowell, T. 2009. *Intellectuals and Society*. New York: Basic Books.

Sowell, T. 2013a. *Intellectuals and Race*. New York: Basic Books.

Sowell, T. 2013b. "Is Thinking Obsolete." TownHall.com., May 1.

Spencer, H. [1899] 1969. *The Principles of Sociology* (3 Vols.) (S. Andreski, Ed.) New York: MacMillan.
Spiro, M. E. 1958. *Children of the Kibbutz*. Cambridge, MA: Harvard University Press.
Steele, C. M., Spencer, S. J., and Lynch, M. 1993. "Self-Image, Resilience and Dissonance: The Role of Affirmational Resources." *Journal of Personality and Social Psychology*, 66(6): 885–896.
Steele, S. 1990. *The Content of Our Character: A New Vision of Race in America.* New York: St. Martin's Press.
Steele, S. 1998. *A Dream Deferred: The Second Betrayal of Black Freedom in America*. New York: HarperCollins Publishers.
Stein, H. and Foss, M. 1999. *The Illustrated Guide to the American Economy, Third Edition*. Washington, DC: AEI Press.
Steinem, G. 1992. *Revolution From Within: A Book of Self-Esteem*. Boston: Little, Brown.
Stoll, D. 2008. (1999) *Rigoberta Menchu and the Story of All Poor Guatemalans.* Boulder, CO: Westview Press.
Stratford, M. 2013. "Poll: Most Americans and Business Leaders Say Graduates Should Be Well-Rounded." *Inside Higher Ed*, September 18.
Strauss, A. 1959. *Mirrors and Masks: The Search for Identity*. New Brunswick, NJ: Transaction Publishers.
Strauss, A. 1978. *Negotiations: Varieties, Contexts, Processes and Social Order.* San Francisco: Jossey-Bass.
Sumner, W. G. 1960. *Folkways.* New York: New American Library.
Suttles, G. D. 1972. *The Social Construction of Communities*. Chicago: University of Chicago Press.
Swartz, D. 1997. *Culture and Power: The Sociology of Pierre Bourdieu*. Chicago: University of Chicago Press.
Tannen, D. 1990. *You Just Don't Understand; Women and Men in Conversation*. New York: William Morrow and Co.
Tattersall, I. 2012. *Masters of the Planet: The Search for Our Human Origins.* New York: Palgrave MacMillan.
Taylor, B. P. 2010. *Horace Mann's Troubling Legacy: The Education of Democratic Citizens*. Lawrence: University Press of Kansas.
Taylor, F. W. 1911. *The Principles of Scientific Management.* New York: Harper and Brothers.
Taylor, M. C. 2010. *Crisis on Campus: A Bold Plan for Reforming Our Colleges and Universities*. New York: Alfred A. Knopf.
Thelin, R. R. 2011. *A History of American Higher Education*. (Second Edition) Baltimore: Johns Hopkins Press.
Thernstrom, S. and Thernstrom, A. 1997. *America in Black and White: One Nation, Indivisible.* New York: Simon and Schuster.
Thernstrom, S. and Thernstrom, A. 2003. *No Excuses: Closing the Racial Gap in Learning*. New York: Simon and Schuster.
Tilly, C. 1998. *Durable Inequality*. Berkeley: University of California Press.
Tilly, C. 2004. *Social Movements: 1768–2004*. Boulder: Paradigm Publishers.

de Tocqueville, A. 1966. *Democracy in America.* Trans. by George Lawrence. New York: Harper & Row.

Toennies, F. 1966. (1887) *Community and Society.* New York: Harper Row.

Trivers, R. I. 1971. The Evolution of Reciprocal Altruism. *Quarterly Review of Biology* 46:37–37.

Turner, R. 1960. "Sponsored and Contest Mobility in the School System." *American Sociological Review,* 26(6), 855–862.

Turner, R. H. 1962. *Role Taking: Process vs. Conformity?* In: Rose, A. M. (Ed.), Human Behavior and Social Processes. Boston: Houghton Mifflin.

Tylor, E. B. 1881. Anthropology: *An Introduction to the Study of Man and Civilization.* London: MacMillan.

US Dept. of Labor. 1991. "Research Summaries." *Monthly Labor Review, December.* Washington, DC. Government Printing Office.

US Dept. of Labor, Bureau of Labor Statistics. 1980. *Occupational Outlook Handbook, 1980–81 Edition.* Washington, DC. Government Printing Office.

US Dept. of Labor, Bureau of Labor Statistics. 2000. *Dictionary of Occupational Titles.* Washington, DC. Government Printing Office.

US Dept. of Labor, Bureau of Labor Statistics. 2001. *2001 National Occupational Employment and Wage Estimates.* Washington, DC. Government Printing Office.

Valentine, C. A. 1968. *Culture and Poverty: Critique and Counter Proposals.* Chicago: University of Chicago Press.

Veblen, T. 1967. (1899) *The Theory of the Leisure Class.* New York: Viking Penguin.

Vedder, R. K. and Gillen, A. 2011. "Cost versus Enrollment Bubbles." *Academic Questions,* Vol.24, No. 3.

Verene, D.P. 2013. "Does Online Education Rest on a Mistake?" *Academic Questions,* Vol. 26, No. 3.

Voegeli, W. 2013. "The Higher Education Hustle." *Claremont Review of Books,* Vol. XIII, No. 2, Spring.

Vollmer, H. and Mills, D. (Eds.) 1968. *Professionalization.* Englewood Cliffs, NJ: Prentice-Hall.

Vonnegut, K. 1998. "Harrison Bergeron." In: *Welcome to the Monkey House.* New York: Dell Press.

de Waal, F. (Ed.) 2001. *Tree of Origin: What Primate Behavior Can Tell Us about Human Social Evolution.* Cambridge: Harvard University Press.

Wallace, J. 1993. *Hard Drive: Bill Gates and the Making of the Microsoft Empire.* New York: HarperBusiness.

Waller, W. 1967. *The Sociology of Teaching.* New York: John Wiley & Sons.

Wattenberg, B. 1990. *The First Universal Nation.* New York: Free Press.

Weber, M. 1947. *The Theory of Social and Economic Organization.* New York: Free Press.

Weber, M. 1958. *The Protestant Ethic and the Spirit of Capitalism.* New York: Charles Scribner's Sons.

Weisberg, R. 2013a. "The Hidden Costs of Journal Peer Review." *Academic Questions,* Vol. 26, No. 2, Summer.

Weisberg, R. 2013b. "Critically Thinking about Critical Thinking." *Academic Questions*, Vol. 26, No. 3, Fall.
West, D. 2007. *The Death of the Grown-Up: How America's Arrested Development is Bringing Down Western Civilization.* New York: St. Martin's Press.
Westermarck, E. 1960. *Ethical Relativity.* Paterson, NJ: Littlefield, Adams, and Co.
Whitehead, B. D. 1998. *The Divorce Culture: Rethinking Our Commitments to Marriage and the Family.* New York: Random House.
Whittier, N. 1995. *Feminist Generations: The Persistence of the Radical Women's Movement.* Philadelphia: Temple University Press.
Whyte, W. H. 1956. *The Organization Man.* New York: Simon & Schuster.
Wiener, P. P. (Ed.) 1951. *Leibniz Selections.* New York: Charles Scribner's Sons.
Wildavsky, B. Kelly, A. P. and Carey, K. (Eds.) 2011. *Reinventing Higher Education: The Promise of Innovation.* Cambridge: Harvard Education Press.
Will, G. 2007. "Farewell, Antioch." *TownHall.* http://townhall.com/Common/Print.aspx
Williams, W. E. 2012. "Too Much College." *TownHall.* http://townwall.com/columnists/walterwilliams.2012/06/27
Willie, C. V. 1979. *Caste and Class Controversy.* New York: General Hall.
Wilson, J. Q. 1997. *Moral Judgment.* New York: The Free Press.
Wolfe, A. 1989. *Whose Keeper?* Berkeley, CA: University of California Press.
Wolfe, A. 1996. *Marginalized in the Middle.* Chicago: University of Chicago Press.
Wolfe, A. 1998. *One Nation, After All: What Middle-Class Americans Really Think.* New York: Viking.
Wolfe, A. 2001. *Moral Freedom: The Search for Virtue in a World of Choice.* New York: W. W. Norton.
Wood, P. 2003. *Diversity: The Invention of a Concept.* San Francisco: Encounter Books.
Wood, P. 2011. "Higher Education' Precarious Hold on Consumer Confidence," *Academic Questions*, Vol.24, No. 3.
Wood, P. and Toscano, M. 2013. *What Does Bowdoin Teach?: How a Contemporary Liberal Arts College Shapes Students.* New York: National Association of Scholars.
Wooden, J. and Jamison, S. 2010. *The Wisdom of Wooden: My Century On and Off the Court.* New York: McGraw-Hill.
Wrong, D. 1961. *The Oversocialized Conception of Man in Modern Sociology.* In: American Sociological Review, Vol. 26, No. 2.
Wuthnow, R. 1987. *Meaning and Moral Order: Explorations in Cultural Analysis.* Berkeley, CA: University of California Press.
Wuthnow, R. 1996. *Poor Richard's Principle: Recovering the American Dream through the Moral Dimension of Work, Business, & Money.* Princeton, NJ: University of Princeton Press.
XU, D. and Jaggers, S. S. 2013. "Adaptability to On-Line Learning: Differences Across Types and Academic Subject Areas." New York: Columbia University teachers College.

Yancey, G. 2012. "Recalibrating Academic Bias." *Academic Questions*, Vol. 22, No. 2.

Zarefsky, D. 1986. *President Johnson's War on Poverty.* University, AL: University of Alabama Press.

Zigler, E. and Valentines, J. (Eds.) 1979. *Head Start: A Legacy of the War on Poverty*. New York: Free Press.

Zinn, H. 2010. *A People's History of the United States* (5th Edition). New York: HarperCollins.

Zorn, J. 2013. "English Compositionalism as Fraud and Failure." *Academic Questions*, Vol. 26, No. 3, Fall.

Zurcher, L. 1983. *Social Roles: Conformity, Conflict and Creativity*. Beverly Hills: Sage Publications.

Index